Chicken Soup for the Soul

心灵鸡汤

最初的你，最后的爱

True Love I

Jack Canfield（杰克·坎菲尔德）
［美］Mark Victor Hansen（马克·维克多·汉森）/ 编著　南溪 / 译
Amy Newmark（艾米·纽马克）

CS 湖南文艺出版社
HUNAN LITERATURE AND ART PUBLISHING HOUSE　博集天卷
CS-BOOKY

图书在版编目（CIP）数据

最初的你，最后的爱：英汉对照 /（美）坎菲尔德（Canfield, J.）等编著；南溪译 .—长沙：湖南文艺出版社，2012.6
（心灵鸡汤）
书名原文：True Love
ISBN 978-7-5404-5416-6

Ⅰ．①最… Ⅱ．①坎… ②南… Ⅲ．①英语—汉语—对照读物 ②故事—作品集—美国—现代 Ⅳ．① H319.4：I

中国版本图书馆 CIP 数据核字（2012）第 036991 号

著作权合同登记号：图字 18-2012-35

上架建议：心灵励志·英语学习

Chicken Soup for the Soul: True Love
101 Heartwarming and Humorous Stories about Dating, Romance, Love, and Marriage
by Jack Canfield, Mark Victor Hansen, Amy Newmark
Foreword by Kristi Yamaguchi and Bret Hedican
Published by Chicken Soup for the Soul Publishing, LLC www.chickensoup.com
Copyright © 2009 by Chicken Soup for the Soul Publishing, LLC. All Rights Reserved.
No part of this publication may be reproduced, stored in a retrieval system or transmitted in any form or by any means, electronic, mechanical, photocopying, recording or otherwise, without the written permission of the publisher.
Chicken Soup for the Soul, P.O. Box 700, Cos Cob, CT 06807-0700, Fax 203-861-7194

心灵鸡汤：最初的你，最后的爱

作　　者：（美）坎菲尔德 等
译　　者：南　溪
出 版 人：刘清华
责任编辑：丁丽丹　刘诗哲
监　　制：蔡明菲　潘　良
特约编辑：沙玲玲
版权支持：辛　艳
封面设计：吕彦秋
版式设计：崔振江
出版发行：湖南文艺出版社
　　　　　（长沙市雨花区东二环一段 508 号　邮编：410014）
网　　址：www.hnwy.net
印　　刷：北京盛兰兄弟印刷装订有限公司
经　　销：新华书店
开　　本：880mm×1230mm　1/32
字　　数：320 千字
印　　张：11.5
版　　次：2012 年 6 月第 1 版
印　　次：2012 年 6 月第 1 次印刷
书　　号：ISBN 978-7-5404-5416-6
定　　价：32.00 元
（若有质量问题，请致电质量监督电话：010-84409925）

目录
Contents

Chapter 2 Adventures in Dating
第二部分 约会篇

Chapter 4 The Proposal
第四部分 求婚篇

Foreword
前言

Kristi: Everyone enjoys a great love story, so we were excited about being part of the Chicken Soup for the Soul family for this wonderful book of true love stories. This is not my first time in a Chicken Soup for the Soul book. I had a story about my early years as an athlete in *Chicken Soup for the Preteen Soul 2* and my mom had a story about my skating career in *Chicken Soup for the Sports Fan's Soul.*

Skating is great, but true love is even better! After all, it's something we all strive for and most of us achieve it at some point in our lives. Bret and I are fortunate to have it all—great careers, a strong marriage, and a wonderful family. But it almost didn't happen...

Bret: We met at the 1992 Olympics when I was playing for the U.S. hockey team and Kristi was figure skating for the U.S. She won a gold medal that year. Nancy Kerrigan and Kristi were walking around meeting some of the other American team members. Kristi made an impression on all of us—she was just excited to be there and happy to be watching the hockey team and the players and be a part of it.

Kristi: There were about twenty-five hockey players and I remembered a few of them, but not Bret. When we met again a few years later in Vancouver, he told me that we had met at the Olympics. I had to go back to look at the photos to see if he was really there.

A hockey player was the last type of athlete I thought I would ever date. Hockey players are just a different breed from figure skaters. We always competed with the hockey players for rink time when I was a kid.

Bret: We had no class.

Kristi: It was pretty funny, because when we were reintroduced, one of my choreographers was with me, and he said there was this cute guy who kept looking over at me. I was so embarrassed, as if I was transported back to grade school.

We dated for about three years before Bret proposed. Bret was playing for the Vancouver Canucks and I was based in the Bay Area so we were only going to see each other over Christmas for a day and half, actually only forty hours! Bret called me and said he had missed his flight. I was not happy. There had been a snowstorm in Vancouver, and Bret's car wasn't working, and there were no cabs available since they are not accustomed to heavy snow in Vancouver.

Bret: We were spending Christmas Day with Kristi's family so I wanted us to have a nice quiet Christmas Eve dinner, just the two of us, so I could propose. But when I arrived, I discovered that Kristi had said that her sister and brother-in-law could join us. I pulled her sister aside and told her I had the ring in my pocket, and that she needed to leave right after dinner.

Kristi: He was still in trouble with me for being late, so it took me a while to figure out what was going on, and then I thought, "Don't do it because I've been so nasty all night." But we ended up at the top of the Marriott in downtown San Francisco, with a 360 degree view of the city, and he proposed. Of course I said yes.

Our parents were thrilled and excited and we decided to have a nice intimate family wedding in Hawaii. My extended family had a tradition of vacationing on the Big Island of Hawaii—25 or 30 of us at the Orchid Mauna Lani. We loved it and thought a small wedding would be nice.

You can guess what happened. We gave everyone more than a year to plan, so they could plan their family vacations around the wedding, and almost 100% of our invites said yes. Over 300 people came. We took over the whole hotel. It was awesome. It turned into a five-day wedding because everyone came early and by the time we had the ceremony on Saturday, everyone knew each other.

Bret: At the reception I scored points by serenading my bride with the Bob Dylan song "Make You Feel My Love." I saw Scott Hamilton quoted in People Magazine saying that every single woman in the room was crying.

Kristi: That was in 2000, and three years later we had our first child, Keara, and two years after that we had Emma. Our daughters are our proudest accomplishments. The minute you become a parent, you become so much closer and it reinforces the bond you have with each other. You become more conscious of the values you want to instill in your family. You also have a better understanding of your own parents – it's a lot of work!

While our marriage is still young compared to many out there, we feel a real affinity to the stories in this latest Chicken Soup for the Soul volume about true love. It's a lot of fun to read about dating, proposals, and weddings and remember our own years of long distance dating and our own wedding. And we love the stories written by long-time couples about how they keep their marriages fresh and their relationships healthy. Some of the stories are so funny, and a few will make you tear up. There is something in here for everyone, even you guys out there. We wives know that you secretly enjoy a good love story too, right Bret?

Bret: Yes, dear.

~*Kristi Yamaguchi and Bret Hedican*

• • • • • • • • •

克丽斯蒂：人人都喜欢伟大的爱情故事，所以能够参与《心灵鸡汤：真情故事》一书的编辑，我们感到十分荣幸。这不是我第一次为《心灵鸡汤》写作，一个关于我早年作为运动员的故事曾在《心灵鸡汤：儿童成长 2》中发表。母亲也曾在《心灵鸡汤：体育迷》中，讲述过我的滑冰生涯。

滑冰是很棒的运动，但是真正的爱情更加美好！毕竟，我们每个人对爱情都有强烈的渴望，并希望在生命中的某一时刻收获爱情。布雷特和我是幸运的。我们婚姻幸福，事业顺利，家庭美满。但是，有可能这一切都不会发生……

布雷特：我们是在 1992 年的奥运会上相遇的，当时我在美国冰球队，克丽斯蒂在美国女子花样滑冰队。那年，她赢得了金牌。南希·克里根（冬奥会花样滑冰明星）和她一起，在赛场上走来走去，和其他的美国队成员打招呼。克丽斯蒂给我们所有人留下了深刻的印象——她非常兴奋，很高兴能观看冰球比赛和认识其他球员，并成为团队的一员。

克丽斯蒂：那时大概有 25 名队员，我记得其中一些人，但对布雷特没有什么印象。几年后，我们在温哥华再次相遇。当他告诉我，我们曾在 1992 年奥运会上见过面时，我非常惊讶，还回去翻了以前的照片看他是不是真的在那里。

我从没想过自己会和一名冰球队员交往。要知道，冰球和花样滑冰不过是冰上运动的不同种类罢了。当我还是个孩子的时候，我们就经常和冰球运动员抢冰场场地。

布雷特： 我们冰球运动比较没地位了。

克丽斯蒂： 说来挺逗的，我们再次遇到的时候，我的编舞导演和我在一起。他跟我说："有个很可爱的家伙一直盯着你看呢。"我当时觉得特别尴尬，就好像回到了小学时代一样。

我们交往了三年左右，布雷特向我求婚了。当时，布雷特在温哥华加人队，而我在旧金山训练。所以我们只有在圣诞节期间——大约一天半的时间，才能见对方。只有40小时！所以布雷特打电话告诉我说他错过航班的时候，我特别伤心。那天温哥华下了很大的雪，他的车子发动不了。而且因为大雪的原因，他也打不到出租车。

布雷特： 我们原本打算同克丽斯蒂的家人一起过圣诞节。所以，在圣诞前夜，我希望我们两个能一起吃一顿浪漫、温馨的晚餐。然后，我可以借这个机会向她求婚。但是，我到达之后克丽斯蒂告诉我，她的妹妹和妹夫也要和我们一起吃晚餐。于是，我把她妹妹拉到一边，告诉她我的口袋里揣着戒指，希望她能在晚餐后离开。

克丽斯蒂： 我当时还在为他的迟到生气，所以，我花了一点时间才弄明白究竟发生了什么事情。我的第一反应是："不要啊，我今天晚上表现得那么恶劣。"但是当我们站在旧金山市中心万豪酒店顶层俯瞰全城的时候，他真的向我求婚了。当然，我答应了。

父母听到我们订婚的消息都替我们感到激动和兴奋。我们打算在夏威夷举办一场甜蜜的家庭婚礼。我们家族有在夏威夷度假的传统——家族里有25到30个人都会选择夏威夷大岛马纳拉尼海岛的兰花酒店。我们很喜欢那里，觉得在那里举办一个小型婚礼会很不错。

你可以想象得出后面发生了什么。我们给所有亲朋好友一年多的时间来准备，让他们的家庭休假安排在我们的婚期前后。几乎所有受到邀请的亲朋都同意这么做。结果，我们的婚礼来了三百多位宾客，几乎占用了整个酒店。那场面真的太壮观了。我们的婚礼持续了五天，因为每位宾客都是提前到达的，等我们周六举行仪式的时候，他们彼此间早都认识了。

布雷特：在婚宴上，我为我的新娘唱了一首鲍勃·迪伦的《感受我的爱》，这给我加分不少。斯科特·汉密尔顿（萨克斯风手）引用《人物》杂志上的话说，房间里的每一个单身女子都感动得哭了。

克丽斯蒂：在 2000 年，也就是结婚三年后，我们有了第一个孩子琪拉。两年后，我们有了艾玛。两个女儿是我们最大的骄傲，是孩子让我们两个紧紧地连在一起。有了自己的孩子之后，你会更注重培养家庭价值观，也会更加理解自己的父母。为人父母，实在不简单呢！

相比其他人，我们的婚姻还很年轻，但是我们的确在《心灵鸡汤：感悟爱情》中找到了共鸣。这些有关约会、求婚和婚礼的故事，读起来非常有意思，也让我想起自己坠入爱情时的那段时光和我们的婚礼。我们喜欢那些老夫老妻写的文章，他们教会我们如何让婚姻健康、富有活力。有的故事让人忍俊不禁，有的则让你泪流满面。每个人都能从故事中有所收获，即使男人也一样。我们做妻子的知道，背地里你们也很喜欢看爱情故事的，对吗，布雷特？

布雷特：呵呵，亲爱的，确实如此。

——克丽斯蒂·亚玛古驰和布雷特·赫迪坎

Introduction
引言

My very thoughtful son, who is a college senior with a long-time fabulous girlfriend, has a wonderful metaphor for relationships. He views a relationship as a machine—a box full of intermeshed gears working together. When the machine is new, the gears are shiny and sharp. They work together, but there is some roughness around the edges and a little resistance as they mesh. Over time, the gears lose some of their shininess, and their edges become a little rounded, but they work together more and more smoothly. A little dirt gets in the machine from time to time, and it must be cleaned out diligently in order to keep the gears working well and avoid permanent build-up.

Once in a while, a major problem may occur, and a piece of metal may fall into the works. But a well-maintained machine with well-matched gears will survive this. The gears will keep moving and the stray piece of metal may get thrown against the side wall of the machine, leaving a permanent dent that mars the machine but doesn't impair its performance. Or the piece of metal may actually damage a gear, bending it or breaking it, but the machine soldiers on, and the gears still mesh better and better over time, albeit with one missing tooth.

Our relationships are like that metaphorical machine. Over time, our gears may darken with age and wear down, and even show some breakage, but if we tend to them they should mesh more and more smoothly. If the machine really suffers irreparable damage, and we break up or divorce, we look to start over with new machines.

Chicken Soup for the Soul: True Love is an inspiring collection of stories about dating, romance, love, and marriage. You will find stories about everything from first dates and falling in love, to proposals and weddings, to second chances and love later in life, to making relationships work over the years. Whether you are looking for new love, basking in the glow of a successful relationship, or working on a relationship that needs a little polishing, you will find fundamental wisdom in these pages, from real people sharing their personal stories with you.

Our Assistant Publisher, D'ette Corona, and I had so much fun reading the thousands of stories submitted for this book. After all, who doesn't enjoy a great love story? We laughed and cried, nodded our heads in recognition, shook our heads in disbelief, and were disappointed when it was all over and the book was finished!

So now it is your turn. "Gear up" for a great read. We hope these stories will help your relationship "machine" work as well as ours, or give you faith that your next box of gears will be the one that operates smoothly for the rest of your life!

~Amy Newmark

Publisher, Chicken Soup for the Soul

• • • • • • • • •

　　我的儿子是名大四学生，他有个很优秀的女朋友，对恋爱也有着独到的看法。他曾将恋爱中的两人比喻为一台由啮合齿轮构成的机器，刚开始的时候，齿轮是崭新锐利的。它们刚开始一起工作，由于齿轮太锐利，它们啮合的时候偶尔会出现摩擦或阻力。但是随着时间推移，齿轮失去了些许光泽，边缘也更加钝化，但它们的配合却越来越好。偶尔，它们也会沾染上一些灰尘，这时候就需要及时清除，保持机器正常工作，避免造成永久性损坏。

　　一段时间后，机器也可能出现一些小故障，比如某个部件不能正常工作。但是如果进行精心保养和护理，它们也能够渡过难关。齿轮运转过程中，被甩出机器侧壁的金属部件可能会在机器上留下永久性凹痕，却不会损害其性能，部件也有可能会弄弯或折断一个齿轮，但是机器维修工会修好损伤的部分。机器上哪怕缺少一个齿牙，齿轮还是能够很好地啮合在一起。

　　恋爱中两个人的关系也正如这个比喻中的机器。随着年岁增长，我们的齿轮可能也会变暗和磨损，甚至有一定的损坏，但只要细心呵护，这台机器便能运转得越来越顺畅。如果机器真的遭受无法弥补的损害，我们就会分手或者离婚，期待着能同新齿轮更好地啮合。

《心灵鸡汤：真情故事》一书收录了有关约会、恋爱、婚姻的各种感人故事：从初次约会到坠入爱河，从求婚策划到婚礼举行，从和好如初到新的爱恋。品味这些故事的同时，相信你能找到让爱情经久不衰的秘诀。无论渴盼下段恋情的成功，还是需要给多年的爱情打磨抛光，这些真实的人和事都会对你有所裨益。

出版助理德·卡罗娜和我在审阅无数来稿时，收获了巨大的快乐。毕竟，谁不喜欢动人的爱情故事呢？我们开心地笑，感动地哭，既会认同地点头，也会微微摇头表示怀疑。当这本书的编辑工作完成时，我们的内心则感到深深的不舍和失落。

现在，轮到你了。"加大油门"开始愉悦的阅读之旅吧。希望这些故事能让你们的爱情"机器"更加良好地运转，或是帮你找到同你默契啮合一生的齿轮。

——《心灵鸡汤》出版人艾米·纽马克

第一部分 相遇篇

Chapter 1
How We Met

You know you're in love when you can't fall asleep because reality is finally better than your dreams.

~Dr. Seuss

当你终于因为现实比梦境更美而无法入睡时，你恋爱了。

——苏斯博士（美国儿童文学家）

Challenged
智力障碍

You don't love someone for their looks, or their clothes, or for their fancy cars, but because they sing a song only you can hear.

~Source Unknown

I was twenty-six, single, and I had just bought my first home. It was my very first "grown-up" purchase. After signing the final paperwork, I decided to stop and visit some friends before heading home to pack.

My friend has never been one for formality, so when I arrived at her house I let myself in. As I came around the corner into her living room, I was a little startled to see a man I had never met sitting on the couch.

As I was introduced to Martin, I could not help but notice that his attire was horribly coordinated. I am no fashion diva by any means, but I had to wonder what this man was thinking when he left his house that morning.

As we sat in the living room engaged in lively

conversation, I noticed that Martin was saying very little. My mother had always taught me that talking over people was not only impolite but very rude. So I tried to incorporate him into our conversation. No matter what I said to him, all I got was stammering and stuttering.

Upon hearing him speak, I mistakenly assumed he was mildly developmentally-challenged in some fashion. This would explain his speech difficulty and his clothing. For some reason, when people find themselves in a situation like this, they tend to talk louder and slower. I was no exception and I must have looked like a complete idiot, given what I learned later.

After a few hours I headed home. I had a lot of packing to do, and moving day was coming up fast.

A few days later, I went shopping for some window blinds for my new home. Once I got there, I realized that my standard screwdriver was not going to do the job. So, I headed over to my friend's house to see if I could borrow a cordless screwdriver or drill from her husband.

When I got there, she explained to me it was no problem to borrow the drill, but her husband had not made it home from work yet and she did not know where he kept it. After pausing for a moment, she said that Martin was in the other room and she would see if he had one.

Within a matter of moments he appeared. This time it seemed that his speech problem was far worse then the last time we had met. Also, I could not help but notice that he had made another not so great fashion choice. Slowly, he told me that not only did he have a cordless drill, but he would come and help me to hang my blinds… and he would drive.

My stomach twisted, not knowing what to say. Although I firmly believed that a challenged individual should be given the same chances as anyone else, I was not sure of the degree of his disability. Could he handle this task? Could he drive? Should I trust him? After all, he was a complete stranger.

I took a deep breath and agreed. I knew that if my friend was okay with this, he must be up to the challenge. Otherwise, she would have pulled me aside and told me. Hoping for the best, I got into his truck and we headed the short distance to my new home.

When we arrived, Martin pulled a tool box from his truck and went inside. I must say I was instantly impressed. Before hanging each blind, he measured and marked, taking extreme care not to damage or mar my beautiful new windows.

As he traveled from room to room hanging the blinds, I followed him. By this time I was more than comfortable with his ability. I just felt I should try to engage him in conversation. During this time I began to notice something. Martin spoke clearly whenever his back was to me. It was only during face-to-face conversations that his speech became difficult to understand.

Then it hit me. Martin was not the least bit mentally challenged. Why then, I wondered, did he have difficulty speaking at times?

At the last window, with his back turned, he told me that he and our mutual friends were going out on Friday. He wanted to know if I would like to come along. Without a moment's hesitation I blurted out yes. I surprised even myself, as that was something I never did.

I would never have guessed in a million years that Martin would be my husband when I first met him, but four months later we were married. By the time we said "I do" the stammering and stuttering came far less often. A few months later, I confessed to Martin my first impression of him. He laughed and said he stammered and stuttered only when he looked at me because he thought I was the most beautiful woman he had ever seen and it made him nervous to be around me. My heart melted… again.

You may be wondering…what about the poor fashion choices? Martin is colorblind.

I guess it goes to show you that you cannot always go by first impressions. If I had, I would have missed out on being married to the most wonderful man on the planet for the past eight years.

~Toni-Michelle Nell

爱一个人可能不是因为他英俊的外表、光鲜的衣着或豪华的轿车，而仅仅是他哼的那首歌，只有你才能听得到。

——逸名

那年，我26岁，单身，刚买了人生中的第一栋房子。这是我"长大成人"后的首次大宗买卖。办完手续后，我决定，回家整理前先到朋友家坐坐。

朋友是不拘小节的人，到她家后，我直接进去。走到客厅拐角处，突然看到沙发上坐着一个陌生男人，这让我有些吃惊。

朋友向我介绍马丁时，我注意到他的装扮很不协调。我并不是什么时尚天后，但还是奇怪，这个家伙早上出门前到底在想什么，怎么会这副打扮。

我和朋友在客厅里聊得不亦乐乎，马丁却不大开口。母亲总教导我，谈话时冷落旁人极不礼貌。所以，我试着将马丁带进谈话。但无论我说什么，得到的总是磕磕绊绊的几个字。

　　这样的回答让我误以为马丁有轻微的智力障碍。只有这样，才能解释他奇怪的打扮和言语表达障碍。出于某种原因，大多数人在类似情况下，都会有意放慢语速、提高音量。我也不例外。考虑到后来发生的种种事情，我当时的表现简直就像个白痴。

　　待了几小时后，我告别朋友回家。要整理的东西很多，搬家日期也逐渐临近。

　　几天后，我买了新家要安的百叶窗。到了之后，却发现带来的标准螺丝刀不合适。于是，我又跑去朋友家，想借她家的充电式螺丝刀或是钻头用用。

　　朋友说借钻头当然没问题，只是丈夫还没回来，她又不清楚东西放在哪里。想了一会儿，朋友告诉我，马丁在隔壁，她过去问问看马丁有没有。

　　很快，马丁出来了。这次他的表达障碍似乎更加严重，穿得还是不伦不类。慢慢地，我听懂了他的意思。他不但有充电螺丝刀，还愿意开车过去帮我安百叶窗。我心里七上八下，不知该说什么。尽管我认为，智障人士应该享有同正常人一样的机会，但我不确定他残疾的程度。他能胜任吗？会开车吗？我该相信他吗？毕竟他是个陌生人。

　　深吸了一口气，我答应了。我知道，如果朋友认为可以，那么马丁一定能够胜任挑战。否则，朋友会把我拽到一边，悄悄告诉我这么做不行。我钻进了他的卡车，前往不远处我的新家，祈祷着一切顺利。

　　到了之后，马丁下了车，拿出工具箱，进了房间。我必须承认，那一瞬间他给我留下了深刻的印象。悬挂每个百叶窗之前，马丁都会仔细地测量、标记，小心翼翼，生怕刮坏我崭新漂亮的窗户。

　　他到各个房间挂百叶窗的时候，我跟在后面，看是否需要帮忙。这会儿，我已经对他充满信心，不再怀疑他的能力。我只是觉得，应该和他聊聊天。我注意到，马丁在背对我的时候，讲话非常流利。只有面对面的时候，他的话才变得磕磕巴巴，难以理解。

突然间，我意识到马丁根本不是智力障碍。奇怪的是，为什么偶尔他会出现表达困难呢？

安装最后一扇百叶窗时，马丁背对着我，告诉我，这周五他要和我们共同的朋友出去玩，想知道我愿不愿意一起去。我想也没想，脱口而出"好啊"。说完，自己都惊讶了，以前的我从来没有这样。

四个月后，我和马丁举行了婚礼。我做梦也想不到，他会成为我的丈夫。婚礼上说"我愿意"的时候，马丁已很少结巴。几个月后，我对马丁坦白了自己对他的第一印象。他哈哈大笑，解释说，面对我的时候说话磕绊，是因为他觉得我是这世上最美丽的女人，在我身边，他会紧张。我的心再次融化。可能你会奇怪，他那不伦不类的打扮又是怎么回事儿？答案是，马丁是色盲。

我想，这个故事告诉我们，有时候第一印象并不准确。如果当时我仅凭第一印象就对马丁下定论，那么过去八年，我就错过了世界上最优秀的男人。

——托尼·米歇尔·内尔

Long Distance Love
异地恋

In true love the smallest distance is too great, and the greatest distance can be bridged.

~Hans Nouwens

"So how did you and your fiancé meet?" My college classmate sat down beside me in the cafeteria, leaning close to look at my emerald engagement ring.

It was a common question when people found out I was just nineteen and engaged, but I always had to fight the urge to wince. I knew that no matter how delicately I tried to answer, they would be wagering on our relationship's demise.

"We knew of each other online…"

"Oh, so this was one of those new Internet relationships?" she asked. This was 1999, and most any news about the Internet boasted that it was great for finding a date and/or a sexual predator.

"No. We knew of each other online, but not well. I was in California, he was in Ohio. We were on the same e-mail list for video game fans, and we knew that we both liked the group Journey. Well,

Jason was going on a road trip to meet people from the e-mail list, and it so happened that Journey was appearing on tour not far from me at the same time. I asked if he wanted to go, and when we met, we just clicked."

"And he was in the Navy then?"

I shook my head. "No. He enlisted about six months later. We were engaged right before he went to boot camp."

When she walked away, her face was composed but I could see she was tabulating the facts in her head: two very young people in a relationship based on the Internet and video games and music; he joined the Navy; they reside on opposite coasts. It sounded like a divorce waiting to happen, if we even made it as far as the altar.

At the same time, I knew how bad it all sounded. So did Jason. He endured the same skeptical reaction from acquaintances and family. There was no way we could defend ourselves and our love with words without sounding silly and immature.

"No," Jason said. "We'll have to show them by making it."

Fairy tales and popular culture make a big deal out of love-at-first-sight, as though the heavens open in celestial chorus. The reality is much more subtle. We met in person, and we were instant friends. This was someone I could trust, someone thoughtful and respectable. To make things even more astounding, Jason made the same impression on my overly-cautious parents. I wasn't allowed to make the ten-minute bicycle ride to my grandma's house unless I called home to let my parents know that I arrived safely, yet this stoic young man instantly earned their trust and respect.

Since we lived thousands of miles apart, most of our initial courtship was done by phone and Internet. Our infrequent reunions were a delightful blur of board games and slow strolls around the local mall while walking hand-in-hand. When Jason came out to visit one final time before joining the Navy, he sold his battered car to buy my engagement ring. There was no formal wedding proposal; we were simply in consensus that we would be married, and the ring made that public. While he was in boot camp, I did the math: we had only been in each other's physical presence for a rough total of three weeks spread over a six-month span. Our engagement probably seemed hasty and foolhardy—and looking at those numbers, I could see why—but I still believed in us. Jason felt the same way, clinging to whatever correspondence I sent his way even as his fellow sailor-recruits received more and more "Dear John" letters as the weeks went by.

Our reunion took place exactly six months after he left for the Navy. It was Christmas, and having Jason in my arms again was the best gift of all. We had both endured other people's doubts about our relationship, but our love was strong. He was still utterly ruthless at Scrabble, too, and as he strategized with his tiles, it gave me ample time to renew my memory of his handsome face. And when it was my turn to play, I would catch him looking at me the same dreamy way.

While we were out shopping for Christmas presents, Jason accidentally knocked a pillow off a high shelf and onto my head.

"Spousal abuse!" cried a fellow shopper on our aisle, a teasing grin on his face. "I was a witness!"

Jason looked at me, beaming. "Spouse!" he said. "He thinks you're my wife."

"I will be," I said, squeezing his hand.

After that visit, it was almost another six months until we were together again. This time, it was for our wedding. I walked down the aisle to an orchestral version of the theme from the Final Fantasy video game series, and Jason was waiting for me, attired in Navy dinner dress whites. The next day, we packed up a Penske truck with all of my worldly belongings and made the long drive from California to my new home in South Carolina.

I didn't expect things to be easy, which was good—they weren't. I hadn't been away from my parents for longer than a week, and quite abruptly, I was 3,000 miles away and living in near-poverty. But I had Jason, and he had me, and Top Ramen noodles are mighty tasty when you're in love. Not only did we stay together, but we were content. Years passed, and we moved from South Carolina to Washington. He began preparations for deployment, and that's when I discovered I was pregnant.

Those six-month droughts without Jason back in our courting days proved to be good practice for deployment. Those same skills—constant letter and e-mail writing, care packages laden with sweets, sleeping with the phone beside my bed just in case—kept us strong while we were apart. Under the turbulent influence of hormones and loneliness, I would cry on cue when certain songs came on the radio, especially our song—Journey's "Faithfully". Jason returned home in time for the birth of our son, Nicholas, and less than a year later he was deployed again. A year after that, Jason left the Navy, and we again hauled ourselves across the country to a new home.

Next year is our ten-year anniversary. We've endured multiple deploy-ments, zigzagged the country in hectic moves, and yet we somehow still like each other. I still get tingles in my belly when Jason comes in the door after a long day at work, and we engage in vicious Scrabble matches on our designated weekly game night. We've worked together to cope with Nicholas's autism diagnosis and special needs. We're still together, against all odds, and still love Journey, video games, and each other. True love doesn't mean that things are easy—it just means the struggle is worthwhile.

And after all this time, I'm no longer afraid of people asking how we met.

~Beth Cato

真爱面前，再近的距离也觉得远，再远的距离也能跨越。

———汉斯·诺文斯

　　餐厅里，大学同学侧过身来看我手上的祖母绿订婚戒指，问："你们怎么认识的？"知道我19岁就订婚的时候，大家常会这么问。一碰到这个问题，我就想打退堂鼓。我知道，不论我回答得多么巧妙，他们总认为我们的恋爱会以失败告终。

　　"我们在网上认识的……"

　　"哦，这么说来，你们这属于时髦的网络爱情了？"她继续问。当时是1999年，几乎所有关于互联网的新闻，都认为互联网是寻找情人，或更准确地说，是寻找性爱对象的好地方。

　　"不，不是这样的。我们通过网络认识，但并不熟。我住在加利福尼亚，他在俄亥俄州。我们两个都是电动游戏迷，而且名字出现在同一份电子邮件名单里。我们也知道，对方和自己一样喜欢旅行。嗯，当时贾森正在旅行途中，去见名单里的另一个人。碰巧我那时也在附近旅行，于是问他想不想来。见面后，我们一拍即合。"

　　"那时，他已经入伍了吗？"

　　我摇了摇头说："不，他是半年之后入伍的。他去海军新兵训练营报到前，我们才订婚的。"

同学走开了，虽然她表情平静，但是我可以看到她脑海中的事实统计表：建立在网络、电玩和音乐基础上的两个年轻人的爱恋；男方参军；两人分住在美国的东、西海岸。就算能结婚，离婚也是必然的。关键问题是我自己也意识到这一切听起来有多糟糕。贾森也有同感。朋友和家人也常对此表示怀疑。我们无法用言语为自身或我们的爱情辩护。无论怎么解释，在旁人眼中，我们的举动都显得愚蠢而且幼稚。

"不，我们一定要永远相爱，用行动证明给他们看。"贾森说。

童话故事和大众文化总喜欢在一见钟情上大做文章，似乎一见倾心，就像置身天国颂歌那样神圣美妙。现实就微妙多了。我们一见如故。他细心周到，值得信任。更令人吃惊的是，贾森给我那小心过度的父母留下了同样的印象。小时候，我被禁止骑车到只有十分钟路程的祖母家，除非答应安全到达之后会给家里打电话，让父母放心。但是这个坚强的小伙子却立刻赢得了他们的信任和尊重。

相隔万里的我们，恋爱初期都是靠网络和电话联系。虽然相聚甚少，但却非常愉快。我们常常一起玩棋盘游戏，或是手牵手在当地的购物中心闲逛。贾森参军前最后一次看我的时候，卖掉了他的旧车，给我买了订婚戒指，但没有正式求婚，我们只是相信我们会在一起，戒指不过是个公开证明。他去新兵训练营报到后，我算了一下，恋爱的半年时间里，我们真正见面的时间加起来不过三周。看到这些数字，我明白了为什么我们的订婚在别人看来显得仓促草率，但我却从未有过丝毫怀疑或动摇。

贾森也是如此。他热切地回复我的每一封信。尽管随着时间推移，越来越多的新兵收到了"分手信"。在他参军整整六个月后，我们重聚了。当时是圣诞节，对我来说，能够抱着他就是世界上最好的礼物。虽然要忍受别人的怀疑，但我们的爱情强大且牢固。他依旧不擅长拼字游戏，趁他苦思冥想的时候，我仔细端详着他英俊的脸庞。轮到我玩的时候，他也同样痴痴地看着我。

有一天，我们外出购买圣诞礼物。贾森出人意料地从高架子上拿了一个枕头，在我头上敲了一下。

"家庭暴力啊！我是证人！"旁边的购物者开玩笑说。

贾森满脸笑容地看着我："他认为你是我的妻子。"

"总有一天，会是的。"我攥紧了他的手。

圣诞节之后，又过了大约半年，我们再次相聚。这次是举行婚礼。伴随着电动游戏《最终幻想》的主题曲，我走进婚礼殿堂。贾森穿着白色的海军晚宴服，在走道尽头等着我。次日，我将所有的家当塞进了潘世奇卡车，驱车从加利福尼亚前往南卡罗来纳州的新家。

我并不期待事情会十分顺利，这点很好。因为适应这一切，对我来说，确实不容易。这么大，我还从来没离开父母超过一周。突然间，我已远在 4800 多公里之外，过着接近赤贫的生活。但我们拥有对方。要知道，相爱的人就连一起吃顿泡面也觉得无比幸福。我们生活在一起，心满意足。几年后，我们从南卡罗来纳州搬到华盛顿。正当贾森为军事调派作准备的时候，我发现自己怀孕了。恋爱初期那段分别的日子锻炼了我，让我能够应付贾森不在身边的状况。那些技巧——不断地写信和发电子邮件，邮寄装满糖果的爱心礼包，睡觉时把电话放在床边方便接听——在分开的日子，维系着我们的爱情。由于孤单，再加上荷尔蒙的作用，一听到电台播放的某些歌曲，尤其是旅途乐队的《忠实》，我就会忍不住掉眼泪。儿子尼古拉斯出生的时候，贾森及时赶了回来。不到一年的时间，他再次被调派。一年后，贾森退役，我们又一次拖着家当，横穿全国到我们的新家。

Chapter 1 How We Met
第一部分 相遇篇

　　明年，就是我们结婚十周年纪念。这十年里，尽管多次分离，四处奔波，但我们的爱只增未减。每次贾森下班回家的时候，我心里还会忍不住激动。我们会在特定的周末游戏之夜，进行激烈的拼字比赛，也一起配合尼古拉斯的自闭症治疗，照顾他的特殊需求。排除万难的我们仍然在一起，仍然爱旅行、爱电动、爱对方。许久之后，我终于明白真爱并不意味着所有事情都要变得简单，而是说为了爱情，同所有困难作斗争都变得值得。

　　许久以后，我不再害怕别人问，当初我们是如何遇到的。

——贝丝·卡托

The Girl for Me
适合我的女孩

Gravitation is not responsible for people falling in love.
~Albert Einstein

People often ask when it was that I knew that my wife of twenty-five years was the girl for me. I always tell them that I knew it before I even knew her name.

It happened on a bright, crisp, autumn afternoon on my first day at college. In fact, it happened in my first class. I was a theater major and was taking Theater Crafts 101. My college advisor had assured me that the class was a great way to meet all the kids who would be in the program with me over the next four years.

So there we were—forty boisterous, nervous, excited teenagers in their first college class. None of us knew what to expect. We didn't know each other. All of us were determined to show off how talented we were. I managed to get to the lecture hall a little early to check out my classmates. There was a pretty blonde over here, a gorgeous redhead over there, and a cute brunette sitting with her best friend towards the back. I slowly strutted my way to the far side of the room and picked a chair by the windows. I was convinced the girls couldn't help but notice my natural "leading man" good looks.

Of course, Theater Crafts 101 wasn't an acting class. It was an "Introductory" class. So, after an hour and a half of being lectured on the history of Western Theater, our professor announced it was now time for some practical experience. We all hoped that meant we'd get on stage. Well, we did get on stage. Then off it again. In fact, our professor marched us downstairs to the main auditorium, up on stage, out the back, and into the workshop. The groans of disappointment could be heard in the lobby.

"All right," our professor said, barely suppressing his laughter, "I know all you future Academy Award-winning actors would prefer to be in front of the curtain right now (ironically, one of my classmates would go on to win an Academy Award), "but here," he declared, "is where the magic starts. This is where you get your hands dirty. Theater isn't just about glamour and applause. Theater is hard work. It's pitching in when things need to get done. And speaking of pitching in, your first assignment is to clean out the storage area and pitch all the trash in the Dumpster out back." People started groaning again.

Now, the assignment didn't really bother me, but some of the girls weren't very happy about it. They'd come dressed to impress. Their make-up was flawless, their hair was carefully sculpted, and their hands were freshly manicured. They hadn't planned on getting dirty in pursuit of their craft. So the guys got to show off by hauling the larger items while the girls stuck to the smaller more manageable pieces.

Since the Dumpster was in the parking lot, and that meant going down a series of hallways and out a fire door, it became apparent that we should form a bucket brigade. One person would grab a piece of scenery, haul it down a hallway, and pass it on to the next person, who would go down another hallway and hand it off to someone else. On and on it would go until the piece reached the guy perched up on the Dumpster who would drop it in. That was me.

I'd been up there about twenty minutes and was getting pretty good at it. The blonde I'd seen in class brought down a two-foot piece of wood that I gallantly tossed one-handed into the Dumpster. The redhead had found a small piece of canvas that I flipped over my shoulder with flair. Then Catherine appeared. Only, I didn't know her name just then.

Catherine was the friend of the cute brunette who'd been sitting in the back of class. She'd actually paid attention during the lecture and had asked several intelligent questions. She was also dressed in a plain flannel shirt and blue jeans. Her make-up was understated and she hadn't groaned when we were told to haul garbage.

Catherine was carrying a two-foot by six-foot flat. Flats are wooden frames covered in canvas. Once painted, a flat could be used to represent anything from a garden wall to a sunny sky. Though not really heavy, they can be cumbersome to maneuver. I was just taken by the fact that she'd opted to pick up something that weighed more than three pounds.

"Thanks, babe," I said as I leaned down and reached for the flat. I think it was the "babe" that impressed her.

"That's all right," she said. "I've got it."

"Hey," I replied with my best Brad Pitt smile. "I'm here; let me help."

Catherine gave me a small shake of her head and then said: "Duck."

"Excuse me?"

Catherine repeated her instruction, slowly. "D-u-c-k."

I was perched on the side of a commercial Dumpster and the lip to the steel container was a good six or seven feet off the ground. I wasn't sure what she intended to do. "Look," I began, "why don't you just let me…?"

Without another word Catherine reached back, grabbed hold of the flat with both hands, and proceeded to swing it around. I dropped down in time to watch the two-foot by six-foot frame sail neatly up over my head and into the Dumpster. The steel container clanged when the wood hit the bottom. I turned in time to spot a hint of a smile on Catherine's face as she gave me a nod, dusted off her hands, and walked away. I remembered crouching there, having nearly been conked in the head by flying scenery, and thinking: "Strong girl."

In that instant I learned all I ever needed to know about my future wife. I learned about her strength (both physical and of character); I learned about her stubborn streak of independence; and I learned about her wicked sense of humor. It would be two more years before we started dating and five till we got married. But on that day, by that Dumpster, I met the girl of my dreams. I just had to wait for my knees to stop shaking in order to realize it.

~Arthur Sanchez

并非万有引力让人们坠入爱河。

——阿尔伯特·爱因斯坦

我和妻子已经结婚 25 年了。人们常常问我，是什么时候认定她就是那个会和我共度一生的人。我总是告诉他们，还不知道她的名字时我就认定了。故事发生在一个明亮、清爽的秋日午后，那是我大学入学的第一天。实际上，发生在我的第一堂课上。我读戏剧专业，选修戏剧工艺品 101 课程。因为大学辅导员对我保证，这门课是了解未来四年同窗的极好方式。

所以我们齐聚在此——40个兴高采烈、紧张兴奋的少年开始了他们大学的第一堂课。没有人知道会发生什么。我们也不认识对方。所有人都下定决心要展现自身的才华。提前来到阶梯教室的我一边等候，一边观察周围的同学。这边有个漂亮的金发女郎，那边坐着一个华丽的红头发女生，后面还有一位可爱的深褐色头发女生，同她的好朋友坐在一起。我大摇大摆、慢吞吞地走到教室的另一边，挑了个靠窗的位置坐下。我十分确信，女孩们一定会注意到我英俊的外表，以及"天生"的领袖气质。当然，戏剧工艺品101课程并不是表演课，只是"入门课"。所以，一个半小时的西方戏剧史介绍后，教授宣布接下来进入课堂实践环节。所有人都期待着，以为我们可以登台表演。嗯，我们确实登台了，但紧接着，又下去了。实际上，教授领着我们去了楼下的大礼堂，走上舞台，转到后面，进入工作室。大厅里怨声载道。

"好的，"教授强忍着笑，"我知道，你们这些未来的奥斯卡金像奖得主更喜欢站在幕布前（讽刺的是，我们中的某一位将来真有可能获得奥斯卡金像奖）。但是这儿，这儿是奇迹发生的地方。在这儿，你的手会被弄脏。剧院不仅仅意味着鲜花和掌声，它更意味着辛苦的工作。要把事情做好，就需要贡献。讲到贡献，你们的第一项工作就是清理储物区，把所有垃圾丢到后面的大垃圾桶去。"话音刚落，又是一片呻吟。

这项任务对我没有多大影响，一些女生却很不高兴。她们过来是为了给人留下深刻印象的——完美无瑕的妆容，精心打理的发型，刚刚修过的指甲。这些女生可不愿意为了舞台道具而破坏自己的形象。所以，男生必须用力拖拽大件物品，女生则拿一些轻巧的小东西。

大垃圾桶摆在外面的停车场上，这就意味着我们需要穿过一系列走廊，还有一扇防火门。显然，我们需要排成一列。一个人拿起布景道具，搬到走廊，递给下一个人。再由他搬到下个走廊，递给另一个人。依次传递，直到道具传给站在垃圾桶旁边的男生——我，由我负责丢进去。

二十多分钟后，我已经很熟悉动作流程。刚在教室里看到的金发女生抱来一块半米多长的木头，我单手轻松地将它扔进垃圾桶里。红头发女生找到了一小块帆布，我凭感觉直接向后丢了进去。然后，卡瑟琳来了。不过那时候，我还不知道她的名字。

卡瑟琳是坐在教室后面那个深褐色头发女生的好朋友。课堂上，她认真听讲，还提了几个很巧妙的问题。和我一样，她也穿着简单的法兰绒衬衣，蓝色牛仔裤。脸上的妆淡淡的，我们被告知搬垃圾的时候，她没有抱怨。

卡瑟琳搬了一块约 1.8 米 x 0.6 米大小的背景板。这种背景板由蒙上画布的木质框架构成。作画以后，既可以用来代表花园的墙壁，也可以表示晴朗的天空。尽管不是特别重，但搬起来却很困难。我很吃惊，她会主动搬一件超过两斤半重的道具。

"谢谢你，宝贝！"说着，我走近，打算接背景板。我觉得那声"宝贝"引起了她的注意。

"没关系，"她回答，"我自己来。"

"嘿！"我脸上露出了布拉德·皮特式的微笑，"有我呢，我帮你。"

卡瑟琳对我摇了摇头："躲开。"

"什么？"

卡瑟琳一字一顿地复述了指令："躲——开。"

我移到了垃圾桶旁边，这个钢制的大家伙足有两米左右高。我不知道卡瑟琳要做什么："我说，为什么不让我……"

话还没说完，就看到卡瑟琳后退几步，两手抓住背景板，转了一下，随即扔出。幸亏我及时蹲了下来。只见这 1.8 米 x 0.6 米的大家伙擦着我的头皮，直直地飞了过去，掉进垃圾桶。木框架沉底的时候，钢制垃圾桶哐当一声巨响。等我回过神，只看到卡瑟琳微微笑了笑，冲我点下头，拍了拍手，走开了。回想起刚才那惊险的一幕，我不禁惊叹："真厉害啊！"

就在那一瞬间，我知晓了未来妻子的一切。我知道了她的强大，她的独立，还有她坏坏的幽默感。两年多后，我们开始约会。五年后，我们结婚了。就在那天，在垃圾桶旁边，我遇到了梦想中的女孩。我只是需要等到膝盖不再打战，才能实现梦想。

——亚瑟·桑切斯

"I'm majoring in English, Math and True Love this term... how about you?"

"我这学期主修英语、数学还有爱情……你呢？"

One Enchanted Evening
一个神奇的夜晚

Happiness often sneaks in through a door you didn't know you left open.

~John Barrymore

After my divorce, I dated a very charming man for several years who, despite all that he had to offer, could never really make a commitment to me or to a future together. We separated and reunited many times, and finally, we found the courage to end the relationship once and for all. It was agonizing, but the healthiest thing we could have done for one another.

After the end of our relationship, I really swore off men. I was the single mother of two small children, trying to balance a full-time career with motherhood, and managing well, most of the time. I didn't have a strong desire to have anyone else in my life, though occasionally I did long for a playmate and lover. Given the situation, it was really just easier not to get involved.

By the spring of 2001, I had been on the Board

of Directors of the American Heart Association in my county for six years. As part of my duties, I volunteered annually with the AHA Annual Gala. Somehow, getting sponsors and auction items for "the Ball" just seemed more glamorous than the other service options, and Lord knows, being a single mother, I didn't have much glamour in my life.

Given that it was my last term, I worked my tail off to make the event as special as it could possibly be. It was set at the new Grand Californian Hotel at Disneyland in California. We had arranged for David Benoit to play for us that evening, and there were terrific silent and live auctions to tantalize all of our guests. My swan song looked complete, but by the night before the event, I couldn't stomach the idea of attending one more gala, especially alone.

I finished the last of my To-Do list and hugged my director, then wished the committee well. My director, realizing that I did not mean to attend the event, looked aghast. I was even more surprised when the refined sixty-something belle told me in no uncertain terms that I would get my tail to the event, OR ELSE. I had never seen her like this, and wasn't quite sure what would happen if I argued with her. I squinched up my face at her, and left the building. I began speed-dialing the sitter I had used, hoping that I could even get someone to take care of the kids at such late notice. After getting a confirmation from the sitter, I headed to the mall. I pawed through the dresses on the rack, doubtful that I would find something in time, and completed the purchase of a deep-blue gown as Security began locking the doors for the night.

By 4:00 P.M. Saturday, I was a wreck. I tried to hold myself together, glaring at the clock with every minute that the sitter was late. A half-hour later, the sitter arrived and I dashed off to the ball. I deposited my car with the valet, strode into the hotel, and tried to scan the crowd for my director. Inside the VIP lounge, I spied her across the room with a few of my close colleagues.

After a brief hug, I told her that I wouldn't be staying for dinner, and she seemed to take no notice. She handed me a glass of champagne and asked my opinion about the auction tables. We talked shop for a few minutes before she asked if I'd met Thom Breslin. "Old, fat, balding cardiologist" is what I thought to myself, knowing that the event was often attended by these types. I told her that I hadn't, and she mentioned that he'd lost his wife to cancer. The image in my mind aged a few more years, and I wondered why she'd asked. She must have caught the expression on my face, because she took that opportunity to suggest that we go join her husband, Roger. As I'd spent Christmas the year before with them, I was pleased that he was attending the event.

As she turned to join Roger's group, I turned away from them to hand the waiter my glass. When I turned back around, in front of me was one of the most handsome men I'd ever seen. I quickly averted my eyes and hugged Roger, clasping his hands. And, with a gentle steer back to the others, Roger asked me, "Have you met Thom Breslin?" That whole "old, fat, balding cardiologist" thing just fell away with his words.

I thought for a moment that I might actually faint. I don't know if it was the form-fitting dress, the champagne gone to my head, or an actual swoon, but I had to remind myself to breathe as he reached out to shake my hand.

We spoke then, about our careers, our lives, and our loves. I shared about my divorce, and he spoke about losing the love of his life to cancer after twenty-one years together. I tried to be empathic and compassionately offered, "I'm so glad that you had so many wonderful years of such deep love." And, to my surprise, he responded, "Yes—but I want to have that again!"

And, with that, we both realized that, while rapt in conversation, the room had emptied and left us in the bubble we'd created with our stories. The dinner bell rang, alerting us to find our tables. We quickly scanned the auction tables, playfully flirting and then headed toward the ballroom. There, this handsome man deposited me at my table at the back of the room and went off to join the head table, as he was a guest of the Director.

As I bit into my salad and pondered what had just happened, something caught my eye and I looked up. There, coming across the room towards me, was Dr. Thom Breslin. "How's your seat?" I asked, knowing that the head table was directly in front of the stage. "Funny," he replied, "there doesn't seem to be a seat left for me." Glancing to my right and left, I was met with open chairs. I lifted my eyes towards his, amazed by their sparkle. I pulled out a chair, and with a smile, he sat beside me. The rest of the evening, for both of us, is now a blur.

It's eight years and three children later, and we still feel blessed to have met in that crowded room. While my director finally confessed to setting us up, so much of our encounter was truly magical. Thom shared with me later that his first date with his late wife, Jennifer, had been at Disney World in Florida. And, so, it seemed simply divine that, in a ballroom, he'd find love again with me, in the "happiest place on Earth".

~Sage de Beixedon Breslin

在你还没发现门敞开的时候，幸福已经悄悄溜了进来。

——约翰·巴里摩尔

离婚后，我同一位非常迷人的男子交往了几年。他做了男朋友该做的一切，却从不给我任何承诺，也绝口不提两人的未来。多次分手又复合后，我们鼓起勇气，决定一刀两断。分手很痛苦，但却是我们能为彼此做的最好的事。

结束这段感情后，我对男人避而远之。作为一名带着两个年幼孩子的单身母亲，我试图在一份全职工作和母亲的角色中找到平衡。大部分的时间，我都处理得很好。尽管偶尔也找玩伴和情人，我却不打算寻找另一半。考虑到当时的情况，还是不要恋爱的好。

到 2001 年春，我已在当地美国心脏协会董事局工作六年。作为职责的一部分，我每年都会到美国心脏协会举办的周年盛典做志愿者。不知何故，为"舞会"寻找赞助商和拍卖品，似乎比其他的工作更有魅力。天知道，作为一位单身母亲，我的生活没有多少魅力可言。

鉴于这是我在职的最后一届，我竭尽全力想把这次大会办得特别一些。大会地点选在加州迪士尼乐园的大加州酒店。我们邀请了美国演奏家大卫·班华作为当晚的表演嘉宾，还安排了现场拍卖以及精彩的默片取悦客人。我的"最后一歌"完成了，但我不打算参加晚会，尤其在没有伴的情况下。

划掉单子上最后一个待办事项，我拥抱了主管，祝愿组委会一切顺利，打算告别。主管意识到我不想参加，非常吃惊。当这位修养良好，年近六十依旧风姿绰约的主管，对我吼"天塌下来你也得过来"的时候，我惊呆了。从未见过她发脾气的我不知道继续争论会产生什么后果。

满面愁容地离开大楼后，我开始迅速地给以前雇用过的保姆打电话，希望这么短的时间内，能找到一个保姆。得到保姆确认后，我又急忙跑到商场，在衣架上乱翻，不知道能否快速找到一件合适的礼服。终于，赶在保安锁门之前，我买了一件深蓝色礼服。

周六下午 4 点钟，我已经急得不成样子。保姆迟到了。我试着保持镇静，眼睛紧盯着闹钟，时间一分一秒地过去。半小时后，保姆终于赶到，我这才急匆匆地赶往大会现场。车子交给代存员后，我大步流星地走进酒店，试图在人群中找到主管。在 VIP 休息室里，我看到了主管，旁边还有几位熟悉的同事。

简单的拥抱后，我告诉她我不能留下来吃晚餐，但她似乎没在意。主管递给我一杯香槟，问我对旁边的拍品怎么看。聊了一会儿后，她问我，是否见过托姆·布雷斯林。我心里暗想"肯定是个又胖又老而且秃顶的心脏病学家"，因为来参加晚会的大部分都是这种类型。我回答说："还没有。"主管就告诉我，托姆的妻子前不久因癌症去世。脑海中托姆的形象又老了几岁，不明白主管为什么和我说这个。她肯定看到了我脸上的表情，因此她趁机提议，到她丈夫罗杰那儿去。因为去年是和他们夫妇一起过的圣诞，所以我很开心能在晚会上见到他。

当主管朝丈夫罗杰走去时，我转身把手中的玻璃杯递给服务员。等我再次转身的时候，我面前站着一个世界上最帅的男人。我飞快地移开了目光，拥抱了罗杰，紧紧握着他的手。罗杰温和地看了看其他人，问我："见过托姆·布雷斯林了吗？"脑海中"又胖又老而且秃顶的心脏病学家"的形象忽然消失了。

我觉得自己快要昏倒了。不知道是紧身礼服的关系，还是因为刚才喝了香槟，抑或是真的头晕。托姆过来和我握手的时候，我不得不提醒自己千万要保持呼吸。

后来，我们开始聊天，谈工作，谈生活，谈爱情。我对他讲述了离婚经历，他也告诉我，和妻子共度 21 年后，因癌症痛失爱妻的哀伤。我试着体会他的感受，充满同情地说："在真爱陪伴下度过那么多美好时光，真让人羡慕。"他的回答让人意外："确实如此，但我还想再次体会真爱！"

我们聊得那么投入，喧闹的大厅似乎突然间变得空无一人，只留下我们在滔滔不绝的对话中编写着属于两人的故事。此时，大厅里餐铃声响起，提醒我们尽快入席。我们快速地扫了一眼拍卖桌，一边俏皮地调情，一边快步向大厅走去。我的座位在大厅靠后的桌子旁，而这个英俊的男人，作为主管的客人，坐在大厅靠前的桌子旁。正当我咬着沙拉，回忆刚才的一切时，一个物体挡在我面前。我抬起头，穿过整个大厅走到我面前的正是托姆·布雷斯林医生。"你的座位呢？"我问，因为贵宾桌就在舞台的正前方。"真奇怪，"他回答说，"那儿好像没我的位子了。"我看了看左右两边的空位，又看了看他，随后拉出一张空椅子。他笑了笑，坐在了我旁边。后来发生了什么，我们已经记不清了。

在一起八年，有了三个孩子之后，我们仍为能在人群拥挤的大厅遇到对方感到幸运。尽管后来，主管承认是有意撮合我们，但我们的相遇仍然充满神秘色彩。托姆后来告诉我，他和已故妻子珍妮弗的第一次约会也是在佛罗里达的迪士尼乐园。所以说，迪士尼乐园似乎真的非常神奇，因为在"最快乐的地方"他又一次在舞会大厅找到了人生的挚爱——我。

——萨哲·得·贝希顿·布雷斯林

"Is the room crowded?
I thought it was Just
you and me in here!"

"房间里很多人吗？我觉得就只有你我两个人！"

Hope Deferred
迟来的爱情

Hope is patience with the lamp lit.

~Tertullian

"Congratulations, girlfriend. I'd love to fly out for your wedding." I dropped the phone, the tears flowing. Not only were three close friends planning weddings, but my brother and sister had each just tied the knot as well. My thoughts turned to Jonathan and our recently cancelled nuptials. It wasn't easy going through heartbreak while those closest to me realized their heart's desires.

Four years earlier a very intuitive friend had shared a profound moment with me. She strongly sensed I would one day have a life partner who would meet my every desire. She warned me, "Be careful and wait for him."

Thrilled that her words confirmed the dreams within my heart, I believed the wait surely wouldn't be longer than a couple of years.

As my twenties evolved into my thirties, that

promise turned bittersweet. The word "spinster", not yet in my vocabulary, began to nag at me. I didn't want to meet just any guy. I wanted the guy, the one who was destined for me—was I too picky? Tall and thin with long, curly blond hair—was I pretty enough? A Bachelor's in Sociology and a Master's in Theology—should I appear less successful, not quite as smart, more relaxed? Why was it easy for others to find someone to love, but so hard for me?

"Martha, I'm hosting a beach party tonight at my place. Would you like to join us?" asked Mark. "Count me in," I replied. I never turned down an opportunity to meet Mr. Right.

That evening a tall stranger with black hair and green eyes approached me. "Hi, I'm Peter. Didn't I meet you at Mark's ranch last summer?"

"You might be confusing me with my twin sister, Mary," I commented.

"That's right, I remember now. So Mary's your twin?" he said.

I wondered, was this slight confusion really destiny bringing us together?

Peter, a successful entrepreneur, invited me to explore with him. We flew kites on a hillside, discovered the back streets of the city, and enjoyed fine dining with international flair. After six months of dating, I was crazy about him. I thought the time had come to take the temperature of our relationship. At the end of a long phone conversation I asked, "Peter, where do you see our relationship going?"

"Martha, I don't see myself getting married for at least five years. And you know I have this ideal picture in my mind of the type of girl I want to spend the rest of my life with. I've really fallen for you, but I don't see marriage in our future."

My heart shattered in a thousand tiny fragments. How could I make sense of this? He wanted to be with me now... but not for a lifetime. Should I continue to date him... and hope his feelings changed? How could I stop the pain without isolating myself from living?

It turned out there were many others in my same circumstance... successful, smart, thirty-something women wanting to start families before it was too late. My roommate came up with the idea of a support group. "Let's meet with other women to navigate through these singles' issues together."

"That sounds like a fantastic idea," I replied.

For two years, fifteen women met twice a month to discuss books like *Men Are from Mars, Women Are from Venus,* and *Love Must Be Tough.* We learned, laughed and cried together as we developed lifelong friendships. One by one the women found their husbands—all except me. I still waited, as doubt encroached on the hope left in my heart.

At forty, directed by a strange sense of destiny, I moved to Colorado. Everything seemed novel and exciting: the mountains, my career in real estate, interesting friends. Within a year I became engaged to a lawyer with three children from two previous marriages.

Friends warned me. "Martha, are you certain you're making the right decision?" Sure enough, within two months his controlling personality chased me away without a backward glance.

I poured myself into the home I had purchased. When the interior design resembled a model home, I studied landscape design and turned my bare slope into a beautiful, shady garden. My Cocker Spaniel, Annie, and my affectionate tabby, Oliver, took the place of children. I entertained groups of friends, traveled abroad, immersed myself in work, and began to write poetry—yet something eluded me. Joy and laughter were not a daily experience. In fact, I found it hard to find humor in anything. Almost fifty, I experienced the Proverb, "Hope deferred makes the heart sick."

One evening, engrossed in the speaker's words at a church dinner, I glanced casually at a guy with an athletic build across the table from me. What a nice-looking man. I wondered what his story was.

As we stood up and walked toward the buffet line, he slid in beside me and introduced himself. "Hello, I'm Paul, a guest of Bob and Huntley. It's nice to be out meeting new people. Tell me about yourself. Are you from Colorado?" We talked, laughed and sparked an interest in one another.

The next evening I received an e-mail from Huntley. "Paul asked for your phone number. May we pass it on?" Not only thrilled, I felt peaceful about him, his character and trustworthiness.

Paul had married his high school sweetheart after graduating from college, so he had never been part of the crazy dating world I knew. He didn't understand about playing games, being afraid to commit, or never calling after saying he would. His last seven years had been focused on taking care of a wife dying slowly of emphysema. His world of oxygen tanks, emergency wards and surgeries had finally ended when she succumbed to the disease. During her last days, she made him promise to carry on with life.

As Paul and I spent time together, my laughter returned. He instinctively knew how to make me feel secure, never comparing me to his spouse, and assuring me, "Martha, you're not the next chapter in my life... you're a new volume." He hugged me until I couldn't catch my breath and I felt our bond tighten.

For my part, I brought Paul back into the land of the living. Together we hiked, camped, occasionally hunted, water skied... and attended my nephew's wedding. As they took their vows, I realized I had fallen deeply in love.

Six months from the day we met, he led me to his hillside prayer spot. "I've never experienced what I have with you. We love the same activities, want the same things in life, and think the same way." He laughed. "You speak the words that are going through my head before I can say them. I can't imagine living life without you."

My heart stopped as I looked down at the emerald-cut diamond he placed on my finger. I flashed back to my friend's admonition to wait for the one who would be my every desire. Paul seemed more of a soulmate than I could possibly have hoped for, more like me than my twin sister. The waiting had paid off, my joy found completion as I envisioned our future together.

~Martha Eitzen as told to Margaret Lang

耐心点燃希望之灯。

——德尔图良

"恭喜啊，一定参加你的婚礼。"放下电话的我早已泪流满面。最亲密的三个好友开始筹备婚礼，弟弟和妹妹也都结婚了。我想起了未婚夫乔纳森还有我们刚刚取消的婚礼。伤心欲绝的时候，听到最亲近的人纷纷找到了他们的人生伴侣，我的日子并不好过。

四年前，一位直觉很准的朋友曾告诉我，未来我一定会遇到一位符合我一切期望的完美伴侣。她提醒我："要耐心等待直到他出现。"

她的话印证了我内心深处的期待，我十分兴奋，觉得不多久我的白马王子一定会出现。

当我从二十多岁的花样年华等到了三十岁的而立之年，朋友的预言变得苦乐参半。尽管"老处女"这个词还没有出现在我的词典里，但我已经开始担心，只是不愿意随便找个人将就。只想要命中注定的那个人，是我太挑剔了吗？高挑的身材、卷曲的金发，我不够漂亮吗？社会学学士、神学硕士，我不够成功不够聪明吗，还是太拘谨？为什么大家都能找到爱人，我却那么难？

"玛莎，我今晚举办海滩派对，你愿意来吗？"马克问。

"算我一个！"我回答。我从不放过任何一个有可能遇到真命天子的机会。那天晚上，一位头发乌黑、有着迷人绿色眼睛的陌生男子走到我身边说："你好，我是皮特。去年夏天，在马克的牧场里，我们是不是见过？"

"哦，你一定是把我和我的双胞胎妹妹玛丽弄混了。"我解释道。

"没错，我这会儿想起来了。这么说，玛丽是你的双胞胎妹妹？"他问。

我心里打鼓，这是上苍有意安排的吗？他就是我要等的那个人吗？

皮特是位成功的企业家。他邀我陪他一起探寻生活的精彩。我们一起到山顶放风筝，探寻城市的穷街陋巷，品尝各地美食。交往半年后，我深深地爱上了他。某天，在一通很长的电话后，我问他："皮特，你觉得我们的感情会发展到哪一步？"

"玛莎，至少五年内，我都不打算结婚。我很清楚自己想要和什么样的女人共度一生。我真的很喜欢你，但我不会娶你。"

我的心碎了一地。我该怎么理解他的话？现在他愿意和我交往……但是同我过一辈子不行。我该和他继续吗，盼着某天他能改变想法？怎么做才能摆脱这巨大的痛苦，坚强地活下去？

事实证明，和我有同样境遇的还有很多人。我们都三十出头，事业成功，头脑聪慧，想趁自己还不算太老的时候结婚嫁人。室友提议成立一个互助小组："这样，我们可以同其他的单身女子一同面对，共渡难关。"

"好主意。"我回答说。

接下来的两年，15名单身女子每个月聚两次，探讨如《男人来自火星，女人来自金星》《爱必须坚强》等。我们一起学习，一起哭，一起笑，建立起终身的友谊。逐渐地，互助小组的成员一个接一个找到了自己的人生伴侣——除了我。我仍然坚持等待，不过内心的希望渐渐消散，取而代之的是无尽的怀疑和困惑。

40岁那年，仿佛受到命运的感召，我搬到了科罗拉多州。一切都新鲜有趣：群山环绕，风光旖旎，房地产工作也蒸蒸日上，新结识的朋友幽默风趣。不到一年，我同一位带着三个孩子的离异律师订了婚。

朋友们纷纷劝我："玛莎，你确定吗？"但没过两个月，我就被未婚夫强烈的控制欲吓得落荒而逃。

之后，我全身心地投入到新家的装修设计中。内部的装修完成的时候，房子看起来就像一栋现代小别墅。随后，我又研究景观设计，将光秃秃的斜坡改造成绿草茵茵的漂亮花园。可卡犬安妮和花斑猫奥利弗就像我的孩子们一样。我结交了很多朋友，常常去国外旅行，全身心地工作，也开始作诗——然而，还是有些缺憾。欢笑和喜悦并不是每天都有。相反，我发现并不是每件事都能变得有趣。在将近50岁的时候，我终于懂得什么叫"迟来的希望，忧愁的心"。

一天傍晚，在教堂晚宴上，听着主讲人发言的我，偶然看到对面那桌坐着一位身材魁伟的男人。真英俊啊，我忍不住好奇他会有着怎样的精彩人生。

当我们起身走到自助餐桌前时，他走到我身边，同我打招呼："你好，我叫保罗，是鲍伯和亨特利的朋友。很高兴认识你，和我讲讲你的故事吧。你来自科罗拉多吗？"我们有说有笑，彼此印象很好。

次日晚上，我收到了亨特利的电子邮件："保罗问你的电话号码，我们能告诉他吗？"我非常开心，更重要的是我觉得内心非常平和。因为保罗品行很好，值得信任。

　　大学毕业后，保罗同高中时代交往的女友结婚。所以，没有疯狂约会的经历。他不懂什么是爱情游戏，不惧怕承诺，也不会答应打电话却再不联系。过去的七年时间，保罗一直悉心照顾患肺气肿的妻子。这其间，他的世界只有氧气罐、紧急病房以及无休止的外科手术。妻子临终之前，要求他保证自己离开之后，会继续开心生活。

　　和保罗在一起，我总是很快乐。他知道如何给我安全感，从不拿我同他前妻作比较，并且安慰我说："玛莎，你不是我生命中的下个篇章，你是崭新的一卷。"他会紧紧拥抱着我，直到我不能呼吸。每当此时，我都会觉得我们之间的感情又加深了一层。

　　从我这方面说，我将保罗重新拉回正常人的生活。我们一起徒步旅行，到郊外野营，偶尔也会出去狩猎，或者滑水……也一起参加我侄子的婚礼。听到新人宣誓的时候，我发觉自己早已深深爱上了保罗。

　　相遇半年后的某一天，他带我走到常常祈祷的山坡。"玛莎，你带给我从未有过的体验。我们热爱相同的体育运动，有同样的生活追求，甚至连想法也一样。"他笑着继续说道，"你常常会脱口而出我想要讲的话，我不敢想象，没有你我该怎么办。"

　　当他为我戴上那枚祖母绿钻戒时，我的心似乎停止了跳动。我想起了朋友的劝诫，耐心等待直到遇到符合你一切期望的男子。保罗甚至比我想象中还要完美，他比我的孪生姐妹更加了解我。这么多年的等待终于得到了回报，想到今后能厮守一生，我的喜悦再无缺憾。

　　　　　　　　　　　　　　　　——玛莎·伊特仁口述，玛格丽特·郎执笔

Love at First Flight
爱在首飞

Nothing compares with the finding of true love; because once you do your heart is complete.

~Anonymous

I wanted an exciting job. Sure, I needed to pay my bills along the way. But money was not the first thought on my mind when I accepted a job as a ticket agent for Midway Airlines. I was sold at the mention of free flights and buddy passes for my friends. I didn't even ask about my hourly wage. I didn't care.

Two days prior to my first day on the job, I called the company to find out a few things—things I couldn't ask the lady who interviewed me.

"Is this job fun?"

"Uh, I guess," replied a baffled male voice.

"Good," I said. "I'm starting Wednesday. What are the other employees like?"

"Well, they are mostly male. A lot of us are in our twenties—except for the boss and a couple of baggage handlers. It's pretty laid back though."

"Perfect. I'll see you then. By the way, what's

your name?"

"Craig," he said. "Craig Face."

I showed up that Wednesday wearing khaki pants and a Midway polo. I had my ID badge made, filled out paperwork, and then my boss, Rizz, introduced me to my co-workers.

"I'm going to have you start training with Craig," Rizz said. "Shadow him for a while as he checks passengers in."

I recognized the name right away. He was the one I had spoken with on the phone. And in case there was a chance he had forgotten, I reintroduced myself.

"I remember you," he said shyly. "You wanted to know if this job was fun."

"Guilty!" I laughed.

"This isn't the fun part. But wait until we go out to meet the planes."

For the next couple of hours, I watched Craig book flights, hand out tickets, and assist with lost luggage. I learned about three-letter airport codes, the list of prohibited items, and how to check baggage. It was interesting—but not exactly "fun".

Since Midway was a small airline, we were also responsible for meeting the arriving planes, guiding them in with glow sticks, and unloading the luggage. That was the next part I needed to learn.

"Let's go," Craig said. "We need to head out to the tarmac before the CRJ gets here."

"What's a CRJ?" I asked.

"It's a type of plane. It stands for Canadair Regional Jet."

Craig handed me a pair of ear protectors as we walked through the terminal. I wondered why I would need them but I put them around my neck just in case.

Once we were outside in the sun, Craig and I sat on a luggage cart and waited for our plane. I was starting to have fun. I felt an adrenaline rush just watching the plane's landing gear meet the runway.

Then, I watched Craig guide the aircraft towards the gate. His tan arms were outstretched and the sun was glistening off his dirty-blond hair. He looked extremely handsome and I realized I was staring at him.

I also realized that I needed my ear protection after all. The jet engines were deafening as the plane approached.

Craig and I (and the other employees) worked together at the airport for about a week. Then our supervisor said she was sending me to Raleigh for training.

"I'm going to send you and Craig," she said. "You guys started around the same time, so it should work out."

It definitely worked out. For two weeks, Craig and I went to class during the day and went out to dinner at night. We tried every restaurant within walking distance of RDU (Raleigh Durham International Airport) and stayed up talking and laughing until the early morning hours.

I was sad when the training was over. Craig and I had gotten to know each other very well and I had fallen for his witty comments and easy-going personality. It was an amazing experience.

But once we returned home, the job wasn't as exciting as it first seemed. It was hot out on the tarmac, the customers were rude, and I was hardly ever scheduled to work with Craig. I quit the job a couple of weeks later.

Some things just aren't meant to be. That job happened to be one of them. It was fun for a while, but I needed to get serious about my life. I needed to go back to school and finish my degree. That's exactly what I did. I enrolled in a summer class and focused on my schoolwork. But I didn't completely abandon fun. I still went out on the weekends and enjoyed the local bands with my friends and classmates. And I dated Craig.

I don't know that I believe that everything in life happens for a reason. But I do believe some things do. I believe that I was meant to work for Midway Airlines. How else would I have met my future husband?

Craig and I have been together for nine years and married for five. We've shared a lot of special memories over the years, but few are as fond as our two-week training in Raleigh.

And he still loves to pick on me about our very first conversation.

"I can't believe you actually called a job to ask if it was fun," he says.

"I know. That was pretty silly of me. But at least I knew what I was looking for."

"I did too," he argues.

"Yeah?"

"Yeah. And I found her."

~Melissa Face

世间最幸福的事莫过于发现真爱，因为真爱的出现将弥补你内心的缺憾。

——逸名

我想找份有趣的工作。当然，付账单也是原因之一。接受中途航空公司代理受票人的工作时，我首先想到的不是钱，而是因为面试官随口的一句话——公司对员工家属及朋友会提供一定优惠甚至免单。我甚至没有问每小时薪水多少。我不在意这些。

正式上班的前两天，我给中途航空打电话了解一些事情——那些我没办法直接问女面试官的事情。

"工作有趣吗？"

"嗯，还算有趣吧！"听筒那边传来困惑不解的男性嗓音。

"很好，"我回答，"我周三开始上班，其他职员是什么样的人呢？"

"嗯，男性居多，大部分都 20 岁左右——除了老板和几个行李员。但是工作非常悠闲。"

"太好了，到时候见。顺便问一下，你叫什么？"

"克雷格，克雷格·费斯。"他回答。

周三，我穿着中途航空的保罗衫、卡其色裤子，到公司报到。做好身份证件，填完表格之后，老板瑞兹领着我，向我介绍周围的同事。

老板："先跟着克雷格吧，他给乘客做登机检查时，你在旁边留心学习。"

我立刻意识到他就是接电话的那个人。但怕他忘了这件事，我又再次介绍了自己。他害羞地回答："我记得你，你打电话问这份工作是不是有趣。"

"认罪！"我笑着说。

"现在还没到有趣的部分。但是等到我们去接机的时候，还算蛮有趣的。"

接下来的几小时，我跟着克雷格，看他预定航班，分发机票，协助处理遗失行李。我学会了三个字母的机场代号，了解违禁物品清单，以及如何检查乘客行李。工作不枯燥，但也算不上"有趣"。

因为中途航空公司的规模并不大，所以我们也同样负责接机，用荧光棒引导飞机降落，装卸行李等。这些就是我接下来要学习的内容。

"走吧，"克雷格说，"让我们赶在 CRJ 之前到达跑道。"

"什么是 CRJ？"我问。

"CRJ 是一种飞机型号，全称 Canadair Regional Jet，即加拿大区域客机。"

经过航站楼的时候，克雷格递给我一副护耳器。我不明白为什么，但还是把它挂在脖子上，以防万一。

走出航站楼，外面阳光明媚，克雷格和我坐在行李推车上等待着即将降落的飞机。我开始觉得有趣了，飞机起落架接触跑道的一刹那，我内心一阵激动。

之后，我看着克雷格引导飞机朝登机口方向降落。他黝黑的双臂直直张开，褐色的金发在阳光下散发出迷人的光彩。他那么英俊，我突然意识到自己看入迷了。

我也明白了为什么护耳器是必要的。飞机靠近时，喷气式引擎的响声震耳欲聋。

我和克雷格（还有其他员工）在机场工作了将近一周。上司告诉我，她打算派我到美国北卡罗来纳州首府罗利市接受培训。

她说："我打算让你同克雷格一起过去。你们两个同时开始工作，应该会配合得很好。"

我们确实配合得不错。接下来的两周，白天我和克雷格一起上课，晚上一起出去吃晚餐。我们吃遍了罗利一都林国际机场附近的每家餐馆，有说有笑，直到次日清晨再次见面。

培训结束的时候，我很伤心。克雷格和我已经熟悉了彼此。他幽默诙谐的话语、随和的个性深深打动了我。

回到本部正式工作后，工作不像起初那么有趣。室外的停机坪温度非常高，有些客人态度十分粗鲁，我也很少和克雷格一起值班。几周后，我选择了辞职。

有些事情并不是那么重要，这份工作就是其中之一。起初工作很有意思，但是我必须对自己的人生负责。我需要重回学校，完成学业，获得学位。

我正是这么做的，我参加了暑假班，认真学习，但也没有完全放弃玩乐。周末的时候，我仍然会和同学或朋友一起出去，听当地乐队的演奏。而且，我开始同克雷格约会。我不知道"万事皆有因"是否正确。但我的确相信，有些事情是命中注定的。我觉得自己就是注定要到中途航空公司工作。不然，我如何会遇到自己现在的丈夫？

我和克雷格相恋九年，结婚五年。这些年，我们留下很多特别的回忆，但都没有我们在罗利机场培训的那两周新奇有趣。

克雷格到现在还喜欢打趣我们的第一次对话。

"真不敢相信，你打电话只是为了问工作有没有意思。"他说。

"我知道，当时挺傻的。但我至少知道自己追求什么。"

"我也知道自己要什么。"他争辩道。

"是吗？"

"当然，而且我已经找到了她。"

———梅丽莎·费斯

"The job may not have been fun... but the benefits were wonderful!"

"这工作可能没什么乐趣……但是却有额外的收获！"

Loathing at First Sight
初见生厌

There's nothing in this world so sweet as love. And next to love the sweetest thing is hate.

~Henry Wadsworth Longfellow

Looking at our wedding pictures always makes me giggle. I recall the young man that my brother brought home to dinner one night well over forty-seven years ago. It was not what one could call love at first sight. It was more like loathing at first sight.

The first time I had met him was a few weeks earlier. It all began with a phone call to my high school principal's office. I was a senior in high school at the time. I worked after school at a local restaurant as part of our school work-credit program.

This particular day, I was not scheduled to work, but Mrs. K (the owner) had called and left a message with the office that I would have to take another waitress's place. Mrs. K was not the nicest person in the world to work for to say the least. She never asked if I was available—she just said in her message to "be there at 4:00 P.M." Since not showing up would affect my grades for graduation, there was no way I could wiggle out of the unplanned shift.

My mother was quite the taskmaster herself, and I found myself caught in a bit of a pickle. My mother expected me to be home immediately after school to start dinner for our family. I tried to call my mom at her workplace to tell her of the change in plans but was unable to reach her. Unfortunately there was no voice-mail in those days. There was no way my mom would just let it slide if she did not know of the change in my work schedule. I could count on being grounded, no matter how good the excuse was, if I did not get my message through to her.

Mrs. K never allowed employees to use the phone while on duty and I knew she would not budge on her rules, even though she was the one who had created the situation. I had to stop for gas so I decided to call my mother again from the gas station. My dad had an account at the local Shell station, where I could sign for gas, and Ed (the owner) would bill my dad later.

I was surprised to see a total stranger running the gas station instead of Ed. The young man was quite a flirt, and took his time putting the gas in the tank, washing the windshield, checking the oil, etc. I tried my best to get him to just put the gas in the tank and forget the other routine services, but he kept on trying to impress me. I tried to be polite, but flirting with a strange guy was the last thing on my mind. He was seriously threatening my job and my big date for the Sweetheart dance the following day if I got grounded.

I finally told him, "Look sir, I am in a big hurry. I have to get to work. Now please put the gas on my dad's credit line in Ed's book." Naturally this lead to more delays as he insisted he had no idea where such a book would be or how to do it, so I had to go inside and find it behind the counter for him. I was beginning to think he wasn't very bright. It was a red ledger, exactly where

I told him he would find it, right beside the cash register.

My next big mistake was in asking him to give me a dime for the payphone, and put that on the ledger charge too. Good grief! He began to lecture me about taking money from a stranger and other nonsense. By that time I was furious and stomped out hurrying to get to work, and decided to try and talk Mrs. K into letting me use the phone at work.

Naturally, with all the time wasted at the filling station, I was late to work and Mrs. K refused my request to use the phone. Not only that, she also said I had to stay late and do clean-up duty to boot. By the time I got home at midnight my mom was fit to be tied and as I had feared, I was grounded. A rude stranger had ruined my life. I hoped I never would lay eyes on him again.

As luck would have it, a few weeks later, my mom called me at school and asked me to pick up an extra pound of hamburger as we were having a guest for dinner. Sounded normal to me, so I was totally unprepared that evening when my brother walked in the door with his new friend named Gene that he had met at the gas station. I wanted to hide in the kitchen as I was still so angry at him, but manners precluded my doing so.

By the time the meal was over, the young man apologized for all the trouble he had caused me and he became a regular visitor in our home. When time for the prom came, my boyfriend and I had broken up, so Gene offered to be my date. From there a loathing at first sight became a love story which resulted in forty-one very happy years of marriage and three beautiful children. Obviously, I decided he wasn't so bad after all.

~Christine Trollinger

世界上，再没有什么比爱更甜蜜。仅次于此的，便是恨。

——亨利·沃兹沃斯·朗费罗

　　每次看我们的结婚照，我都会情不自禁地笑。47 年前的一个夜晚，弟弟带了这位年轻人到我家吃晚餐。我们不是像大家想的那样一见钟情，相反，我们一见面就讨厌对方。因为他就是我一周前遇到的那个讨厌鬼。这一切都始于高中校长办公室的一个电话。当时，我正念高中。课余时间，到当地的一家餐馆打工，这也是学校实习项目的一部分。当天，我并不需要上班，但是 K 女士（餐馆主人）给学校办公室打来电话，留言给我让我替另一位女服务生代班。K 女士当然算不上世界上最好的雇主——她从来不问我有没有空，留言中只说"下午四点上班"。如果不去，会影响到我的学分，所以尽管这次换班是临时通知，我还是要过去。

　　我母亲也是个严格的"监工"。她希望我放学后能立刻回家，为家人准备晚餐。真是进退两难。我试着给母亲办公室打电话，通知她计划有变，但电话始终无法接通。遗憾的是，那时还没有语音信箱。在不知道我工作安排有变动的情况下，她是绝不会放过我的。不管我的理由多么充分，只要没有知会母亲，我一定会被关禁闭。

K女士从来不允许员工在工作时间打电话。我也知道，就算事情因她而起，她也绝不会为我破例。因为要去加油，所以我决定到加油站再给母亲打个电话。父亲在当地加油站有一个账户，每次我加完油后，爱德华（店主）会把账单寄给父亲。

但当时爱德华不在，负责加油的是一位陌生的小伙子。我稍微有点吃惊。这家伙真会卖弄风情，不紧不慢地把汽油加进油罐，擦洗挡风玻璃，检查是否装满等。我费了好大劲让他忘了其他例行服务，只把油加满就好。但他一直试图给我留下深刻印象。我试着礼貌待人，但同一个陌生人调情是我最不想做的事。他正在耽误我的宝贵时间，也严重威胁到我的工作，还有明天我同心上人的约会。要知道，再不打电话，我极有可能要被母亲关禁闭了。

最后，我终于忍不住对他说："听着，我现在真的很急，要赶着去上班。你能把油钱先记在爱德华的本子上吗，那上面有我爸的账户。"很自然的，这又耽误了一些时间，他坚持说不知道账本在哪儿，也不知道该怎么办。我只好走到里面，替他找出了放在柜台后面的账本。我开始觉得他不是很聪明，红色的账本就放在收银台旁边，我已经说得够明白了。

接下来我犯了一个巨大的错误。我想向他借一个10美分硬币，打付费电话。他可以把这笔钱也记在红色账本上。他却开始对我说教，教育我不该随便拿陌生人的钱，还有其他很多废话。那时候，我已经火冒三丈，愤愤然离开加油站赶去工作，决定请求K女士借我打个电话。当然，在加油站浪费了那么长时间后，我上班迟到，K女士也拒绝了我的请求。不仅如此，她还要求我下班后留下来打扫。回到家的时候，已是深夜，母亲自然十分恼火。果不其然，我被关了禁闭。我的生活就这样被一个粗鲁的陌生人毁了，但愿再不要让我看到他。

几周后的一天，母亲给我打电话，要我在回家的路上多带一斤牛肉回来，因为有位客人要。我觉得很正常，所以弟弟带着他在汽油站新结交的朋友吉恩回来时，我完全没有准备。我还是很生气，真想躲在厨房不出来，但出于礼貌，我不能那么做。晚餐结束的时候，吉恩为他给我带来的麻烦道歉。后来，他逐渐成了我家的常客。舞会来临的时候，我已经和男朋友分手，所以吉恩邀请我，作为他的舞伴出席。从那以后，初见生厌的开端演绎出了一段动人爱情。现在，我们已经共同度过了41 年的美好时光，并育有三个孩子。显然，他不像我一开始认定的那样糟糕。

——克里斯汀·托灵格

My Hot Italian
意大利帅哥

The art of love... is largely the art of persistence.
~Albert Ellis

Rich man, poor man, beggar man, thief, Doctor, lawyer, Indian chief. I never dated an Indian chief, but that was probably because they're hard to come by in suburban New Jersey.

I dated a lot. I just never found anyone I liked.

My mother once said, "If a knight in shining armor came riding down the street on a white stallion, you'd say, 'But he has a red plume in his helmet. I wanted one with a purple plume!'" She couldn't understand what there was to think about. To my mother, love came after finding someone appropriate to marry. She'd say things like, "He's in med school. What do you mean you don't like him?"

Truthfully? I feared boredom. I just couldn't imagine spending the rest of my life with anyone I ever went out with. Wasn't there supposed to be a spark or something? All of these guys seemed interchangeable—same guy, different name.

Maybe I needed to broaden my search.

Teaching did afford me summers off and I was able to spend some of my vacation time in Europe. Men were so romantic there. They looked at women in a way that I had never been looked at before in my life. Was it the wine or exotic locales that made them so attractive? What ever it was, they should bottle it and sell it as souvenirs at the airport. They'd make a fortune.

Of course, September brought me back to reality.

On the first day of school there was an Italian boy in my class. This wasn't unusual. I taught in a large, inner-city school where most of the kids were from either Europe, South America, or the Caribbean. This boy's first words to me were, "You know, you'd be perfect for my big brother."

Honestly? It wasn't the first time I heard that from a student, but there was no way I would ever take anyone up on that offer. Too weird.

But Rocco never let up. Not a week went by that I didn't hear how much his brother and I had in common. This kid was relentless. Even the other kids in class were getting in on it. "You gotta meet him, Miss Maddalena. You'd like him."

And let me tell you, the big brother wasn't bad-looking. Rocco brought a picture in. You could tell it was taken without him knowing it, but the guy was a hot Italian just about my age. This was 1977, and Prospero was the spitting image of John Travolta as Vinnie Barbarino.

"How old is he?"

"Nineteen."

"Nineteen? He's way too young." I was twenty-three heading towards twenty-four. Dating younger men wasn't fashionable. Yet.

"He acts older." This coming from a fourteen-year-old.

Still, it was really too weird. I'd stick with hitting the clubs with my girlfriends, but it was getting old.

Kissing too many frogs and hearing, "What's your sign?" too many times made me decide to go on a self-imposed dating strike. I had a better time staying home and reading than standing around talking to the desperado disco-babies in three-piece suits.

Then boredom hit. Spring was in the air, hibernation time was over, and I needed to get out. Nothing serious, just a little fun. The school year was almost over. Could I? Should I? We had nothing in common. He was way too young. But we were just going out, not getting married.

"Rocco," I said, "do you think your brother is still interested in meeting me?" To tell you the truth, I wasn't even sure if he knew anything about it. I just figured that since Rocco was so persistent with me, he was doing the same thing at home. I guessed right. It turns out that Prospero had been sending his own friends past the school at dismissal to check me out. I slipped the kid a piece of paper. "Tell him to call me."

Our first date was April 30, 1977. What can I say? When I looked in his eyes it felt as if I had known him forever. Before we knew it, we were spending all of our time together. Everything was more fun when Prospero was around. Although we came from very different backgrounds, we shared the same sense of adventure and common values. We took the time to grow together.

Like the song says, we fooled around and fell in love.

Rocco was best man at our wedding in 1980 and made a lovely toast taking credit for the fix up. I still run into some of those kids from my class. They're married now, with kids of their own, and they never fail to remind me that if it wasn't for them, I wouldn't have met my husband.

If anyone ever told me that I would marry Rocco Menna's big brother, I would have laughed like crazy. But what can I say? It was the best thing I ever did. Since the day I met him, Prospero has been my knight in shining armor. And his plume is absolutely perfect.

~Lynn Maddalena Menna

爱情的艺术，很大程度上是坚持的艺术。

——亚伯·埃利斯

　　富人、穷人、乞丐、窃贼、医生、律师、印第安酋长。哦，错了，我从来没有同印第安酋长约会。这大概是因为印第安酋长在新泽西州市郊实在不多见。

　　总而言之，我同很多人约会。却从未遇到过自己喜欢的人。

　　母亲曾打比方说我："就算你遇到穿金甲、骑白马的英俊骑士，你也会挑剔，'为什么他头盔上的羽毛是红色的，我理想中的是紫色羽毛！'"母亲不明白我到底在想什么。对她而言，找到适合的结婚对象比爱情更重要。比如，她会说："他读医学院，你为什么不喜欢？"

　　说实话吗？是因为我害怕无聊。那些曾经的约会对象，我根本无法想象要如何同他们共度一生。难道爱情不应该有些火花或者激情吗？那些男生对我来说都一样，不过名字不同罢了。

　　或许，我应该拓宽寻找范围。

　　教师工作的确提供了一些闲暇时间，我趁着暑假到欧洲旅游。那儿的男士特别浪漫。他们总会用一种欣赏的目光注视你，这是我从来不曾经历的。究竟是酒精作用还是异域风光让他们如此迷人呢？不管哪个，他们真应该将此包装作为纪念品在机场出售。一定赚钱。

9月的到来，将我拉回了现实世界。

新学期第一天，班里来了一名意大利男孩儿。这算不上什么新鲜事儿。我在一所大型市中心学校教书，班里的孩子很多来自欧洲、南美洲，还有加勒比海地区。这个意大利男孩对我说的第一句话是："你知道吗？你和我哥哥简直是天生一对。"

说实话，我并不是第一次听到这样的话。但无论如何，我也不会接受这样的邀请，太奇怪了。

但是洛克不肯放弃。接下来的一周，他一直对我讲，我和他哥哥有多少共同点。这孩子真是百折不挠。班上的其他学生也开始参与进来："玛塔莲娜小姐，你一定得见见他。你会喜欢他的。"

老实说，洛克的哥哥普洛斯佩罗并不难看。洛克带了他的照片过来。一眼就可以看出，洛克是趁他哥哥不注意的时候偷偷拍的。看起来他和我年纪相当，是个很帅的意大利小伙子。当时是1977年，他看起来就和饰演《寇特，欢迎归来》中飞尼巴巴利诺的美国影星约翰·特拉沃尔塔一模一样。

"你哥哥多大？"

"19岁。"

"19岁？太年轻了。"我已经23岁了，即将步入24岁。那会儿，还不流行姐弟恋。

"但他很成熟。"这是一个14岁小男生的评语。

对我来说，同自己学生的哥哥约会还是太奇怪。我宁愿和女性朋友一起去俱乐部消磨时光，尽管没有什么新意。

　　亲吻了那么多丑男人，听过无数次"你觉得怎么样"的问题后，我终于决定进行约会罢工。宁愿自己一个人待在家里安静地看书，也比在嘈杂的舞厅里听"衬衣——马甲——西服"的三件套先生讲话有趣。

　　就这样冬天过去了，美好的春天即将来临。冬眠结束，我也该到外面走走，找些乐趣。已经到了学年末，我能同洛克的哥哥约会吗？这么做没关系吗？我们没有任何共同点。他太年轻了。但只是一起出去玩而已，又不是要结婚。

　　于是，我问洛克："你觉得你哥哥还愿意见我吗？"说实话，我都不确定他哥哥是否知道这事儿。但我猜，如果洛克在我身上下了这么大工夫，那么他肯定也会游说他哥哥的。我猜对了。事实上，普罗斯佩罗也派了自己的朋友到学校，趁下课的工夫，悄悄看了看我。我递给洛克一张字条："让他打电话给我。"

　　1977 年 4 月 30 日，我们第一次约会。怎么说呢？初次见面，就有种似曾相识的感觉。我们常常待在一起。因为普罗斯佩罗，身边的一切都变得非常有趣。尽管背景差异很大，但我们有着同样的冒险精神和价值观。我们愿意共同成长。

　　就像歌中唱的，"我们四处游玩，坠入爱河"。

　　1980 年，普罗斯佩罗和我举行了婚礼。洛克担任伴郎，并作了一篇可爱的祝酒词，称自己是给我们牵线搭桥的大功臣。偶尔，我也会遇到以前的学生。他们现在已经结婚，有了自己的孩子。但总不忘提醒我，当年多亏了他们，我才遇到现在的丈夫。

　　如果当时有人告诉我，我会嫁给洛克·门纳的哥哥，我肯定会哈哈大笑。但我能说什么呢？这是我一生中最正确的决定。从我看到普洛斯佩罗的第一眼，他就是我身穿铠甲的骑士，当然，头盔上的羽毛也正合我意。

——林恩·玛塔莲娜·门纳

Miracle by Chance
再次邂逅

Love isn't something you find. Love is something that finds you.

Fifteen years ago I hung out at a country bar called the Club Palomino. I loved listening to good bands there, and dancing to their country rock music. I used to drag my friend out to see my favourite band, Cheyenne, who were amazing and always packed the place. My friend and I used to get up and dance to their songs.

I was interested in the rhythm guitar player in the band. To me, he was the best looking one, and I loved his voice along with his rhythm guitar sound. Yes, I had the "hots" for him and would gaze at him playing his guitar and singing while I was on the dance floor or at the bar. Cheynne played at Club Palomino for a long time. I went there as much as I could to see them, and of course, to watch my favourite player. The sad part about it was I used to see him with a short blond girl, his girlfriend or wife

I assumed.

When the Club Palomino was closed down, to be replaced by a real estate development project, I wanted to ask the band where they would be playing in the future. But I didn't have enough courage to do that.

Time went on. I met someone and got married. That was a mistake. Eventually we got a divorce. I starting going out to bars again but I didn't meet anyone decent enough. I wasn't crazy about the bands playing at other bars either.

Later, a friend told me to join a particular dating site on the Internet, which I thought I would never do. I checked it out for fun. I had a few dates but didn't find the right person. I gave up on it until one night, after getting home from a bar that I hated, I logged in to that site again. I got an interesting e-mail from a guy and liked his picture. We started e-mailing each other and seemed to have so much in common. We chatted every night as often as we could.

And then, a miracle happened. We started chatting about music. I told him I liked country music and used to frequent Club Palomino. He was really surprised and told me he used to play there. I wasn't sure whether to believe him or not! He said he would send me a picture of his band that played there. I thought "yeah right" to myself as I waited patiently in front of my computer for the picture. Lo and behold, a huge picture came up on my screen. He was the rhythm guitar player in Cheyenne! And he had married, and then divorced, that short blond girl I used to see with him at the club.

We finally met three weeks later, and on our first date, he got up on stage and started playing his guitar and singing in front of an audience. That did it for me. I was hooked. The guy I admired fifteen years ago was performing in front of my eyes and was my date! I was in heaven.

We have been together more than five years now, and the final surprise occurred after we bought a condo and moved in. We looked out the window, and there was the office building of the dating site where we met!

~Jeannette Gardner

爱情是无法被找到的，它却可以找到你。

——洛丽塔·扬

15 年前，我常去一家名叫帕洛米诺俱乐部的乡村酒吧，因为很喜欢那里的乐队，也喜欢跟着乡村摇滚乐摇摆起舞。我常拉上好友，一起去看最爱的夏延乐队。他们真的很棒，常常在帕洛米诺酒吧演出。朋友和我总会和着音乐起身跳舞。

我尤其喜欢夏延乐队中的吉他手。在我看来，他是乐队中最英俊的成员，优美的嗓音在吉他伴奏下显得格外动听。是的，我"喜欢"他，无论在吧台喝酒还是在舞池跳舞，我都忍不住地偷偷看他，他边弹边唱的样子，实在是太迷人了。很长一段时间，夏延乐队都在帕洛米诺酒吧演出。为了看演出，尤其是我喜欢的吉他手，我常常到酒吧。令人伤心的是，我曾看到他和一位金色短发女生在一起，可能是他女朋友或妻子吧。

后来，帕洛米诺酒吧倒闭了，取而代之的是一项房地产开发工程。我想问夏延乐队以后会到哪里表演，却没有勇气开口。

时间慢慢过去，我恋爱了，也结婚了。但那是个错误，我们的婚姻以失败告终。在那之后，我又重新光顾酒吧，却没有遇到合适的人，也不喜欢那些表演乐队。

后来，朋友告诉我一个交友网站。虽然认为自己绝对不会网恋，出于好奇我还是登录了。我试着约会过几次，但没有遇到中意的对象。本来已经放弃交友网站，直到一天晚上，我从一家糟糕的酒吧出来，心情很坏，回家后再次登录。我收到一封有趣的邮件，而且非常喜欢他的表述。于是我们开始邮件往来，发现原来我们有这么多共同之处。后来，基本上每晚我们都会抽出时间和对方聊天。

某天我们聊到音乐的时候，奇迹发生了。我告诉他，自己很喜欢乡村音乐，曾是帕洛米诺酒吧的常客。他大吃一惊，告诉我他曾经在那儿表演过。我不知道该不该相信他。为了证明自己，他说发一张乐队在帕洛米诺酒吧表演的照片给我。我心想"好啊"，就在电脑前静静地等他发照片。屏幕上出现一张巨大的照片。天哪！他就是夏延乐队的吉他手！他结过婚，后来离婚了，他的前妻就是我在酒吧看到的那个短发女子。

三周后，我们终于见了面。就在我们第一次约会的时候，他走上舞台，在那么多观众面前，为我弹奏。我简直入迷了。15年前我喜欢的那位吉他手就在我的面前，而且是我的约会对象。太幸福了！

现在，我们在一起已经五年多。当我们搬进新买的公寓时，最后的惊喜出现了，窗外，赫然矗立着那家交友网站的办公大楼。

——珍妮特·加德纳

第二部分 约会篇

Chapter 2

Adventures in Dating

Take a chance! All life is a chance. The man who goes the furthest is generally the one who is willing to do and dare.

~Dale Carnegie

....

冒险一试！整个人生就是一场冒险。走得最远的人，通常是愿意去做并勇于冒险的人。

——戴尔·卡耐基

Dating at the Speed of Light
闪电约会

Two things are aesthetically perfect in the world—the clock and the cat.

~Emile Auguste Chartier

Speed dating sounds interesting, at least in theory. You sign up for an evening of dating and fork over some money, though less than you'd spend on dinner for two in a restaurant that doesn't feature a drive-through window. Then you show up at a predetermined location—a coffee shop or bar—to play musical chairs.

Only in this case, every time the music stops, you meet a new person. And there begins your date.

After reading a couple of articles on it, I decide to check it out. Not that I am actually going to do it, mind you, but I am curious. Okay, more than curious, I am tempted.

A trip to a website for one company sponsoring these events makes for enlightening reading. The main reason for this fast-growing industry appears to be "too many frogs, too little lip balm" .Of course, the company states it more diplomatically.

According to the website, people are interested because it's fast, cheaper than joining a dating service, and safer because you decide whom you want to meet. You meet Mr. or Ms. Possible at a supervised location and there are no matches unless both parties say they're interested. At that point, the agency contacts you with phone numbers. After that, you're on your own.

It costs $49 which covers up to nine dates in one evening as well as coffee and a dessert. Not cheap but if it's a really good dessert, with lots of chocolate, it might be worth it.

I continue to read. The "events" offered by this particular establishment are organized into four different age groups. The most popular is the twenty-five- to thirty-five-year-olds, with their next two events already sold out. That is followed by the thirty- to forty-year-olds, the thirty-five- to forty-five-year-olds, and then the forty-two plus category.

That brings up an interesting point. Do I sign up based on my own age or on the age of men I want to meet? After hearing so much about hot, steamy older women/younger men relationships, I'm tempted to shave off a year or two and run, not walk, to the thirty-five- to forty-five-year-old group. Maybe even the thirty- to forty-year-old group if I remember to take my Geritol before I go and if the bar is dark.

Or do I thumb my nose at our youth-worshiping culture and proudly sign up for the forty-two plus category, hoping to meet a suave, debonair mature man with a touch of gray at the temples and the butt of a thirty-year-old. Hey, I'm only human.

Though with my luck, I'll sign up for the forty-two plus category only to find every male under the age of ninety has signed up for younger categories.

The process is simple. You show up at the location and get a name tag with your first name, last initial and a number as well as a confidential response card on which you indicate if you'd like to go out with that person again. Oh, if you're stuck for words, there's a list of conversation starters to get the ball rolling.

As a woman, you also get your own little table for two, where every nine minutes or so another Mr. Possible is supposed to plunk himself down and start chatting. The organizers ring a bell to let you know when it's time to move on. Nine minutes? That's eight minutes too long with some men and a lifetime too short with others. But in speed-dating, all dates come in one size—short.

I'm not so sure about this table thing. Why do men circulate while women sit and wait to be chosen? Having long hair, pouty red lips and a D cup makes it pretty certain that you will get chosen. But what about the rest of us? What if no one comes to your table? Can you get up and drag someone over? Or, do you pull out a book and pretend you've wandered into this meet-and-greet exercise by mistake?

Even if Mr. Right doesn't make it to your table, all is not lost. According to the organizers, you're allowed to corner him, that is, to mingle during the break or after the event. Remember, though, stalking is a crime.

Since the last time I had a date was when the Titanic sank, the real one, I'm becoming more interested. I don't like to use the word desperate—it's such an ugly word. I have my credit card out and I'm just about to hit enter to e-mail the form when I notice something. There, in the small print, it says for every man you register they'll reduce the fee by $10. If I bring five men, I don't have to pay a thing. Hey, I might even get a dollar back.

Alarm bells start going off in my head. First of all, if I knew five single men whom I wouldn't be embarrassed to bring to an evening like this, I wouldn't need to pay for a date-a-thon to begin with. And second, that tells me right away that the ratio of men to women is not in my favor.

Still, you never know. Mr. Almost Right, or at least Mr. Not Entirely Wrong in Dim Light, could be just one cup of coffee away. On the other hand, $49 is one and a half large bags of specialty cat food, enough to feed Thomas for a whole month. And as long as I'm the only one in this house with an opposable thumb who can open the cat food container, I know he'll never leave me.

So it's coming down to feeding one big, fat, not too bright orange tabby cat or a chance to meet Mr. Right. A cat or a man? A man or a cat? Well, that's easy.

Thomas, come here. It's time to rub your tummy. You're such a good boy.

~Harriet Cooper

从美学观点看，这世界称得上完美的事物只有两件——时钟和猫。

——埃米尔·奥古斯特·沙尔捷

闪电约会听起来非常有趣，至少理论上如此。先报名，再缴纳一笔费用。当然，这笔钱比两个人去饭店少，不是那种汽车快餐哦。然后赶往指定的地点，咖啡厅或者酒吧，开始进行抢座位游戏。

每当音乐停止的时候，你会看到一位新朋友。他就是你的约会对象。

读了几篇闪电约会的介绍文章后，我决定亲自试一试。顺便说一下，我只是好奇，并不打算真报名参加。好吧，我承认，不仅仅是好奇，是非常动心。

其中一家活动赞助商在公司网站上放了一些启蒙读物。根据介绍，闪电约会这一行业快速发展的主要原因似乎是"低素质的男人太多，高素质的女人太少"。当然，这家公司用了更加婉转的表达。

网站表示，闪电约会得到人们的青睐，主要是因为相较于普通的交友服务，闪电约会更加快捷、便宜且安全，参加者可以自主选择心仪对象。约会在第三方的监督下进行，只有双方均有意继续交往时，公司才会告知另一方的手机号码。之后，二人可自主联系。

49 美元的花费包括 9 位约会对象、咖啡，以及一份甜点。算不上便宜，但如果甜点是浓浓的巧克力蛋糕，倒也可以接受。

继续往下读。公司提供的"活动安排"将参与对象按年龄划分为 4 个小组。最受欢迎的是 25~35 岁小组，这个小组接下来的两场活动入场票已经提前售完。仅次于此的，是 30~40 岁小组，再次是 35~45 岁小组，最后是 42 岁以上小组。

这倒是挺有趣的。我应该根据自己的年龄报名呢，还是根据自己理想对象的年龄报名？听过那么多大龄妇女同年轻小伙子的恋爱故事后，我真想给自己减去一两岁，冲进 35~45 岁小组。要是来之前，再吃点巨力多（一种营养补充剂），酒吧比较暗的话，或许我可以加入 30~40 岁小组呢。

还是应该向崇尚年轻的社会勇敢说"不"，骄傲地报名参加 42 岁以上小组呢？或许能遇到一位温文尔雅、两鬓斑白的成熟男士。没准儿，他还有着 30 岁男人的翘臀呢。嘿，我又不是圣人！

尽管依我的运气，参加 42 岁以上小组，只能遇到些 90 岁以下的老头。

过程非常简单。先来到指定地点，再戴上标有名字、姓氏首字母以及序号的胸卡。记得拿上反馈卡，通过它，你可以告诉主办方自己的心仪对象是谁。哦，也不用担心自己一时紧张说不出话，主办方早已为你准备好了一堆话题，保证谈话顺利进行。

作为女士，你将坐在一张二人餐桌后面等待，大约每九分钟就会有一位男士过来，坐在对面，开始和你聊天。主办方会通过摇铃，来提示时间。九分钟？同某些男人，只待一分钟也觉得长；而对另一些人，你就是同他过一辈子也觉得不够。但是，闪电约会里，所有的爱情都只有一种型号——小号。

我不理解桌子的安排。我的意思是，为什么男人可以四处走动，女人只能坐在桌子后等着被挑选？如果你长发飘飘，嘟嘟的嘴唇透着性感，还有着 D 罩杯的傲人胸部，当然你能被选中。但剩下的人该怎么办？要是没人愿意坐到你面前，你能起身从旁边拽人过来吗？还是，你该拿起一本书，假装自己是误打误撞来了约会现场？

根据主办方的说法，就算真命天子没有坐在你的桌前也没什么损失。你也可以趁休息时间或者在活动结束后主动结交。但是，要记得，跟踪他人可是犯法的。

我的上段恋情，已经是泰坦尼克号沉没时候的事儿了，属于遥远的过去。我不喜欢"饥渴"这个词——太丑陋了。填好表格后，我拿出信用卡，正当准备点击"发送"时，我注意到网页下面的一行小字，上面写着参加者每动员一位男士加入，即可免除 10 美元费用。按这个说法，如果能动员 5 名男士，我一分钱都不用付。要是能带来更多的人，我是不是还能拿到一些钱呢？

我开始有些怀疑。首先，要是真能找到 5 名愿意参加约会的单身男士，我根本没必要参加这场马拉松式的约会。其次，它表明这次约会活动绝对是女多男少。

但你永远不知道，或许你的真命天子和你只隔着一杯咖啡呢。另一方面，49 美元可以买托马斯一个月的猫粮。只要我是这个屋子里唯一能打开猫罐头的人，托马斯一定不会离开我。

所以，我是该去喂一只又大又肥的黄褐色花斑猫呢，还是去参加闪电约会期待遇到真命天子呢？选猫，还是男人？选男人，还是猫呢？嗯，很简单。托马斯，过来，该挠挠痒了。真乖！

——哈瑞特·库伯

First Date, First Dent
第一次约会，第一次撞车

One forgives to the degree that one loves.

~La Rochefoucauld

Crunch! I knew the sickening sound of metal on metal, and it wasn't the sound I wanted to hear as I was pulling away from one of the most unusual and yet promising first dates I'd ever had.

I jumped out of my car and tried to assess the damage in the inky blackness. All I could tell was that I had officially backed into my date's 1988 Mustang. Ugh! I couldn't believe what I'd just done! I trudged back to his door, dreading the confession I was about to make. As I stood waiting for him to answer my knock, I reviewed the events that had led up to this moment.

The night had started just fine. My darkroom partner from photography class had finally asked me out. I really liked this guy. He seemed genuine and caring, but he could both give and take a joke with the best of them. Definitely my kind of guy.

Since I lived off campus, I parked at his dorm, and he drove us to the movies in his Mustang, a car he was extremely proud of. The conversation flowed freely, as we had plenty to talk about, from our classes to our similar upbringing. I was truly enjoying myself.

We finally pulled up to the movie theater, but it looked abandoned. I worried that we were out of luck, but he thought there was a chance it was open. Sure enough, his positive spirit prevailed: it was open! We purchased tickets and went inside, only to find that I was also right: the place was deserted! Literally, we were the only people there, aside from the ticket-taker and the projectionist (and, truth be told, I wouldn't be surprised if they were the same person). Anyway, we settled in and watched our private screening. Then the fun really started.

About halfway into the movie, the screen started to flicker, and we heard the flapping of the film as the projector broke. We stared at the blank screen. My date took charge. He went to see what the problem was and ended up making friends with the projectionist. Soon we were receiving a tour of the projection room and enjoying an insider's view on how movies are shown.

I have to admit it was kind of fun. And even more interesting was to see how this man acted under pressure. In fact, I was starting to really admire him. As we watched the rest of the movie, my mind began to wander. Maybe we might have a chance—maybe we would end up married with lots of little children who are fascinated by how things work and who could see the possibilities and not the problems in life. I could just see Junior taking apart my blender and making a time machine....

But truly I was getting ahead of myself. Plus I had no idea at that point what a tragic (for the Mustang!) ending our date was fated to have. So the movie ended and we drove back to the dorms, happily chatting, oblivious to the impending disaster.

We said good night and bang! There I was knocking at his door again to tell him I'd ruined his muscle car. I was sure then that I'd ruined my chances as well. But he answered the door, slightly surprised to see me standing there only moments after we had said goodnight. I sheepishly confessed my crime, hung my head and waited for the worst.

But it never came. Instead, that patient man went out to see the car, barely glanced at it in the pitch black and pronounced it fine. I was shocked. And also interested. I know my reaction would have been much different had our roles been reversed. In fact, I am certain it would have involved shaking heads, wringing hands and loud voices, yet there he stood, smiling and telling me not to worry. It was at that moment that I knew I'd found a good man.

And guess what? Somehow, despite all my mistakes, he saw something in me, too. Two years later we drove away in that Mustang with a sign that said "Just Married" covering up a slightly scratched and dented bumper. It's been nearly eighteen years now, and while we no longer own the Mustang, we do have a rich history together, complete with fun stories of our adventures, beautiful twin boys and a future that's brighter than any shiny chrome bumper you could imagine.

~Lisa Tiffin

爱对方的程度，就是能宽恕对方的程度。

——拉·罗切福柯德

砰！耳边响起令人厌恶的金属撞击声，这是我最不愿意听到的，因为我刚刚结束一场意义重大且前景美好的约会。

Chapter 2 Adventures in Dating
第二部分 约会篇

　　跳下车，我在一片漆黑中检查车子的受损程度。能确定的只有一点，就是我倒车时撞到了约会对象那台产于 1988 年的野马牌汽车。天哪！我都干了些什么！我拖着沉重的脚步，来到他家门前，心里忐忑不安，想着该如何忏悔。在等待他开门的时间，我脑海中闪现着刚才约会的一幕幕情景。

　　约会的开端非常顺利。摄影班暗房的搭档终于约我出去。我真的非常喜欢这个男生。他看起来既真诚又体贴，非常幽默，也开得起玩笑。绝对是我喜欢的类型。

　　住校外的我，把车子停在了他宿舍门口。我们开着他引以为豪的"野马"车，出去看电影。谈话非常顺利，从班级情况到自己的成长经历，无所不聊。整个过程，我都十分开心。

　　终于，我们在一家电影院门前停下车，但电影院看起来就像废弃了一样。我十分担心，怕不走运碰到关门歇业的影院。但他安慰我说，去看看吧，有可能正在营业。果然，他的积极态度胜利了：营业中！于是我们买了票，直到走进去才发现，原来我也是对的，这家影院破破旧旧，确实像是废弃的。毫不夸张，除了售票员和放映员外（说实话，就算二者是同一个人，我也不会有丝毫惊讶），整个影院就只有我们两个。无论如何，我们还是坐下了，享受这专属的私人银幕。之后，有意思的部分来了。

　　电影演到一半左右的时候，银幕开始闪烁，之后传来了混乱的胶片传动声，我们意识到放映机出故障了。看着空白的电影银幕，他起身去看看问题出在哪里，最后竟然和放映员成了朋友。之后，我们参观了放映室，了解了电影放映原理。

　　我必须承认，这非常有意思。但是更有趣的是看到了他在紧急情况下的真实反应。事实上，我开始爱上他了。电影后半段的时候，我思绪飘飞：或许我们真能在一起呢；或许我们会结婚，并且生一大堆孩子，孩子们对事物背后的原理深深着迷；他们乐观向上，能看到生活中的希望，而不是一大堆难题。我甚至能够想象孩子们拿着我的搅拌器，制作时光机……

事实上，我的确想太多了。此外，我怎么也想不到约会竟以我撞坏他的车悲惨收场。电影结束后，我们开车回到宿舍，愉快畅谈，浑然不觉灾难即将来临。

我们互道晚安，而突然砰的一声，撞车了。此刻我再次敲响他的房门，为的是告诉他，我撞坏了他的大功率汽车。我确定我毁了我们之间的一切可能。他打开房门的时候，稍微吃了一惊，不明白刚刚告别的我为何突然回来。我怯怯地向他坦白了自己的罪行，低着头，等待最糟的结果。但是，什么都没有发生。相反，这个耐心的男生只是走出去，在漆黑中，大略看了一下车子的情况，然后告诉我说："车子还好，没关系。"我震惊了，也更加好奇。我知道，如果我是他的话，结局可就大不相同。事实上，我认为他一定会皱着眉头，攥紧拳头，冲我大吼大叫。但他只是站在那儿，微笑着告诉我不要担心。就是这一刻，我知道自己找到了一个善良的男人。

你猜怎么着？尽管我做了那么多蠢事，他还是看到了我的优点。两年后，我们开着贴有"新婚"的"野马"出行，纸条正好盖住了刮花的保险杠。现在，已经是我们在一起的第18个年头，尽管"野马"已经转手，我们仍然有着丰富的回忆，有探险趣事，也有漂亮的双胞胎儿子，还有一份比任何熠熠发光的保险杠都要灿烂的未来。

——丽莎·蒂芬

The Doberman Dates
一场关于杜宾犬的约会记忆

You can discover more about a person in an hour of play
than in a year of conversation.

~Plato

Ah, Randi. Randi of the smoldering eyes and
skin that's marble smooth. Randi, in whose black
hair a man could lose his way. A cyclone of a
woman, that Randi. And one magical night in 1972
Randi chose me.

She picked me out of at least two hundred
desperate L.A. singles who had paid good money
to jam into a bad restaurant and yell their hopes and
dreams at each other. It started with a nod, followed
by a compliment about my smile, delivered in a
voice whose every syllable aroused. Randi's praise
migrated to my eyes and, after we swapped a few
sentences, my brain. "Ivy League," she purred when
I answered the "what college" question, and her
exquisite fingers touched my hand. Wesleyan is not
an Ivy League school, but before I could correct
her, Randi said that she too had been expensively

educated.

She invited me to dinner at her home the following Friday night. She
wanted to try out her gourmet cooking. Now I knew this exquisite creature and
I could harmonize our lives, and I spent the week dreaming of the white hot
passion that awaited me.

Friday. The night was drizzly, perfect for a quiet dinner in Randi's
apartment. But she had not put out any hors d'oeuvres. Worse yet, her kitchen
looked spotless, with no indication of a meal in progress. Randi steered me into
a bedroom whose purple walls matched her bedspread. "There," she said, and
pointed to at least a dozen diplomas hanging over a stainless steel headboard.
She was expensively educated, all right, at one-week academic wonders
like Perpetual Savings and Loan's Seminar on Financial Institutions, the
Bellefontaine Academy for Wealth Accumulation, The Culinary Institute of the
Arts, and the Summertime School for the Humanities. I said I was impressed,
while my eyes traveled from her stiletto heels to the mirrors on her ceiling.

Randi squeezed my hand. "I'd like to see a movie first," she said, and
added that a theater was close by. On its one screen was *The Doberman
Gang*, the immortal, unforgettable yawn (I mean yarn) about a dog trainer
who taught Doberman Pinschers to rob banks. Each canine got the name of a
famous outlaw. Bonnie. Clyde. Baby Face Nelson. Pretty Boy Floyd. Dillinger.
Someone booed when it was over. I would have joined him but was too focused
on my hunger pangs. I had skipped lunch in anticipation of Randi's gourmet
cooking.

We drove back to Randi's apartment complex and spent ten minutes
hunting for a parking space. It was raining hard now, but she wanted to show
me the grounds, especially the recreation room where, it just so happened,
there was a crowd. "Oh, a party," she said without sounding surprised. "Let's
go in for a minute." Before I could answer, Randi passed through the sliding

glass doors. As I followed her, some bruiser in an open shirt with a gold charm hanging on his hairy chest demanded ten dollars. That's ten 1972 dollars. "Guys pay," he said, in a tone of voice you would reserve for an imbecile. I lingered at the door, wondering if Randi would return before this brute shoved me out into the rain. When she re-appeared, she held a half-eaten French dip sandwich from which juice dribbled to the floor.

Randi asked, "Don't you want to stay?"

I stammered, "I thought we were going…"

"I want to go to the party," she interrupted. "We can say good night here." Flakes of French dip clung to the hand that Randi thrust forward. "Good night, young man." All sensuality had vanished from her face, like vitamins going out of stale orange juice. Seconds later, Randi was gone.

My landlord served a free brunch every Sunday. At least ten of us were gorging ourselves on bagels, lox and cream cheese. Someone asked what I had done over the weekend. Randi was worth a story if nothing else, but after three sentences there was an echo: "Ivy League." "Ivy League." "Dinner." "Dinner." "Mirrors." "Mirrors." "Diplomas." "Diplomas."

It wasn't an echo. The words kept coming after I paused. "Bad movie." "Party." "Ten dollars." Someone at the coffee urn across the room was describing to another group of my neighbors what had occurred on his date the night before.

"Excuse me," I asked the owner of that voice. "Were you out with a girl named Randi?"

Indeed he was. Jonathan had been treated to Randi's world of purple walls, diplomas, and mirrors. Like me, he had not been treated to her cooking. Instead—you guessed it—she wanted to see *The Doberman Gang*. Jonathan had gone home without his supper. I respected him because he too had refused to pay the ten-dollar entry fee for the rec room party, and I conceded that Randi must have preferred him over me, because Cornell—his alma mater—actually belongs to the Ivy League.

Thanks to our shared experience with Randi, Jonathan and I became fast friends. We palled around L.A., made some investments together, and double dated with women who actually did want to eat when darkness fell. Ten years later, I danced at his wedding.

Although it's been more than thirty years since we met her, Jonathan and I confess to a lingering admiration for Randi. She was special. Anyone who can sit through *The Doberman Gang* two nights in a row has to possess some unique quality that sets her apart from the rest of us. Woof.

~Anthony J. Mohr

和一个人玩一小时对他的了解，胜过一年的交谈。

——柏拉图

啊，兰迪！她的眼睛温情脉脉，肌肤如大理石般光滑，乌黑的秀发瀑布般柔顺，让每个男人都意乱情迷。啊，尤物兰迪！正是这样的女人在1972年的某天夜晚选择了我。

洛杉矶举办了一场有近200名单身人士参加的聚会，参加者花了大价钱，只是为了在一个差劲儿的饭馆朝对方吹嘘自己的希望和梦想。我就是其中一个。就在这儿，我遇到了兰迪。她冲我点了点头，称赞我笑起来的样子很好看。她的嗓音犹如天籁般动听。交谈了几句之后，兰迪对我的表扬已经让我幸福得飘飘然起来。当我回答"你在哪所学校"的问题时，兰迪悄声低语"是常春藤联盟啊"。与此同时，她玲珑的指尖轻轻触碰了我的手。我还没来得及纠正她，卫斯理学院不属于常春藤联盟时，她紧接着告诉我，自己也接受了昂贵的教育。

兰迪邀请我下周五晚上到她家吃晚饭。她说自己在尝试烹饪美食。由此，我确信这个精致漂亮的人儿将来肯定是位贤妻良母。接下来的一周，我都心情澎湃，热切地期待周五来临。

终于到了周五晚上，天空飘着毛毛细雨。我并不介意，反而觉得宁静浪漫，和兰迪共进晚餐再合适不过。让我意外的是，兰迪并没有准备任何餐前点心。更糟的是，她家的厨房看起来一尘不染，丝毫没有在煮饭的迹象。兰迪带我到她的卧室看，紫色的墙壁很配她的床单。"看那儿。"她指着一个不锈钢床头架说。那儿摆放着至少十多张学位证书。好吧，她的确接受着昂贵的教育，例如，参加金融机构举办的为期一周的永久储蓄和贷款研讨会，贝尔方丹学院组织的财富积累课程，去烹饪学院学习烹饪艺术，到暑期学校学习人文科学。我一边告诉她，这给我留下了深刻印象，一边将目光从她的细鞋跟移到天花板的镜子上。

听了我的话，兰迪紧紧握着我的手说："我想先去看部电影"，并补充说影院就在附近。影片是《六犬大盗》，讲述一位传奇的驯狗师，训练杜宾犬抢劫银行的故事。影片中，每只杜宾犬都以闻名遐迩的绿林好汉命名，有鸳鸯暴徒邦妮和克莱德、娃娃脸尼尔森、美少年弗洛伊德、大盗狄林杰。影片结束的时候，有观众喝倒彩。要不是饥饿难忍的话，我也会加入。要知道，为了品尝兰迪的厨艺，我中午都没有吃饭。

等我们开车回到兰迪家所在的公寓大楼，花了十分钟终于将车子停好后，她说想带我看看房子周围的庭园，尤其是文娱室。外面的雨越来越大，我们走到文娱室的时候，那儿已经聚集了一群人。"有派对，"她看起来毫不惊讶，"我们进去玩一会儿吧。"没等我回答，她已经穿过了滑动玻璃门。等我想跟着进去的时候，一个衣衫敞开、露着胸毛、脖子上挂着金色护身符的彪形大汉拦住了我："10 美元。"要知道，当时可是1972 年呢。大汉像看着傻瓜一样看着我："男生付钱。"我在门口徘徊着，不知道在被丢进雨中之前，兰迪会不会回来。她再次出现的时候，手里拿着一块已经吃掉一半的法式蘸酱三明治。我看到诱人的汁水滴落在地板上。

"你不愿过来吗？"兰迪问我。

我结结巴巴地回答："我以为我们要去……"

"我想参加派对，"兰迪打断了我，"那我们就在这儿道晚安吧。"兰迪同我握手，拿着三明治的手中一些碎渣掉落，"晚安，年轻人。"她脸上的性感光泽在此刻瞬间消失，就像失去了维生素的陈旧橙汁一样。

几秒钟之后，兰迪转身离去。

房东为我们提供免费的周日早午餐。正当我们十多个人对着可口的面包圈、熏鲑鱼和奶油奶酪狼吞虎咽时，有人问我，周末是怎么过的。我想，虽然同兰迪的约会并不成功，但至少是个不错的故事。我刚讲了几句，便似乎听到了回音："常春藤联盟""常春藤联盟""晚餐""晚餐""镜子""镜子""学位""学位"。

这不是回音。但我停顿的时候，总会响起相同的声音："糟糕的电影""派对""10 美元"。原来，房间那头，坐在咖啡壶边的男生正向另一帮室友描述自己昨天的约会。

"打扰一下，"我问那位男生，"你是同一个叫兰迪的女孩约会吗？"

果然，乔纳森也参观了兰迪的紫色卧室、学位证书，还有天花板上的镜子。当然，同我一样，他也没有吃到晚餐。而且，正像你猜的那样，兰迪约他一起看《六犬大盗》。乔纳森也是饿着肚子回来的。同我一样，他拒绝付 10 美元去参加娱乐室的派对，这点我很是敬佩。我暗地里认为，兰迪肯定更喜欢他才是，因为他所就读的康奈尔大学的确属于常春藤联盟。

由于相同的经历，乔纳森和我成了很要好的朋友。我们结伴同行，游览洛杉矶的名胜，合伙投资做生意，也一起参加四人约会。当然，我们的约会对象是那些夜幕降临的时候，的确想吃东西的女子。10 年后，我在他的婚礼上跳舞。

尽管遇见兰迪已经是三十多年前的事情了，乔纳森和我都承认，我们对她仍是念念不忘。兰迪是很特别的女生。一个连续两晚都愿意看《六犬大盗》的人，身上必然有着我们缺乏的独特品质。汪、汪。

——安东尼·J.摩尔

Adventures in Online Dating
网恋奇遇

"I'm not looking to meet someone. I have a great life. A man would just mess things up. Besides, if God wants me to marry, don't you think He will bring along the right person at the right time?"

My friend looked skeptical as she eyed me through the steam rising from our cappuccinos. "Did it ever occur to you," she said, "that God wants you to be looking? Sure, you have your teaching career, your house, your Beagles, and your independence. Perhaps a good relationship would add further richness to an already great life."

I filed that last statement somewhere deep in my brain. In the weeks that followed I occasionally took it out, studied it, prayed about it, and then returned it to its hiding place. One day, while in the middle of this ritual, I noticed that my friend's words had increased in size. Taking root, they had spread like mint in a garden and, as such, could no longer be ignored. I was reminded of the Biblical account of Abraham, who sent his servant in search of a wife for his son, Isaac. Abraham did not sit around and twiddle his thumbs, waiting for a young woman to knock on the door of his tent. His plan involved deliberate action.

"Okay, Lord," I prayed. "If you want me to look for a man, then please tell me where and how to begin my search, as I assume bars, nightclubs, and the underside of rocks are not your preferred venues."

Rewind to 1970. I was sixteen years old and clueless when it came to flirting and dating. The only piece of advice my mother gave me on the subject of boys was, "Don't you ever call a boy on the phone! You don't want him to think you're fast."

Fast at what? Long division?

I heeded her advice, though I disagreed. It was a new era. The 60s mantra of "Free Love" still resonated amidst the disco balls; women burned their bras in Double D-sized bonfires; and Virginia Slims claimed we'd come a long way, baby. Yet there I sat, juxtaposed in time, imprisoned by my pink Princess telephone as I waited for Dream Boat to call. The Pill has been credited with setting women free, but I believe the credit belongs to the microchip. My mother may have told me never to phone a boy; she never said anything about e-mail.

Fast forward back to the twenty-first century. Here began my adventures in online dating, with its freedom to initiate contact regardless of gender. I decided I would not be found sitting in front of a pink Princess computer waiting for a mailbox icon to announce, "You've got male!" I resolved that when and if I came across an attractive profile, I would have no qualms over sending the first e-mail. The anonymity of cyberspace gave me opportunities to communicate with men without revealing my name or address until I felt comfortable doing so, if at all.

I was off, both excited and scared by this self-imposed journey. Occasionally, upon initiating contact, that first e-mail was also the last. This gave me insight into the risk-and-rejection factor that men have experienced for eons. It is not fun. However, taking these risks also brought some fascinating people across my path, which explained why I never met for dinner on the first date. I needed to know I could beat a hasty retreat if we had nothing to talk about, or if he wanted to spend the evening discussing his passion for nude motorcycling in Alaska. For these reasons, and because I love good coffee, I decided to stick with cafés for first meetings. First, however, I established some "Ground Rules". The slightest utterances of "ex-wife", "estranged wife", or "my wife's sleazy lawyer" were grounds for ordering my coffee to go.

I met a plethora of men who could not seem to talk about anything but their broken marriages and messed-up kids, and who had so much emotional baggage they could have used their own personal bellhops. These people were common, but I encountered a few who were downright bizarre. Take the man who, after several e-mail exchanges between us, called me on the phone to chat. During the course of our conversation I mentioned how impressed I was that he was not bothered by our age difference, and by the fact that I was older. His response: "Oh, that's a turn-on for me. Also, you being a teacher really clinched it. You know, it's part of the whole naughty-older-teacher-thing." I mumbled something about having to grade my students' papers and hung up, feeling as if I needed a shower.

Another man, upon seeing the two wood boxes that contain the ashes of my deceased dogs, proclaimed that I was involved in "Satanic animal worship". He added that I could not love both animals and people; I had to choose. So I did. My Beagles and I waved goodbye as he drove off.

One day I came across the profile and photos of someone with whom I believed I had a lot in common, and I sent him an introductory e-mail. Within five minutes I received a reply in which he stated that while I "seemed very nice", unfortunately I was too short for him. (I hail at five feet, three inches.) He was tall and the woman of his dreams had to be at least five foot six. I thought this so ludicrous I decided to write again. By this time my sarcastic sense of humor was running in high gear. "As you seem to be a mature professional, I am rather surprised that you would be concerned with a relatively trivial matter such as height. For a tall person you seem to have some shortcomings." Suffice it to say he sent back a tirade that rivaled Mussolini's speech from the balcony.

As for physical attributes, online dating gave me but a glimpse of someone's true appearance. Some photos were blurred, some revealed only half a face, and others were so morose that they looked as if they were taken just moments before the walk to the death chamber. On the other hand, I viewed bulging biceps, washboard abs, and full heads of hair, only to later encounter clones of George Costanza. I wanted to tell these men that if middle age spread had moved in, and their hair had moved out, look at these changes as signs of experience and wisdom, rather than attempting to begin a relationship under false pretenses. In addition, I wanted to scream, "Please don't try the 'comb-over' in an attempt to look younger! It doesn't work!"

Despite these experiences, I am very glad I embarked on this cyber-dating adventure. I downed a lot of coffee, but that was merely the froth on the cappuccino. In June of 2007 I read the profile of a man who was a committed Christian, lived only fifteen miles away, and who had also never been married. Intrigued, I positioned my fingers over my computer keyboard to send him a message. Then I saw it. He was forty-five years old and I was fifty-three. A full eight years stretched between us. Experience had taught me that men under the age of fifty typically were not interested in women who had crossed that great divide. I decided not to set myself up for disappointment and so did not contact him.

Two days later there was mail in my online box. I clicked it open and received the surprise of my life. "It's that guy!" I exclaimed, although no one but my dogs and God could hear me. "It's the forty-five-year-old-Christian-fifteen-miles-away-never-been-married-guy!" I wrote back and a correspondence began, followed by telephone conversations. One week before my online dating subscription was set to expire (I had resolved not to renew it), on July 30, 2007, we met in person over lattes and scones. We had no trouble recognizing each other, as both of us had posted current photographs. We talked for hours and agreed to meet again; then again; and yet again. We slowly got to know each other as friends. I was taken by his kindness, the respect with which he treated me, and the fact that he liked my dogs. We shared many common interests, yet willingly accepted one another's differences.

On Christmas Day, 2008, he asked me to marry him, and we were wed on April 4, 2009.

All of this transpired because we chose to step out from the familiar and the traditional, to trust God, and to risk walking the fiber optic line of computer dating, gigabytes from my pink Princess telephone.

~Laurel Hausman

为什么不去冒险呢？难道成功不就是从中得来的吗？
——弗兰克·斯库利

"我不想找男朋友。我一个人过得很好，男人只会把事情弄糟。另外，要是上帝希望我结婚的话，你不觉得他会在合适的时间让我遇到合适的人吗？"

透过两杯冒着热气的卡布奇诺，朋友用怀疑的目光上下打量着我："难道你从来没有想过，上帝希望你自己寻找吗？没错，你生活得很好。教师是很棒的职业，你也有自己的房子，养着可爱的小猎犬，还有可贵的独立。但是，一段动人的爱情可以锦上添花。"

我把朋友的最后一句话放在心底。接下来的几周，我会偶尔把这话拿出来想一想，品味琢磨，祈祷爱情的来临，然后重新放回心底。但某天，进行这个仪式的时候，我忽然发现这话的分量加重了。它已经生根发芽，就像院子里的薄荷一样长势凶猛，不容忽视。我想起《圣经》中对亚伯拉罕的描述，他派仆人外出，为儿子伊萨寻找妻子。亚伯拉罕并没有无所事事地坐着，等待年轻姑娘走进他的帐篷。他的计划包含着缜密的行动。

"好的，上帝，"我祈祷着，"如果你希望我寻找伴侣，那么能不能给我些指引，告诉我从哪里开始。我想酒吧、夜店、岩石区的桥墩下应该不是您的首选场地吧。"

现在，让我们先回到 1970 年。那时，我 16 岁，对调情和约会一无所知。关于男生，母亲给我的唯一建议是："永远不要主动给男生打电话！那样，他会认为你太快。"

什么叫"太快"？是做长除法的速度吗？

尽管不同意母亲的看法，但我还是听从了她的建议。这是一个新时代。迪斯科舞厅中重新响起了 60 年代的"自由恋爱"颂歌；在熊熊烈火中，女人烧掉自己的胸罩；维珍妮牌香烟喊出了取得重大进步的口号。然而，我却静静地坐在这儿，仿佛囚禁在粉色公主电话的牢笼中，等待梦中情人的来电。避孕药有解放女人的美誉，但我觉得女人真正的解放应该归功于电脑芯片。母亲告诉我不要主动给男生打电话，但是没说不能主动给男生发邮件。

快速回到21世纪。下面就是我网上约会的开端，它最大的好处就是不分性别，任何一方都可以采取主动。我决定不能坐在粉色电脑面前，等着邮箱小图标提示"你有一个新男人！"我决定，看到有趣的简历，一定毫不犹豫地发送第一封邮件。互联网的匿名，让我可以在不透漏任何个人信息的前提下，同男士开始交往。当然，如果交往顺利的话，我愿意告知对方我的名字和住址。

关掉电脑，我对这种自我主导的约会旅程感到既兴奋又忐忑。偶尔主动发送的第一封邮件，往往也是最后一封。这让我注意到女性主动的风险以及男性对此类举动的排斥。这并不好玩。这些冒险，让我遇到了很多有趣的人，也让我意识到初次约会最好不要选择一起吃饭。如果两人无话可聊，或者他一个晚上大谈特谈阿拉斯加裸体摩托车赛多么惊险刺激，我一定得知道怎样溜之大吉。出于以上考虑，加上对咖啡的喜爱，我决定初次见面地点一律安排在咖啡馆。但首先，我要建立一些"基本规则"。只要提到"前妻"、"夫妻不和"或者"前妻雇用的卑劣律师"，我就立刻端起咖啡走人。

我遇到过很多男士，他们张口闭口都是破碎的婚姻和顽劣的孩子。这样的人思想包袱太重，还是让他们自己在咖啡馆冷静一下吧。这些还算普通，我也曾遇到过几个彻头彻尾的怪胎。比如，几次互传邮件之后，他打电话过来同我聊天。对话过程中我惊讶地发现，他丝毫不在意我们之间的年龄差距，要知道是我比他大。问他的时候，他的反应是："哦，那更能挑起我的性欲。你的教师身份也增色不少。你知道，就像中年女教师色诱学生。"我含糊地讲了几句，借口要批改学生作业，挂断电话。

实在是太醍醐恶心了，真需要洗个澡。

　　还有一位男士，在看到盛着两只爱犬骨灰的盒子时，指责我是"撒旦式的动物崇拜"。他认为，我不能既爱动物又爱人类，我需要作出选择。我选择了。他离开的时候，我带着小猎犬，朝他挥手道别。

　　一天浏览资料时，我看到了一位同自己有很多共同点的人。于是，我给他发了一封邮件，简单介绍了自己的情况。不到五分钟就收到了他的回复。他在邮件中写道，觉得我"人很好"，但对他来说太矮了（我身高一米六）。因为他很高，所以理想中的另一半身高至少要在一米六八以上。我认为他的理由实在是荒唐可笑，决定再次写信过去。信中，我的幽默和讽刺表露无遗——"作为一名成熟的专业人士，你对琐碎小事比如身高的重视程度真让我感到吃惊。身材高大的你，想必也有不足。"

　　对于他的回复，我只想说，他的长篇大论足以和当年墨索里尼在剧院的演讲媲美。

　　至于外表，通过网络约会很难准确判断。有些照片模糊不清，有些只露半张脸，还有一些照片忧郁得就像刚刚走出行刑室的囚犯。有时，照片上的人也会有健硕的肱二头肌、洗衣板般的腹肌、浓密的头发，但等到真正见面的时候却发现不过是个像乔治·克斯坦撒一样的白痴。我真想告诉那些男士，如果人到中年开始脱发，就将此看成经验和智慧的标志吧。不要试图蒙混过关。另外，我真想大喊："别再把稀疏的头发拢过头顶装年轻了，根本不管用！"

　　尽管经历了这些不愉快，我还是很庆幸自己能开始这次网络约会之旅。我喝了很多咖啡，虽然很多时候刚尝了卡布奇诺上面的泡沫，就要转身离开。2007年6月，我注意到一位男士的资料。他是一名虔诚的基督徒，住在离我24公里远的地方，而且从未结婚。在好奇心的驱使下，我开始敲打键盘，给他发送了一封邮件。后来我才注意到，他45岁，而我53岁，整整大他8岁。经验告诉我，通常50岁以下的男士会喜欢更年轻的女士，不会对50岁以上的女士感兴趣。要知道50岁是一个很大的分水岭。为了避免再次失望，我决定不再联系他。

两天之后，我看到邮箱里有未读邮件。点开邮件，没想到巨大的惊喜在等待着我。"是那个人！"我惊呼，尽管只有上帝和我的爱犬能够听到，"是那个住在24公里外、年纪45岁、从未结婚的基督徒！"我给他写了回信，之后，我们开始邮件往来。后来，我们开始打电话聊天。网上约会许可证到期（我决定不续约）前的一周，也就是2007年7月30日，我们决定见面。由于我们两个材料上贴的都是近期照片，所以很快就认出了对方，我们点了拿铁和一些小烤饼，边吃边聊。第一次见面聊得很投机，所以有了接下来一次次的约会。慢慢地，我们成了很好的朋友。我喜欢他的善良和对我的尊重，重点是他也喜欢我的狗。我们有很多共同爱好，也愿意接受彼此间的差异。

2008年圣诞节，他向我求婚。2009年4月4日，我们举行了甜蜜的婚礼。

这一切的发生只因我们愿意打破常规，在上帝的指引下，愿意相信光纤线的网络约会和千兆字节的粉色公主电话。

——劳雷尔·豪斯曼

My Final Date with Veronica
我同维罗妮卡的最后一次约会

A happy person is not a person in a certain set of
circumstances, but rather a person with a certain set of
attitudes.

~Hugh Downs

It was dumb. The dumbest thing I've ever done.
Maybe the dumbest thing any human being has ever
done. No one at school knew about Thistle. It was a
dark secret that had never seen the light of day and I
cringed at the thought of anyone ever finding out.

Can you blame me? Thistle was a logging town,
a piteous patch of ground where cars were dented,
teeth were missing, and haircuts resembled a pre-op
lobotomy. It was a disheveled place, a wide spot in
the road where lumberjacks drank beer and chopped
trees, and sad women with two first names listened to
long, complaining ballads about two-timing men and
the rocky road of life. The last thing I wanted was for
any of my college friends to discover the ugly truth:
Thistle was my home.

You might wonder then, why did I tell Veronica?

To which I can only reply: I'm not sure.

My girlfriend, Veronica, was attractive. No doubt about it. She was sleek and tall and wore her dark hair in an expensive razor-cut blow-dried unisex coiffure. Oddly enough, though, it wasn't her beauty I was interested in.

She also came from a wealthy family. Veronica had a closet stuffed with Dior dresses and a MasterCard with an unlimited line of credit. Yet I could have cared less about her money.

What impressed me most about Veronica was her mind. She was smart, a straight-A student, senior class president and an avid environmentalist. She used words so big they made me flinch.

So I fell in love with her. For a while there I was on cloud nine. Had I known a little more about Veronica, though, I might have chosen cloud seven.

You see, she had a dark side about her, a sourly intense, pursed-lipped, preoccupied air, and a sometimes rude temper. When angered, she had a way of staring at you that was downright creepy.

But I enjoyed Veronica's company. Night after night I found myself sitting beside her at the library reading literature not just meaningful, or deep, but positively gravid with meaning. Whitehead. Camus. Sartre, for God's sake!

All that liberal cant must have caused a serious time warp in my thinking because that's when I told her about Thistle.

Her "Huh?" was punctuated by a frown. "You're kidding," she said.

"I'm afraid not," I replied.

"Thistle? That sounds almost anthropological, like an African tribe or something."

Obviously Veronica was not simpatico. She arched an eyebrow when I described the tobacco-chewing women and the tow-headed children. Her face puckered with distaste when I told her about the people I knew who had dropped out of school in the seventh grade to attend monster truck rallies.

"You had me fooled," she said. "I thought you were smarter than that."

"It's not that bad," I explained.

"Well, it sounds dreadful," she said. "And I want you to take me there this weekend so I can see it for myself."

Omens and portents were everywhere if only I'd been alert. "Are you sure," I asked? "I mean, it's awfully Middle American."

"Of course, I'm sure. It'll be fun to see how the other half lives."

There was no stopping her. One way or another, I was out to prove Thomas Wolfe wrong: you can go home again, especially when someone is holding a knife to your ribs.

It was a long and dusty drive to Thistle, and Veronica complained all the way. Mom greeted us at the door when we arrived, wearing her usual flowered dress without a waistline and a plain white apron that looped over her head. She pecked me once on each cheek, then held me at arm's length as if to check the merchandise for damage.

"You smell good today, Ma," I said.

"You saying I don't always smell good?" she replied.

"No, I'm just saying you smell nice. You got someone special to come calling?"

She chuckled. "You silly boy."

Veronica kicked my leg. "Oh," I said, "where are my manners? Ma, this is Veronica."

My mother studied her, pursing her lips. "Lord Mercy," she said, "she's a half-cooked little fritter, but a fellow'd have to be coated with Teflon not to let her stick to his pan."

I blushed. "Y'all stop talking like that," I said.

Veronica threw a long measured look in my direction.

"Y'all?" she said. "Did you just say 'y'all'?" I felt the blood vacate my face.

We made our way through the kitchen where supper was cooking. Mom had pots on all four burners, timers ticking, and food covering every inch of countertop.

Veronica, though, was not impressed. The look on her face said, "under this roof lives a family that is one hundred percent pure white trash, probably descended from a long line of cousins."

Our living room was done in a sort of "junkyard" motif. There was a stone fireplace, a coffee table holding copies of hook and bullet magazines, and a mounted deer head hanging above the fireplace. Dad was asleep in front of the TV, out like a side of beef on Thorazine.

"Wake up, Arnold," Mom shouted. "We've got company."

"I'm up," he muttered, pulling his false teeth out of his pocket.

Dad was dressed for dinner. And work too, for that matter. He wore a blue shirt with elbows that looked like they had been dynamited away, Can't Bust 'Em pants, and clunky, black boots—the same clothes he wore everywhere.

I went into the kitchen to check on dinner. When I returned, Veronica and my father were already deep in conversation.

"What do you do for a living, Mr. Hebley?" she asked.

"I'm a logger."

Uh-oh, I thought, here comes trouble. I felt my spirit start to belly over, like the Titanic on its way down.

"A logger," she said. "Is that a fact?"

Dad shrugged. "It's no big thing. I mean it ain't half as excitin' as it sounds."

Mom came out of the kitchen holding a long handled fork. "Don't let him kid you, honey," she said. "That man loves to cut trees. He'd just go on forever, cutting every last tree if you didn't stop him."

Veronica's smile was a fresh wound in scar tissue. "Every last tree, you say?"

"Oh, I love the smell of sawdust," said Dad. "Besides, somebody's gotta cut down the trees before those damn environmentalists put the kibosh on it."

That did it. Without another word Veronica snatched up her coat and headed for the door.

"Wait!" I yelled, but it was too late. She climbed in my truck and sped off, vanishing in the proverbial cloud of dust.

It took a long time for my sorrow to dissipate. Like, say about five minutes. Then I grabbed a beer and sat down in front of the TV. There was a terrific wrestling match on. A fellow in a snake suit was jumping on his opponent's neck. I settled back and smiled, feeling the way a guy does when he knows he's finally home.

~Timothy Martin

一个人快乐与否，不在于环境的好坏，而在乎心态的好坏。

——休·道恩斯

真是愚蠢。这是我这辈子所做过的最蠢的事。也许是有史以来人类所做过的最蠢的事。学校里没有人知道蓟草镇这个地方。它像一个见不得光的黑暗秘密，一想到有可能被人发现，我就提心吊胆。

但你能怪我吗？蓟草镇是个以伐木业为主的小镇，坑坑洼洼的路面上停靠着破烂的汽车，路上的行人要么少颗牙，要么就是梳着额叶切除手术前的发型。这里乱糟糟的，喝着啤酒砍树的伐木工在路边厮混，也有弄了个名字当姓氏的怨妇，听着冗长又哀伤的流行歌，歌中的故事无非是脚踩两条船的负心汉，或者人生之路的艰难险恶。我最不愿意同学发现的真相就是：蓟草镇是我的家乡。

那么，你可能奇怪，为什么我会主动告诉维罗妮卡？答案是，我也不知道。

我的女朋友维罗妮卡非常有魅力。这点是毋庸置疑的。她打扮时髦，身材高挑，留着昂贵修剪、精心吹烫的中性发型。奇怪的是，我不是被她的美丽所吸引。

维罗妮卡来自一个富裕的家庭。衣柜里塞满了迪奥时装，还有不限额度的万事达卡。然而，我看重的也不是她的钱。

我最在意的是维罗妮卡的头脑。她聪敏过人，功课全优，担任高年级班长，同时也是位狂热的环保主义者。她常爱用些令人心生敬畏的大词。

就这样，我爱上了维罗妮卡。有一段时间，我幸福得仿佛置身九重天。不过，如果我对维罗妮卡再多些了解的话，我可能只会飞到七重天。

要知道，她也有不好的一面：性格乖张，爱发脾气，斤斤计较，有时十分粗鲁。她生气的时候，会恶狠狠地盯着你，简直让人毛骨悚然。

但我喜欢维罗妮卡的陪伴。夜复一夜，我坐在她身边，在图书馆里阅读文学作品，看那些内容深刻、意味深长却态度积极的作品。天哪！那会儿我已经在读怀特海、加缪和萨特。

一定是这些文人的伪善之言让我在思考上出现了严重偏差，因为就是在这时，我告诉了维罗妮卡有关蓟草镇的事。

"嗯？"她皱了皱眉，"你是在开玩笑吗？"

"不是。"我回答。

"蓟草镇？听起来就像人类学术语，像非洲原始部落之类的。"

很显然，维罗妮卡不是好相处的人。听到口嚼烟草的女人和头发蓬乱的孩子时，她的眉毛挑成了拱形。知道有些人小学七年级就辍学去开卡车的时候，她更是满脸厌恶。

"我上当了！"她说，"我以为你要比这好。"

"也没有你想得那么糟糕。"我解释说。

"但是听起来糟透了！"她说，"我想让你这周末带我过去，亲自看一下。"

这么多坏兆头，如果我够警惕的话，早该注意到了。"你确定吗？"我问，"要知道，那可是可怕的美国中西部人。"

"当然，我确定。看看其他人如何生活也不错。"

没有什么能阻止她。事实证明，托马斯·沃尔夫是错误的：你可以回家，尤其有人拿刀抵住你肋骨的时候。

回蓟草镇的路程漫长，又一路尘土飞扬，所以维罗妮卡一肚子抱怨。

到家的时候，母亲已经站在门口接我们。她一副家常打扮，穿着没有腰线的碎花裙，套着白色围裙。她亲了亲我的双颊，然后伸开双臂拥抱了我，那架势就像在检查商品有没有损坏。

"妈，你今天身上很香。"我说。

"你是说只有今天吗？"妈妈反问。

"不，我只是觉得你身上的香味特别好闻。要去见特别的人吗？"

母亲笑了："傻孩子。"

维罗妮卡踢了我一脚，我这才想起来还没有向母亲介绍，于是赶忙对母亲说:"哦,妈,这是维罗妮卡。"

母亲打量着维罗妮卡,撅起了嘴:"主啊,她真是个半生不熟的小油条,一个男生需要铁氟龙涂层才能让她不粘锅。"

我满脸通红:"妈,你别这么说话。"

维罗妮卡向我投来意味深长的一瞥。

她问:"你刚才是不是用了'y'all'(黑人惯用语)?"我难堪得脸都白了。

我们经过厨房进入客厅。厨房里正在准备晚餐。四个炉灶上都放着煎锅,计时器也在滴滴答答响,厨房台面上堆满了食物。

但维罗妮卡毫不领情。她脸上的表情似乎在说:"住在这儿的一家人真是百分百的废物,他们的白人血统肯定来自八竿子打不着的远方表亲。"

客厅就像一个"废物堆放处"。石制壁炉上面挂着一个鹿头,旁边的咖啡桌上摆着一些鱼钩和杂志。父亲坐在电视机前打瞌睡,看起来就像打了镇静剂的牛肋肉。

"醒一醒,阿诺德!"母亲大声地说,"来客人了。"

"醒了。"父亲边迷迷糊糊地回答,边从口袋里摸出假牙戴上。

父亲已经穿戴整齐。蓝色衬衫让他的胳膊肘看起来好像被炸飞了一样,腿上是永远磨不破的裤子,脚上一双笨重的黑靴。不论吃饭还是工作,他永远就这一身衣服。

在我跑到厨房查看饭菜是否准备好了的时候,维罗妮卡已经同我父亲聊了很多。

"你是做什么工作的,赫伯利先生?"她问。

"我是伐木工。"

糟了,我暗想,麻烦来了。我觉得我的灵魂已经触礁翻船,仿佛泰坦尼克号沉没一般。

"伐木工，"维罗妮卡问，"这是真的吗？"

父亲耸耸肩说："没什么大不了的。实际上并没有听起来那么有趣。"

母亲从厨房里出来，手里还拿着一把长叉。"可别上当，亲爱的，"她说，"他呀，最喜欢砍树了。要是不阻止他，他一定能把每棵都砍了。"

维罗妮卡脸上的笑容就像伤疤组织上的新创口。"每一棵树吗？"她问。

"我喜欢碎木屑的味道，"父亲回答，"另外，总得有人赶在那些环保人士胡说八道之前，把树给砍了。"

她终于发怒了，抓起外套，一言不发地夺门而出。

"等一下！"我在后面大喊，但已经晚了。她钻进我的卡车，加大油门，飞驰而去，消失在飞扬的尘土中。

我花了很长时间才不再伤心。嗯，大约五分钟吧。之后，我拿起一罐啤酒，坐在电视机前，上面正演着一场精彩的摔跤比赛。穿着蛇纹衣的家伙跳到了对手的脖子上。我往后靠了靠，脸上露出了微笑，我知道这才是回家的感觉。

——蒂莫西·马丁

My Worst—and Best—Easter
最坏却也是最好的复活节

Easter spells out beauty, the rare beauty of new life.
~S.D. Gordon

They always say, "You just know, and it will happen when you least expect it," but I never believed them. Especially in L.A. In ten years of living there, dating was among my favorite—and least favorite—of hobbies.

After yet another handful of bad dates—which included a guy who told me he does coke ("but just quarterly"), a guy who said he is getting better in regard to his last break-up ("though we might get back together"), and a guy who proceeded to flirt with everyone except for me at a party I took him to ("I had a great time," he said—little did I know I had set up a speed dating event—just for him)—I had had enough. And that was all in the same week. And, in L.A., this was typical. Quantity, not quality, and I was tired of it. Having grown up in the Midwest, where were all the guys with Midwestern manners? I

Chapter 2 Adventures in Dating
第二部分 约会篇

had the best boyfriend ever before I moved to L.A. and was convinced all these bad dates were payback for my breaking his heart ten years earlier.

"They" also say to meet someone through friends. But guess what? The above three examples prove "them" very wrong.

This last date, the speed dating one, took place on Easter, with a guy from church at a post-Easter brunch. And I didn't think of his behavior as anything more than un-Christian. The previous year, I had given up dating for Lent; now, I wondered why I hadn't this year, too.

Easter night, a group of my non-Christian friends were meeting for dinner as they did every Sunday night. After the above, being in another group situation was the last thing I wanted to do. But since I was all dressed up and had nowhere else to go, I thought, "Why not?"

For the next hour, I sat parked in front of the restaurant, on the phone with my friend Courtney debating whether or not to go inside. At the time, it was more fun to complain about my day and why not to go in.

"I'm not dating anymore," I told her. "It's too hard. I'm just going to focus on my writing," I added. "Yeah, but that's hard, too," Courtney said. "Yet you keep doing it." True, I thought. "Just forget about them, truly forget about them," Courtney added. "You know that everything happens for a reason, and there is someone better out there for you than a flirty guy who wants his ex-girlfriend back and does coke quarterly," she said. I couldn't help but laugh; I knew she was right.

I decided to go into the restaurant, only to realize I had left my driver's license in a drugstore across town, one that was closing in a half-hour. I drove back to get it, then drove back to the dinner, wondering if it was even worth going in anymore, over an hour later.

Outside the restaurant, I saw a guy at the valet, Tyler, whom I had known six years prior, one whom I had had a crush on. He asked if I wanted to go have a drink. Though it was tempting, I knew my friends were waiting for me, and I wanted to see them, so I declined. I secretly thanked God for the ego boost as I stepped inside.

Once there, I saw another guy I knew, Paul, one I had met a couple years ago, one of those people you meet and have chemistry with, yet neither of you are single, so you say you'll stay in touch, but don't. Yet here he was, alone. We talked for a few minutes, and he told me he would find me before he left. Fair enough.

I thanked God for the second ego boost, and finally met up with my friends. After we caught up a bit, a guy and girl whom I did not know joined our table. The guy, David, was sitting next to me, and we soon started talking... and talking... and talking. A few minutes in, I started to like the guy—he was just so... normal, didn't flirt with everyone in the room, and had no ex-girlfriends or coke habits to speak of. I couldn't remember the last time I had clicked with someone so immediately.

However, I had no clue if the girl David arrived with was his girlfriend. I certainly didn't want to talk to him so much if she was, like the speed dating guy had done to me. I asked David about the girl: they were just friends. Phew.

David and I then remembered we had first met eight months prior, at a friend's birthday party. I had even taken a group photo at the party, with him in it. We also discovered that we had been at the same Halloween party months before, yet never saw each other at it (back then, I had a boyfriend, so checking out other guys wasn't on my radar). Finally, David and I realized we shared a best friend, Jeremy.

I suggested we each text Jeremy to tell him we had met. I had given up texting for Lent, so this was my first post-Lenten text. Jeremy wrote right back. I opened my phone for David and I to read at the same time, without reading the text myself first. It said, "Hey, I was thinking of setting you two up. He seems like your type." I don't know who turned more red, me or David. "This will be a good story someday, of how we started dating," we said in unison, a little perplexed, yet intrigued.

Jeremy had also texted David, asking how we had met. "J-Date," David wrote back jokingly. The funny thing was, just the other week, I had told Jeremy I was going to go on J-Date, for another Christian girl I know went on and ended up marrying a guy from there. Little did Jeremy know that David was kidding. (If you are reading this now, Jeremy, I guess the secret's out.)

Now, hundreds of dates later, "they" were right. You do just know, and when you least expect it. After my long-term, Midwestern college boyfriend, I never thought I would find love like that again. But after meeting David, I realized that I could. And I had. A few months after we started dating, I told David, "Thanks for being at that non-Easter dinner." "Thanks for being," he replied.

~Natalia K. Lusinski

复活节阐释了美，阐释了新生活不可多得的美。

——S.D. 戈登

人们常说"爱情总是出人意料，不期而至"。但我从不相信。尤其是在洛杉矶住了十年之后，这其间，约会一直是我最不喜欢的爱好之一。

一连串糟糕的约会后，我再也无法忍受。其中一个家伙告诉我他吸毒（"但只是季度性的"），一个家伙说他已经从上次失恋的阴影中走出（"但我们有可能复合"），还有一个家伙在我带他参加的派对上，和除我以外的每个人调情（他告诉我说"今天很愉快"，我没想到自己帮他安排了一次快速约会）。但所有这些不过是上周的事。在洛杉矶，到处都是这样的约会。只有数量，没有质量。我已经厌烦了这样的约会。在美国中西部地区长大的我总忍不住想，有着中西部气质的男人都哪里去了？搬来洛杉矶之前，我有世界上最棒的男朋友。我总觉得，这些年来所有的糟糕约会，都是对我十年前伤害他的惩罚。

"人们"也常说通过朋友介绍可以遇到不错的交往对象。但是，以上三个例子证明"人们"是错的。

最近的这次约会，也就是快速约会那位，发生在复活节。从教堂出来后，我们一起吃了节后早午餐，他的行为一点不像个基督徒。前年，因为四旬斋，我没有约会。我想，为什么今年不这么做呢？

复活节当晚，我一些不信基督的朋友像平常周日一样，聚在一起吃晚餐。经历过白天的一切，再参加另一个小组的聚会是我最不愿做的事。但既然我已经装扮好，又无处可去，为什么不参加呢？

一小时后，我把车子在餐厅前停好，然后给好友卡特尼打电话，问她我该不该进去。这是我抱怨白天遭遇以及解释为什么不愿进去的大好时机。

"我再也不约会了，"我告诉她说，"太难了，我以后要专注写作。""写作也很难啊！"卡特尼反驳，"你要坚持下去。"这倒是，我心里暗想。卡特尼继续说道："忘了他们就好，真正忘记。要知道万事皆有因，你会遇到一个更好的人，而不是一个季度性吸毒或者想和前女友复合的家伙。"我忍不住笑了，我知道她说得对。

正当我决定走进餐馆时，却发现刚才把驾照落在镇里的一家药店，

那家店大概半小时后就要关门。于是我开车返回药店，找回驾照又开车
回到餐厅，心里打鼓还值不值得进去，因为我已经晚了一个多小时。

在餐厅外的停车场上，我遇到了泰勒。我们是六年前认识的，那时
我很喜欢他。他问我要不要一起喝一杯。虽然很有诱惑，但我知道朋友
们都在等我，所以拒绝了泰勒。走进餐厅的时候，我暗暗地感激上帝赋
予我的勇气。

刚进入餐厅，我就看到了保罗，我们在几年前见过。他是那种让人
看到就喜欢的男人，但当时我们两个都不是自由身，所以尽管我们说保
持联系，却再没联络。但是现在，他出现了。我们交谈了几分钟后，他
告诉我，他会在离开之前过来找我。很合理。

我再次感谢上帝赐予我勇气。终于，我见到了朋友们。聊了一会儿
之后，一对陌生男女加入我们这桌。男生大卫坐在我旁边。很快，我们
开始交谈，兴致盎然。几分钟后，我喜欢上了大卫——他，怎么说呢？非
常正常，不会和房间里的每个人调情，没有前女友，也不吸毒。我真不
记得，上次遇到这么合适的人是什么时候的事。

但我不知道同大卫一起的女生是不是他女朋友。如果她是的话，我
不该和大卫聊这么多。因为我不想自己像那些快速约会男一样。我问大卫，
他和那个女生的关系。原来，他们只是朋友。咻！白担心了。

之后，我们想起来，我和大卫早在八个月前一位朋友的生日派对上，
就曾经见过。我还拍了一张派对的合照，其中就有他。后来又发现，几
个月前的万圣节派对，我们也都去了，不过当时没有认出彼此（因为当
时我有男朋友陪着，并没有太在意其他男生）。后来，大卫和我发现，我
们有一位共同好友杰瑞米。

我提议，我们两个人同时给杰瑞米发短信，告诉他我们遇到对方。

因为四旬斋，我一直没发短信。所以这是四旬斋过后我的第一条短信。杰瑞米很快回复。我并没有先读短信，而是打开手机，和大卫一起看。短信上写着：嘿，我正想着撮合你们两个，他似乎很喜欢你这种类型的。我不知道我们两个谁的脸更红，我还是大卫。"将来谈到我们怎么认识的时候，这肯定是个不错的故事。"我俩异口同声地说。

杰瑞米也给大卫发短信，问他约会进展得怎样。大卫半开玩笑地回复："犹太约会。"最有趣的是，一周前，我曾告诉杰瑞米说要去参加犹太约会，因为我之前有位女性基督教朋友就是在那儿遇到了现在的丈夫。杰瑞米一点也没想到大卫是在开玩笑（杰瑞米，要是你在看的话，就露馅了）。

经过了数百次约会，我知道"人们"是正确的。爱情总在不经意的瞬间悄然而至。和大学时期的男友分手后，我再没期待能获得那样深刻的爱情。我对大卫说："谢谢你参加那次非复活节晚餐。""谢谢你也来了。"他回答。

——纳塔利亚·K.卢辛斯基

Flour Power
面粉的力量

The great doing of little things makes the great life.
~Eugenia Price

Picture this: a slim, tow-headed nine-year-old boy is sitting on a kitchen counter next to a plate of just-baked cookie cutouts awaiting their adornment. The front of his red, footed, fleece pajamas is smudged with flour, as is the tip of his nose. His gray-green eyes look serious as he contemplates the task before him. Standing on a chair nearby is his sister. Splotches of red and green icing cling to the sleeves of pajamas identical to her brother's except they are pink. Her enormous blue eyes glow when she beholds the culinary bounty before her, and her lightly-freckled cheeks are powdered with the confectioner's sugar used to make icing for the stars, bells, trees, and Santas her brother and she are decorating with red and green tinted sugars and multi-colored sprinkles.

A small, dark-haired woman supervises this

baking extravaganza, ping-ponging between the two children while offering encouragement and assistance as needed. Decorettes are scattered everywhere. Flour dust permeates the air and settles on the counters, stovetop, and linoleum.

Emanating from the kitchen is an aroma so delectable that a man in gold-rimmed spectacles is drawn to the doorway to investigate the merry, if messy, proceedings. "Dad," his son calls out, "Look what we're doing!"

The man smiles and steps closer to admire the cookies, iced liberally and gobbed—some to the max—with multi-colored sprinkles. He selects several conservatively decorated ones to munch while he finishes reading the daily newspaper in the living room.

But I'm getting ahead of myself.

Rewind to several weeks earlier, when mutual friends called the man and woman to arrange a dinner party where she, a childless widow in her late thirties, and he, a forty-something widower with two young children, could meet. Though both had nearly given up on finding suitable mates in their small college town—including the university where they taught—they agreed to the setup.

"I'll have to get home by nine to finish grading essays," the woman said before attending the dinner.

"I won't be able to stay late. I have to get the children into bed at a decent hour," the man told the hostess.

At 12:30 A.M., the woman helped the man carry his daughter, now sound asleep, out to his Jeep; his drowsy son followed close behind. "He intends to call," the friends told the woman.

A day, then two, went by. The third day extended past dinnertime with still no phone call. "I guess he's changed his mind," the woman thought with regret, for the man was everything she'd always wanted—children and all.

The phone rang several hours later. It was the man who, amidst an intensely hectic schedule, finally had time to call. The two talked comfortably for an hour before he asked her to dinner at a local Italian restaurant.

They arrived at the restaurant slightly before 7:00 P.M. and ordered wine to sip as they perused the menu. Then they began to talk, really talk, as if no one else in the universe, much less the restaurant, existed. Sometime after 9:30 P.M., they ordered meals. Patrons of the restaurant came and went until the man and woman were the only diners remaining. By this time, their waiter was sipping a beer at the bar.

When the couple detached from their verbal communion, they were astonished to find that the other tables in the restaurant were cleared and empty. Though their waiter assured them they could stay as long as they liked, it was after 1:00 A.M. and time to depart; the man had considerable driving to do before he'd arrive home to relieve the babysitter from her duties. While helping the woman into her coat, his lips met her forehead. At her door, he gave her a real kiss.

The woman entered her dwelling, feeling as if everything around her was electric. Though she'd scoffed when people in love described themselves as "floating on a pink cloud," exactly that was now happening to her. She tried to undress but ended up sitting on the corner of her bed, contemplating the events of the evening.

Her phone rang. It was the man, who declared, "I almost got arrested, and it's all your fault!" While driving home, he'd been so deep in thought that his Jeep kept drifting across the centerline of the nearly deserted highway. A trooper had noticed his erratic driving and pulled him over. The man had talked his way out of getting a ticket by explaining to a sympathetic—and slightly amused—officer that he'd just come from a very intriguing date.

The next day, the man invited the woman to join his children and him at the Sunday matinee of *Ernest Saves Christmas*. The following afternoon, he brought her to his home: a spacious 1940s Colonial furnished beautifully in earth tones and situated picturesquely on five acres of meadowland and woods. So harmonious was the environment that contentment—more like bliss— enveloped the woman. She wanted to sing; she wanted to dance.

After dinner at his house that night, the woman asked if she could bake Christmas cookies with his children.

Which brings us back to the opening scene.

The man reappears in the doorway and scrutinizes the floury footprints crisscrossing the kitchen. "Dad," the little girl pipes up, "Come see this cookie! I made it just for you!" He picks his way across the floor to gaze upon a cookie so covered with icing and decorations that its Santa shape is obliterated. Though inedible by adult standards, it is a six-year-old's dream. The man's eyebrows arch then relax. He turns to his daughter. "Are you sure you have enough sprinkles on that?" he asks.

She giggles. "Doesn't it look good?"

"It's a masterpiece. And you've worked so hard decorating it, I think you should be the one to eat it."

Directly, glasses of milk are poured. Numerous cookies are eaten; dozens more are stored. With bedtime approaching, the children wash up and change into clean pajamas. While the woman tidies the kitchen, the man reads a story to the children. Afterwards, the adults retire to the living room, where a fire dances in the fireplace. Wine is poured, and the man and woman toast the success of the evening. "This is the first time they've ever baked cookies," the man tells the woman beside him on the sofa. "They were too young before their mother died." With arms around each other, they talk—or don't talk—until the fire burns down to tiny embers.

After twenty years of marriage and counting, my husband still maintains that he was set up: somehow I knew that, if I positively wanted to hook him, all I'd have to do was bake Christmas cookies with his children. The ambience created by such a joyous activity made him realize that I was the right woman for him and his difficult years as a single parent were about to come to an end. All he could do after that was completely fall in love with me—and I with him. The rest, as they say, is history.

~Catherine Grow

做好琐碎小事，也能成就伟大生活。

——尤金妮亚·普莱斯

请试着想象这样一幅画面：头发蓬乱的瘦小男孩儿坐在厨房柜台边，上面摆着一盘刚刚出炉、未加修饰的饼干。他红色连脚羊毛睡衣的前面沾满了面粉，连鼻尖儿上也是。思考着眼前的任务，他灰绿色的眼睛看起来特别严肃。站在旁边椅子上的是他妹妹。她穿着和哥哥同样款式的粉色睡衣，袖子上沾满了红色斑点和绿色糖衣。她和哥哥一起，用各色糖汁为星星、铃铛、树木和圣诞老人做装饰。蓝色的大眼睛出神地看着面前的烹饪用具，微带雀斑的脸上沾满了五颜六色的糖汁。

一位身材娇小的黑发女人，监督着这烘烤盛况。在两个孩子间来回穿梭，给他们鼓励和帮助。装饰用的糖衣掉得满地都是。面粉的飞尘弥漫在空气中，飘落在柜台、炉灶和油毡上。

戴金丝边眼镜的男人被厨房飘散的诱人香气吸引过来，来看看这欢乐的、当然也有些凌乱的活动。"爸爸，"他的儿子叫着，"看看我们做的！"

男人微笑地走过去，欣赏着这些饼干——它们被抹上了糖衣，撒上了各色的糖屑。当然，有些饼干显然是过度装饰了。他拿了几块不算太夸张的饼干带到客厅，打算读完报纸的时候吃。

不过，我好像说太多了。

几周前，男人和女人的朋友分别打电话给他们，说想安排一场晚宴。女人三十多岁，寡居，没有孩子；男人四十多岁，鳏居，两个孩子，朋友们想让他们见个面。尽管他们已经放弃了在小镇上、包括他们教书的大学里寻找到合适对象的希望，但二人还是同意见面。

"我9点之前就要回家，批阅学生论文。"女人出席晚宴之前说。

"我不能待太久，要哄孩子上床睡觉。"男人告诉女主人。

午夜12点30分，女人帮着男人把他熟睡的女儿抱上吉普车。他昏昏欲睡的儿子紧随其后。"他会打电话的。"朋友告诉女人。

一天过去了，又一天过去了。第三天的晚餐时间，女人还是没有等到电话。"我猜他改变了主意。"女人满是遗憾，这个男人符合她的所有期待——孩子及所有一切。

几小时后，电话铃响了。正是这个男人。他在繁忙的日程中，终于抽出时间打电话。两人愉快地聊了一个多小时。之后，男人约她到当地的一家意大利餐厅共进晚餐。

晚上7点，他们来到餐厅，点了红酒，边喝边看菜单。然后，他们开始交谈，真正的交谈，好像忘了宇宙的存在，更不要说餐厅。9点30分，他们开始就餐。餐厅的顾客来来去去，直到男人和女人成了唯一的食客。此时，餐厅的服务员已经靠在吧台开始喝酒。

亲密的谈话终于结束，他们惊讶地发现，餐厅已经空无一人且已整理干净。虽然服务员向他们保证，想待多晚都可以。但已是夜里1：00，他们不得不离开。男人赶回家结束保姆的工作前，他还要开很久的车。帮女人穿好外套后，他亲吻了女人的前额。他把女人送到家门口后，给了她一个真正的吻。

女人回到住处，感觉周围的一切都令人兴奋不已。尽管平日总嘲笑那些恋爱中的人说的"恋爱就像浮上云端般美妙"，但她发现这正是自己现在的感受。她本想脱衣睡觉，却最终坐在床边，回想今晚发生的一切。

此时，她的手机响了。是男人的电话，他说："我几乎被逮捕，这都怪你！"原来，开车回家的路上，他一直沉浸在刚才美好的约会中，吉普车早已不知不觉地开到旁边废弃高速公路的中心线。交警注意到他飘忽不定的驾驶，将他拦了下来。男人解释自己刚从一个美妙的约会中回来，被他逗乐的交警没有给他开罚单。

第二天，男人邀请她和孩子们一起参加周日的《拯救圣诞老人》音乐会。第二天下午，他邀请她到自己家做客：房间很宽敞，大地色系，浓厚的20世纪40年代殖民时期风格，房子外面风景如画，有大约两公顷的草地和树林。这一切是如此和谐。知足——更像是幸福感——笼罩着女人。她快乐得想唱歌，想跳舞。

晚餐后，女人问，能不能同孩子们一起做圣诞饼干。

这就有了我们刚开始看到的那一幕。

男人再次来到门口，看着厨房地板杂乱地沾满了面粉的脚印。"爸爸，"小女孩高兴地喊道，"快来看看这块饼干！我特意为你做的！"他走过脏乱的地板，目光落在了一块沾满糖衣和各种点缀、已经看不出圣诞老人形状的饼干上。尽管按成年人的标准，这样的饼干是不能食用的，但它却是一个 6 岁女孩儿的梦想。男人挑起的眉毛渐渐舒缓下来。他转向女儿说："你确定你洒了足够多的糖屑吗？"

女儿咯咯地笑起来："好看吗？"

"真是杰作。既然你那么辛苦地装饰它，我想这块饼干应该让你吃。"

他们喝了很多牛奶，吃了很多饼干。剩下的饼干被储存起来。临近就寝时间，孩子们洗漱完毕，换上干净的睡衣。男人给孩子们朗读睡前故事，女人则整理厨房。

之后，他们回到客厅休息，壁炉中火苗舞动。他们端着酒杯，庆祝今晚的成功。"这是他们第一次烤饼干，"男人告诉坐在他身旁沙发上的女人，"妻子去世的时候，他们都还很小。"他们靠在一起，聊天或者沉默，直到壁炉里的火苗只剩微小的余烬。

二十年的婚姻生活和相互依靠后，我的丈夫仍认为他上当了：不知怎么，我也这么认为。如果真想让他爱上我，我要做的只是和他的孩子们一起做圣诞饼干。这样的活动能营造出一种欢乐的气氛，让他意识到他作为一个单身父亲的艰难岁月即将结束。那之后，他会全身心地爱上我，我也一样深爱着他。后面的情况，不用说，大家也都猜到了。

——凯瑟琳·格瑞

The One Who Never Was
从未爱过的人

'Tis better to have loved and lost than never to have loved at all.

~Alfred Lord Tennyson

It was Thursday, around 5:30 P.M. on a perfect spring day; I was sitting in the patio section of a restaurant across the street from a busy train terminal, waiting for Marie to arrive. Every couple of minutes the terminal would unleash a fresh batch of homebound commuters. The seemingly endless waves of commuters served as a good distraction as I continued battling the army of butterflies in my stomach. I am not accustomed to being nervous but it seemed appropriate to feel anxious before my first date with the girl who I didn't want to remember and could never forget.

One week before, I had seen Marie for the first time since graduating college three years earlier. I had finally revealed the truth that had been haunting me since the first moment I ever saw her, a truth I had spent years trying to ignore, a truth which had to be confessed, a truth she deserved to hear, a truth she needed to believe—Marie is the standard against which I measure all other women. Another train pulled in and the terminal started producing a new mob of commuters when Marie called to tell me she had arrived.

The butterflies kicked into high gear as I looked across the street. This wave of commuters contained the woman who forever changed the way I look at all other women. Marie stood out from the crowd like a rose in a barren desert. She wore an unforgettably bright smile and casually walked with an elegance that was as surreal as it was intoxicating. My breath was taken away at the first sight of her beautiful smile. Somehow Marie found a way to make her smile even more alluring when she spotted me from across the street and started walking over.

Little did I know, this date would be the start of an enlightening journey that would ultimately leave me with the knowledge that following your heart will prove insufficient if you allow your fears to create even the slightest bit of hesitation or restraint.

The next two years were a roller coaster. During good times we talked for hours, laughed and enjoyed being together as if our ups and downs and everything else in the world were completely irrelevant. I found myself totally at peace with the job I created for myself—making her feel as comfortable, safe and happy as possible. I thought her eyes revealed that she reciprocated my feelings.

It was not only Marie's physical beauty that captivated me; it was something infinitely more rare and significant. By my standards, nothing can compare to a person who effortlessly exudes an energy that eases the mind of all stress, while simultaneously enabling all that truly matters in life to be displayed with brilliant clarity and joy. The women I had dated in the past all possessed the attributes I wanted (intelligence, humor, physical/inner beauty and compassion) but those characteristics were never enough to make me content—I needed more. I needed a woman with the unique ability to profoundly strengthen and inspire me, a woman who forced me to become a better person simply because I knew she deserved the absolute best I could offer, a woman whose well-being I viewed as being equally or more important than my own.

Eventually we drifted apart, leaving me wondering why the vicious hot/

cold cycle had continued for those two years. Was it because I hadn't been assertive enough about what I wanted? Was it because we are both afraid to trust each other with the inherent responsibility that a deep connection like that requires? Maybe my instincts were all wrong and she never felt the same way for me as I did for her. Regardless of what the real reason was, I don't feel any differently towards her or see her in a lesser light. In a strange way I don't care what the reason was; all that matters to me is that she is happy and safe. Regardless of how much I want to be the one to make her smile like no one else can, I'd be content knowing she is smiling and being treated like gold (as she deserves to be) by someone else.

Even though things turned out much differently than I believed they would, I learned valuable lessons from my experiences with Marie. Truth be told, although I have called Marie "the one who got away", the fears and hesitations which I believe to have ultimately kept us apart made Marie "the one who never was" more than anything else.

Even though I would love to go back in time and change how things unfolded between us, I have no regrets. I followed my heart, and although she never truly returned my feelings, she deserved the kindness I gave her nonetheless. I learned that when a person as special as Marie comes into your life you owe it to yourself and to her to follow your heart and put it all on the line. Otherwise you'll allow your fears to restrict your future, leaving you with nothing but memories of "the one who got away" or even worse, memories of "the one who never was".

~Jeffrey Nathan Schirripa

在爱过后失去某人，总比从未爱过好。

——阿尔弗雷德·罗德·坦尼森

一个美好的春日下午，也就是周四下午 5：30，我坐在街对面的露天餐厅，看着对面繁忙的火车站，等着玛丽的到来。每隔几分钟，火车站就会涌现一批新鲜的面孔，他们都是些盼着回家的上班族。络绎不绝的乘客，正好可以缓解我的紧张与激动。我平日里很少紧张，但这是我同玛丽的第一次约会。她是那种我不愿意想起却又无法忘记的女孩。

一周前，我遇到了玛丽。这是大学毕业三年后的首次见面。后来，我终于对她说了实话，从我看到她的第一眼起就想告诉她的实话，这么多年一直试图掩饰的实话，一个需要坦白和忏悔的实话，一个她有权听到的实话，也是她需要相信的实话——她是我心目中最完美的女人。此时，又来了一班车，车上涌出一批新鲜面孔，这时玛丽打电话给我，告诉我她到了。

我在街对面搜寻她的身影，心里小鹿乱撞。人流中的这个女人，永远改变了我衡量其他女人的标准。玛丽在人群中那么亮眼，就像荒芜的沙漠中突然出现了一朵娇艳的玫瑰。她脸上挂着令人难以忘怀的灿烂微笑，随意的走姿散发出率性的优雅气质，如梦似幻，让人心醉神迷。看到她明媚笑容的刹那，我似乎停止了呼吸。玛丽看到我，朝我走来的时候，脸上的微笑似乎更加迷人。

我一点也不知道，这次约会将会变成一场启蒙教育。它最终教会了我，如果你任由恐惧带来哪怕一丁点儿犹豫或抵触情绪，那么再忠实于自己的心意也无济于事。

我们接下来两年的交往，就好像过山车游戏。感情亲密的时候，一聊就是几小时，一起开怀大笑，享受着两人厮守的美好时光，仿佛之前的争吵从未发生。我很满意自己所做的一切——尽可能给她所有的舒适、安全以及快乐。她的眼神让我觉得我们心有灵犀。

我爱玛丽不仅是因为她的美丽，更是因为她身上罕见而特别的品质。

有她在，你会觉得一切压力都消失了，生命中最重要的事变得清晰明快。过去的约会对象，也具备我喜欢的品质（聪明、幽默、外在美、内在美、激情），我却从不满足。我需要更多，我需要一位可以影响我、激励我的女人。一个让我愿意为她做得更好的女人，一个我视她比自己更重要的女人。

最后，我们分手了，只留下我在想为什么这两年的感情总是忽好忽坏恶性循环。是因为我不够确定吗？还是因为我们害怕信任对方，害怕稳定后随之而来的责任？或许，是我理解错了，可能她从未像我爱她那样爱我。但无论什么原因，我对她的感情还是一样。很奇怪，我不在乎真正的原因。对我来说，只要她健康快乐就足够了。不管我多想成为那个让她笑得最开心的人，只要知道她现在过得快乐，有人真正爱她疼她（她值得这样），我就别无所求。

尽管同玛丽恋情的发展和当初设想的不同，但我还是从中学到了很多宝贵经验。说实话，尽管我称玛丽为"那个离开的人"，但是导致我们分手的那些犹豫和抵触，实际上让玛丽成了"那个从未爱过的人"。

假如时光可以倒流，我愿意重回过去，弥补我们之间的所有误会。但我并不遗憾。我追随着自己的心意，哪怕她从未真正爱过我，她仍然值得我这样深爱。我知道，当有一位像玛丽一样的女人走进了你的生活，你应当好好把握，不恐惧不逃避，让她也爱上你。否则，陪伴你的只有"那个离开的人"留下的回忆，或者更糟的是"那个从未爱过的人"留下的回忆。

——杰弗里·纳桑·迟锐帕

The Rainbow
彩虹

And as he spoke of understanding, I looked up and saw the rainbow leap with flames of many colors over me.

~Black Elk

1995 was a bad year; my husband of forty-eight years died in August, then four months later my mother died. What was I supposed to do now after caring for him for ten years, and helping with Mother's care? Lonely days and nights stretched endlessly. Dark and dreary thoughts constantly filled my mind. If I slept at all, I had nightmares. One day my pastor invited me to his Grief Support Group and I went, reluctantly, and met others who shared their feelings, how they coped. Finally, in an effort to dispel the depression that threatened, I resolved to turn my mind to other things, to seeing the beauties of nature, beginning with my first ocean cruise. I was hesitant to travel alone, so I invited four of my teenaged granddaughters for company. On a lovely sunny day in June we boarded Holland America's *Nieuw Amsterdam* in Vancouver and headed for

Alaska. The two older girls, sisters, shared one cabin. The other two bunked with me.

Each morning I awoke before the girls, walked the decks, and savored the sights, smells, and sounds of the ocean. The girls and I took in all the shows, went on three shore excursions, marveled at hundreds of bald eagles in the wild, and even walked on the Mendenhall Glacier. When they were occupied with teen activities, I relished my moments on deck and tried to banish the dark thoughts and nagging concerns. Watching the soothing waves helped.

For weeks I had debated and prayed about what was happening in my life. My greatest concerns were about the nice widower I had met in the Grief Support Group. I saw him at church each Sunday. He phoned occasionally to chat. We went to dinner and a movie once, riding in the red Firebird he was so proud of. He tolerated my depressed moods and bouts of tears and even managed to make me laugh a few times. But was I being fair to take up so much of his time? I couldn't forget that my husband had been dead less than a year. What was I doing? I was almost seventy. What would my children think? I needed a sign, but the rolling waves of the Inland Passage never showed me any.

The morning our ship sailed into Glacier Bay, I dressed quietly and hurried to the Promenade Deck. Alaskan time was four hours earlier than at home, so despite the ship's clock saying it was 4:00 A.M., my built-in clock insisted it was 8:00 A.M. I walked briskly around the deck and watched the ocean and the lightening sky. On my first turn around the bow I spied a brilliant rainbow spanning the western sky. I was almost afraid to hope, but I couldn't help wonder if this were the answer to my prayers.

Martha, another widow, joined me on my next lap. She also had a knotty problem: deciding whether to surrender her independence and move in with her lonely sister, who had recently lost her husband. We had discussed our respective dilemmas two or three times on previous days without coming any closer to conclusions. Now as we rounded the bow, we admired the intense colors of the rainbow.

"Martha, I wonder—do you think this could be God's sign for us? You know, like when he showed the rainbow to Noah?" I asked.

"I don't know," she said, "but if it's still there on our next lap, I'll consider it."

Our rainbow continued to brighten the sky on subsequent laps, fading only when we went inside for breakfast. We ate in silence, but I felt more relaxed and at peace than I had in weeks.

I spent the entire day on deck, drinking in the glaciers, the blues and greens of the ice, each from different decades, even different geological ages. The summer day was warm, the sky a clear cerulean, the water a mirror, as if posing for reflecting pictures and broken only by the occasional otter splashing playfully in the ocean. Ice walls towered above the ten-story deck, their beauty demonstrating once again God's majesty.

When we docked in Ketchikan, I phoned my widower friend, Cal, but didn't mention what had happened. He was cordial and offered to pick me up at the airport on my return. Cal is a retired engineer, an avid woodworker, and a bicyclist who loves to travel. He and his late wife had not been able to do so during her many illnesses any more than I had been able to travel during my husband's illnesses.

When I returned from our cruise, he visited my house often and I soon realized I was developing strong feelings for him. But I never put a name to our relationship until the night my daughter phoned. When I mentioned I had been out to dinner with Cal, she exclaimed, "Mother! You never told me you were dating!" She sounded happy.

During the rest of that year we attended plays and the ballet and took day trips to state parks in the area in his Firebird. He often brought me flowers; he became very affectionate. In January, Cal knelt down on one knee and proposed marriage. I accepted. After consulting with our pastor, we set a date in April, sold our homes and bought one together. Our wedding arrangements were overseen by the watchful eye of the congregation, some of whom even threw us a shower. In our joy, we invited the entire church membership to attend the ceremony.

Tennessee's spring in 1997 was at its most glorious. The redbuds and dogwoods put on a spectacular show for our northern guests while Southern magnolias and azaleas burst with crimson and white blossoms. All seven of our children flew in from distant parts of the country to participate; his sisters and their families drove down from the Midwest; two of his cousins came from Ohio and Missouri. My late husband's brother and his wife drove in from across the state.

On the day of our wedding, it rained lightly at intervals, but the sun finally showed itself in time for our evening ceremony. When my brother arrived to escort me to the church, we both marveled at the glorious rainbow in the eastern sky. I may have had doubts that the rainbow I saw in Glacier Bay was a sign, but I firmly believe that this one on our wedding day was showering God's blessing on us.

Cal and I have been married for twelve years now and each day our joy and love grow deeper. He still brings me flowers. No more dark thoughts plague me.

We spent our honeymoon on a Caribbean cruise, trying nightly to count the millions of stars and watching the Hale-Bopp comet process regally across the sky. Together, we experienced both the rough Atlantic and calm Pacific oceans on our recent voyage through the Panama Canal. On the last night aboard, we had the rare pleasure of viewing a full lunar eclipse away from all city lights. One year we plan to share the beauties of a different Alaskan cruise. God has been good to us.

~Elsie Schmied Knoke

当他谈到理解的时候，我抬起头，看到了一抹彩虹缤纷绚烂。

——黑麋鹿

　　1995年是我人生中最灰暗的时光。这年8月，共同生活了48年的丈夫去世。四个月后，母亲也撒手人寰。照顾丈夫、照顾母亲近十年后，现在的我茫然无措。那些寂寞孤单的日夜，我无法入睡。就算终于睡去，也是噩梦不断。有一天，牧师邀请我参加他所在的悲伤互助小组，我很不情愿地去了，结识了一些人，听他们分享自己的故事以及走出伤痛的经验。最后，为了摆脱抑郁，我决定做些其他事情来转移自己的注意力。我要领略大自然的美。就这样，我开始了人生第一次海洋之旅。因为害怕独自旅行，我邀请了四个豆蔻年华的孙女陪我一起。6月的一个阳光灿烂的日子，我们在温哥华登上了荷美邮轮公司新阿姆斯特丹号邮轮，驶向阿拉斯加。两个年纪稍大的女孩在一个船舱，另外两个和我一起。

　　每天清晨，孩子们还没醒来时，我都会走到甲板上，吹吹海风，看看辽阔无际的海，感受海洋的声音和气息。我和孩子们一起观看了所有的演出，也上岸作短途旅行。荒野里，数百只秃鹫聚在一起的奇观，让我们赞叹不已。我们甚至还在门登霍尔冰川上走了一遭。她们玩一些小孩子的游戏时，我会开始回忆甲板上的美好时光，试着驱走那些悲观想法和无尽的烦恼。看海能帮我舒缓情绪。

连续数周，我一直在同自己辩论，也为自己祈祷。我最关心的就是那个在悲伤互助小组遇到的鳏夫，他看起来人很好。每周日，我都会在教堂遇到他。偶尔，他也会打电话同我聊天。他曾开着引以为傲的红色火鸟汽车，载我一起去吃饭、看电影。他总能容忍我低落的情绪、突然掉落的眼泪。有几次，他甚至成功地让我破涕为笑。但占用他那么多时间，这么做公平吗？我无法忘记丈夫去世一年不到的事实。我到底在做什么？要知道，我已是近 70 岁的人。孩子们会怎么想？我需要一个指示，但波浪翻滚的内陆航道并未给我任何迹象。

早上，船航行到冰川湾，我轻手轻脚地穿好衣服，来到甲板上散步。阿拉斯加的时间比在家早了 4 小时，所以尽管船上闹钟显示的是早上 4 点，我自己的生物钟却认定现在已是 8 点钟。我轻快地走到甲板上，看着大海，还有蒙蒙发亮的天空。在船艏门周围散步的时候，我忽然发现一道亮丽的彩虹挂在西部天空。我不敢奢望，却禁不住怀疑，这是不是上苍回应了我的祈祷。

玛莎在我转第二圈的时候加入进来。她同我一样，是个寡妇。但她还面临着一个更棘手的问题：是否要放弃独立，搬到新近失去丈夫的姐姐那儿。之前，我们也讨论过几次，但没有得出任何结论。现在，我们一起在船头散步，看着天空绚烂的彩虹。

"玛莎，我想知道，你觉得这是上帝给我们的指示吗？就像让诺亚看到彩虹那样?"我问。

她说:"我不知道,但如果我们转下一圈的时候,它还在,我就认真考虑。"

随后的几圈,彩虹一直都在,明亮地挂在天空,直到我们进入船舱吃早餐的时候,才慢慢消失。吃饭的时候,我们都沉默着,但是相比几周前,我觉得心情轻松平和了许多。

我在甲板上待了整整一天,陶醉于美丽的蓝绿色冰川,每块都来自不同的年代,甚至不同的地质时期。夏季的天总是暖暖的。天空一片蔚蓝,海静得像面镜子,只有调皮的水獭偶尔嬉戏的时候,才会打破这平静。耸立的冰墙大约有十层甲板高,它壮阔的美再次证明了上帝的威严与神奇。

当船在凯奇坎停靠时,我给鳏夫朋友卡尔打了电话,没有提彩虹的事。他非常热情,并提出等我回来的时候到机场接我。卡尔是位退休工程师,平时喜欢做木工,也爱骑自行车旅行。因为此前他妻子多病,同我和丈夫的情况一样,他们也很少出去旅行。

结束了海洋之旅,回到家后,卡尔常常过来玩。我很快发现自己喜欢上他了。但我从未正式承认我们之间的恋爱关系,直到有一天,女儿打电话给我。当我提及曾和卡尔一起吃饭的时候,她惊呼:"妈!你从没说过你在约会!"女儿听起来很开心。

其他时间,我们一起看话剧,欣赏芭蕾演出,他也会开着"火鸟"带我到附近的州立公园散心。卡尔经常送花给我,也变得十分深情。1月,他单膝下跪,向我求婚。我答应了。咨询过牧师后,我们将婚期订在4月的一天,各自卖了房子,合买一处新居。婚礼的安排是在教会的监督下进行的,一些人还给我们带来了礼物。为了和更多的人分享喜悦,我们邀请了全部教会成员。

1997 年春，正是田纳西州最美的时刻。南方的木兰和杜鹃绽放着深红、浅白的花朵，北方紫荆和山茱萸的美也让我们南方的客人赞叹不已。七个孩子都从全国各地赶来参加我们的婚礼。他的姐妹和家人也从中西部赶来。卡尔的两个表兄弟，一个来自俄亥俄州，一个来自密苏里州。我已故丈夫的弟弟也带着妻子穿越了大半个国家，特意赶来。

婚礼当天，天空中飘着蒙蒙细雨，但傍晚婚礼仪式前，天空放晴了。当我在兄长的陪伴下，赶往教堂的时候，我们看到了东部天空的那道彩虹。所有人都惊叹不已。虽然不敢肯定冰川湾看到的彩虹是上帝的指引，但这次出现在我们婚礼上的彩虹，一定是上帝对我们的祝福。

现在，卡尔和我结婚已经 12 年了。我们在一起的每一天，都充满了幸福和快乐。我们的爱情也随着时间的推移越发深厚。他现在仍然送花给我。那些阴郁消极的想法已离我远去。

我们的蜜月旅行是游览加勒比海。晚上一起躺在甲板上数星星，看海尔—波普彗星划过天空。穿越巴拿马运河的时候，我们一起领略大西洋的粗犷，欣赏太平洋的宁静。昨晚，在远离城市灯光的海洋上，我们观看了罕见的月全食。明年，我们计划来一次不同寻常的阿拉斯加之旅。愿主保佑。

——艾斯·西米德·可诺克

Go for It

努力追求

You come to love not by finding the perfect person, but by
seeing an imperfect person perfectly.

~Sam Keen

In 2007, I turned fifty, was recently divorced,
and had been disabled since age thirty-six. "Well,
Debbie," I said in a pep talk to myself, "you still
wear the same size jeans you wore decades ago.
Age has made you interesting. Maybe someone will
develop a romantic interest or take a second look."

Who was I kidding? I was middle-aged and
disabled...unworthy, damaged, broken, a burden.
How could I socialize, let alone explain my bizarre
disability? Did jeans really matter?

In 1994, I was diagnosed with a rare neurologi-
cal disorder, Stiff Person Syndrome (SPS). It occurs in
one in a million people. My compromised neuroinhi-
bitory system has a heightened response to external
stimuli, i.e., touch, sound, emotion, and movement,
eliciting severe body spasms and frozen rigidity,
predisposing me to injury from unprotected falls.

Turning on my computer, my spirits lifted at

an e-mail from John, my best friend. I lived in Colorado. He lived in Florida, but we were close. Telephone and e-mail communications with him were stimulating, fun, and deep. Candidly, I shared my insecurities with him in a phone conversation.

"John, nobody will want me. I am very limited in what I can do. It wouldn't be fair of me to ask any man to take on my physical baggage."

"Debbie, I believe God will have someone for you. You still have so much to offer," he replied in an attempt to boost my confidence.

"I just don't think so. I want to live my life alone. I can't go through another divorce. I'd rather be alone by choice than lonely in a marriage," I sighed.

John reminded me about his late wife, Donna. "I wasn't looking for anyone when I met her, content living alone and occupied with my business. Donna poked her head into Sunday school class one day. Obviously, God had plans for us. It was a good marriage. Trust me, it is possible for you."

Pondering his encouraging words, I still had serious doubts, especially considering the uncertain and frightening possibilities of my SPS diagnosis.

During my next phone conversation with John, I told him my daughter, Jaime, and I had tentative plans to go to Clearwater and Disney World. "Let me know when you are sure and I will help you book arrangements. I think I can schedule a free day to come and have dinner with you and Jaime," he offered.

A few months later, Jaime and I were waiting at our Disney World hotel to have dinner with John. After months of phone conversations, Jaime and John had become close and were anticipating meeting one another. Jaime understood my nervousness over John seeing my disability for the first time. When he phoned to let us know he was in the lobby, I asked my daughter for a few minutes alone with John, leaving my walking stick in the room.

Thoughts of seeing John excited and intimidated me. Talking about a disabling condition is different than actually seeing the reality. Would he think differently of me when he saw me?

The elevator doors opened to a paparazzi flash, John taking my picture. Aside from the shock on my face, the picture is of a seemingly normal woman with dark brown hair, black capris, and a stylish print shirt.

I absorbed every detail of John: receding hair, portly build, twinkling blue eyes, black pants, white shirt… and his cane, since John has SPS too. Taking a seat on a nearby settee, we looked into each other's eyes for the first time and embraced. Inhaling the subtle masculine scent of his cologne, I was surrounded by his warmth.

After the Florida trip, our phone conversations became five-hour marathons, a couple of times a day, every day. Our friendship had evolved into something so much deeper… and so very complicated. John is almost fourteen years older than me and has other major health issues along with Stiff Person Syndrome. I have insulin-dependent diabetes with my SPS. We discussed our feelings versus the reality. Should we?

I became Mrs. John Crawford in 2008 and relocated to Jacksonville. Our life is rich, full, and unique. Reality stalks us but experiencing wonderful is worth it.

~Debra A. Crawford

爱一个人，并非因为你发现他完美，而是因为他的不完美在你的眼中很完美。

——萨姆·凯恩

36 岁的时候，我残疾了。现在是 2007 年，我已将近 50 岁，又刚刚离了婚。"嘿，黛比，"我给自己打气，"你牛仔裤的尺码一直没变，岁月让你变得更加迷人，会有人爱你的。"

我在骗谁呢？中年、残疾、失败、负担，这就是我的标签。我怎么能够正常交往，更别说解释我奇怪的残疾了？难道穿小号的牛仔裤真的重要吗？

1994年，我被诊断出患有一种罕见的神经系统疾病——僵化综合征。这种病极其少见，百万人中只有一例。丧失免疫力的神经元抑制系统会对外界的刺激，如触摸、声音、情绪和运动等刺激作出强烈反应，从而引发身体严重痉挛和僵化，造成意外摔伤。

我打开电脑，看到好友约翰的邮件时，心情为之一振。我住在科罗拉多州，他住在佛罗里达州，但我们非常亲密。无论是电话还是邮件，同约翰聊天总是非常有趣，而且很有意义。和他电话聊天的时候，我向他倾诉了自己的不安全感。

"约翰，没有人喜欢我。我能做的事情非常少。我不能要求任何男人接受我这个包袱，这么做太不公平。"

"黛比，上帝一定为你准备了合适的另一半。你仍然可以做很多事情。"他试着鼓励我，帮我恢复自信。

"我不这么认为。我宁愿独自生活，不想再次离婚。我宁愿有选择地孤单，也不愿在婚姻里寂寞。"我叹了口气。

约翰对我讲起了他已故的妻子唐娜："遇到她之前，我很享受一个人的生活，每天埋头工作处理业务。但当她把头伸进主日学校课堂的那一刻，我知道，上帝已经安排好一切。我们的婚姻很幸福。相信我，你也能做到。"

我琢磨着他的话，但仍心存疑虑，尤其是想到自己病情的不确定性和可能出现的可怕后果。

在和约翰的一次通话中，我告诉他，自己和女儿杰米准备去清水镇和迪士尼乐园游玩。"等你决定下来的时候，记得通知我。我可以帮你们预定，而且我应该能抽出一天时间，陪你和杰米吃顿饭。"

几个月后，我和杰米在迪士尼乐园酒店等待约翰，准备和他共进晚餐。经过几个月的电话交流，杰米和约翰已经变得很熟，非常期待和对方见面。约翰将第一次看到我的残疾，杰米很理解我此刻的紧张心情。当他打电话告诉我们他在大厅的时候，我让女儿先等一会儿。因为我想和约翰单独待几分钟，我下去的时候并没有拄拐杖，而是把它留在了房间。

一想到马上就要见到约翰，我既兴奋又害怕。我知道谈论残疾和亲眼看到的感觉是不一样的。看到我的时候，他会改变主意吗？

电梯门打开，迎面一阵耀眼的闪光，约翰在给我拍照。除了吃惊的表情外，画面中的女人看起来再正常不过，深褐色的头发，时尚印花 T恤，配黑色紧身裤。

我记住了约翰的每一个细节：后梳的头发，魁梧的身材，蓝色眼睛炯炯有神，黑裤子，白衬衫……还有他的手杖，约翰也有僵化综合征。到附近的沙发上坐下后，我们第一次注视着对方的眼睛，并紧紧拥抱。沉醉在他古龙香水的男士气息中的我，感受到特别的温暖。

佛罗里达之旅后，我和约翰的电话交谈成了五小时的马拉松赛，而且每天都会打好几次。我们的友谊已经演变为一种更深更复杂的情感。约翰比我大将近 14 岁，除了僵化综合征外还伴有其他严重健康问题。我的僵化综合征的并发症是胰岛素依赖型糖尿病。我们讨论了感情与现实的冲突。我们该怎么做呢？

2008 年，我成为约翰·克劳福德夫人，并搬到杰克逊维尔市。我们的生活丰富、完整且独特。现实牵绊着我们，但为了体验生命之美，这一切都值得。

——黛布拉·A.克劳福德

Another Forever
另一个永远

For it was not into my ear you whispered, but into my heart.
It was not my lips you kissed, but my soul.

~Judy Garland

I sat at my desk on the third floor of our office building. My desk was covered with promotional materials and items that called for my attention as the associate director of public relations for our large denomination. There were two new roles in my life now—widow and public relations specialist.

After serving nearly fourteen years as a missionary in the Caribbean, my husband's untimely death from cancer had certainly changed the direction of my life. Left with my youngest son to finish high school, living and working in Atlanta was a far cry from our ministry amid the simplicity of life on the beautiful island of Grenada!

Focused on my latest project, I was interrupted when a secretary from one of the departments walked into my office and tossed a professional resumé on my desk. "You'll be interested in this," she smiled.

"Our newest guy—he's a widower!"

I was courteous, but miffed. One thing I did not need was the concerted interest that had been shown in my "aloneness". At age forty-seven there was certainly, in the back of my mind, the idea that I would not remain single forever; I had enjoyed a good marriage and considered that "someday" that might be my pleasure again. But not right now!

As I opened the folder to consider which news sources would get the latest press release that I would prepare, I glanced at the profile. What? Coming to Georgia from Oklahoma was Ed Onley, age fifty-one, with... six children!

Forget that one! What in the world was my friend thinking? I had three sons, all spaced an orderly four years apart.

In the following two weeks I did my professional duty. I interviewed "the widower" and sent the proper media outlets his most impressive work history, extolling the benefits of his having left his home missions assignment to join us. I admit that I was readily impressed with the native Virginia accent that he had not lost while he established community ministry centers, medical care clinics and chaplain programs in Mississippi, Arkansas and then Oklahoma. I cheered him on as he began to do the same thing in Georgia.

Then it happened.

One day Ed stopped me on the balcony walkway as I was leaving the director's office. With a strange combination of shyness and boldness, he asked if I had just a minute. I stopped, and he posed his first non-professional question to me: "I was just wondering... have you come to the place in your life where you would care to go to dinner with a gentleman?" He must have seen the surprise on my face, as he quickly added, "And that gentleman is me!"

That day in January was the beginning of a sudden, unexpected and delightful friendship that soon blossomed into much more. I found underneath my superficial judgment one of the finest and most loving men I had ever known. An example of his goodness was expressed as he let me talk about my personal loss, and he shared openly about his own marriage. In conversation with him I found that I did not have to put my twenty-seven years of marriage out of my life, and he could continue to nourish the thirty-one years he had with his late wife.

Just one example of his generous spirit was shown after he heard me complain about not being able to get any grass to grow on the gravesite where my late husband was buried in a country churchyard. Unbeknownst to me, on one of his days off he drove some thirty miles to the site, tilled the surface and laid sod. He would show it to me later when we made a visit to the cemetery.

After only a few months of dinners and walking the various malls together, it was obvious that we two adults with such similar ministry backgrounds had much more going for us than "friendship". But how could we move from one level to the ultimate when we had such wonderful histories with our separate families?

That was resolved one evening when, after dinner at a favorite Atlanta restaurant, Ed looked at me with what I had come to call his "baby blues"— eyes that reflected honesty, care, and love. With what he still says was an uncommon courage, he took my hand. "I know that you had a wonderful husband, and that you loved him very much. I know that you promised to love him forever." He paused, then continued, "I was just wondering, do you think that maybe you could love me for another forever?"

He was not asking me to forget my first love, but asking that I consider extending my love to include him. I did not hesitate. I said yes.

Less than six months after that first encounter on the balcony when I agreed to "go to dinner with a gentleman," Ed and I were married, surrounded by family and friends who celebrated the gift of our unexpected union.

So, here we are, nearly twenty-five years later, a blended family of nine children and fifteen grandchildren. We have walked through valleys, celebrated mountaintops, experienced joy and tears, gains and losses—all that have served only to make us stronger.

And we keep on walking together—for another forever.

~Elaine Herrin Onley

你轻轻的话语不是说在我的耳际，而是说进我的心田；你的吻不是印在我的双唇，而是印在我的心灵。

——朱迪·加兰

　　我的办公室位于公司办公楼三层。现在我正坐在桌前，上面堆满了需要处理的宣传材料和物品。这就是我作为公司公关部副主管的工作。我现在只有两个身份标签——寡妇兼公共关系专家。

　　丈夫在加勒比地区做了 14 年传教士之后，过早地因癌症去世，这也改变了我的人生轨迹。我带着小儿子来到亚特兰大。他还在读高中。这儿的生活和工作，同美丽的格林纳达海岛上简单的牧师生活，大不相同。

　　正当我专心工作的时候，另外一个部门的秘书打断了我，她把手里拿着的一份专业简历放在我面前。"你会感兴趣的。"她笑着说，"是我们的新成员，他是个鳏夫！"

　　虽然心里恼火，但我仍然表现得十分礼貌。

Chapter 2 Adventures in Dating
第二部分　约会篇

目前，我最不需要的就是别人对我"孑然一身"的强烈兴趣。47岁的我知道，自己不可能一直单身。总有一天我会遇到合适的人，他会再次带给我幸福和快乐。但绝不是现在！

当我打开文件夹，思考正在写的那篇新闻稿该用哪条消息来源时，我瞥了一眼放在旁边的材料。艾德·昂雷，51岁，从俄克拉何马来到佐治亚……什么，他竟然有6个孩子！

忘了他吧！朋友究竟怎么想的？我已经有3个儿子，他们彼此间隔4岁。

接下来的两周，我一直努力工作。我采访了那位"鳏夫"，将他最出色的工作经历发给适合的媒体，歌颂他离开家乡加入我们的高尚行为。我承认在参与了密西西比、阿肯色、俄克拉何马那么多社区中心、医疗诊所和牧师项目后，他仍能保留正宗的弗吉尼亚口音，这点给我留下了深刻印象。当他在佐治亚州开展同样的工作时，我为他欢呼加油。

然后，故事发生了。

一天，艾德在楼厅过道拦住了我。当时，我刚从主管办公室出来。他看起来既羞怯又勇敢，问我有没有时间。我停了下来，他向我提出了第一个非专业性问题："我只是想知道……嗯，你是不是已经准备好和一位绅士共进晚餐？"他一定注意到我脸上惊讶的表情，因为他很快补充说，"那位绅士是我！"

1月的那天，成了一段愉快友谊的开端。很快，这段友谊发展到另一个阶段。我发现自己以前的判断太肤浅了，他是我所认识的人中最善良也最有爱心的。其中一个例子，就是他让我谈谈自己的个人得失，而他也和我分享了自己的婚姻。在同他的交谈中，我发现自己并不需要抹杀过去27年的幸福婚姻。他也可以保留同已故妻子31年美满婚姻的回忆。

听到我抱怨没办法让丈夫的墓地周围长出任何草后，他再次展示了他的慷慨大度。我不知道的是，他专门拿出一天的休息时间，开车到30公里外的公墓，平整土地并铺设草皮。为的是后来一起到墓地纪念的时候，可以指给我看。

接下来的几个月，我们一起吃晚餐，一起逛商场。显然，作为有着相似背景的成年人，我们之间的情感已经不仅仅是"友谊"。但是，我们该如何走到一起，尤其是各自都同以前的家庭有着精彩的历史？这个难题得到了解决。一天，在亚特兰大一家不错的餐厅用过晚餐后，艾德用我称之为"婴儿蓝"的眼睛看着我，眼里流露着诚实、关怀和爱。他鼓起勇气，握住我的手。"我知道你有一个很棒的丈夫，而且你非常爱他。我也知道你曾承诺爱他到永远。"他停顿了一下，然后继续说，"我只是想知道，你是否也能够爱我到另一个永远？"

他没有要求我忘记自己的爱人，只是要求我把他也纳入这份直到永远的爱。没有犹豫，我答应了他。

从在楼厅走道答应同"一位绅士共进晚餐"后，不到半年，艾德和我结婚了。对于我们的意外结合，家人和朋友纷纷送来了祝福。

现在，我们已经结婚25年，我们的大家庭里有9个孩子，15个孙子孙女。我们曾走过崎岖的峡谷，也曾在山顶振臂高呼。这些年来有欢笑，有泪水，有得也有失。所有这些，让我们的感情变得更加牢固。

我们会继续走下去——直到另一个永远。

——伊莱恩·赫林·昂雷

The Frog Prince
青蛙王子

I'd kiss a frog even if there was no promise of a Prince
Charming popping out of it. I love frogs.

~Cameron Diaz

To all the single girls out there who want to
find their prince, I want to let you know it's possible
to find him. All you need is a frog. Seriously. Pretty
much any kind of frog will do. Let me tell you about
my frog and how he led me to my prince.

One Saturday morning I was shopping at my
favorite garden store. I was wandering through the
section that housed the garden statues. I hadn't dated
anyone in quite a while and was feeling sorry for
myself. I was in my thirties and desperately wanted
to meet the man of my dreams and have a family.
However, there were no prospects in sight.

I was about to leave the area when I saw him.
He was short and squat and wearing a crown. My
frog prince. That's right, a statue of a frog with a
crown. I reached down to pick him up and started to
chuckle to myself. I wondered if this was a practical

joke God was playing on me. Was this my Prince Charming? Somehow, he cheered me up and I decided to buy him as a reminder to not take myself and life so seriously.

He went outside in one of my flowerbeds and I smiled every time I saw him, thinking, "Someday I WILL find my prince." He was my little secret, my hope for what was to come. I eventually met someone and we began dating. I wondered, "Is this my Prince Charming?" Eventually I realized he wasn't the one I was looking for and the search began anew. Meanwhile, I kept accumulating frogs. You see, I had broken down and told my family about my secret frog prince and soon I was getting a frog from my mom for each birthday and Christmas. She had high hopes for me as well.

After a while, I decided that I needed to step up my efforts to find Prince Charming so I put a profile up on Match.com. I went on a lot of first dates and even kissed a few frogs along the way. Meanwhile, I never gave up hope that I would find him. Then it happened.

My brother and his fiancée gave me a special ornament for Christmas. It was a very small but ornate frog wearing a crown. Since I received it at Christmas and it was almost time to take the tree down, I didn't put the ornament on my tree that year. The following year, I put my tree up the day after Thanksgiving as I usually do. It was also the day I updated my profile on Match.com with a new picture. On Sunday, I realized that I had forgotten about my new frog ornament that my brother and my now sister-in-law had given me. That night, I placed it at the top of the tree, right under the star.

The next day I checked my profile on Match.com and I had received a wink from a guy who sounded really interesting. The rest, as they say, is history. After two months we were engaged. No, Mom, I wasn't pregnant. We both just knew that we were meant to be together. We have now been married for five years and I have three terrific step-kids and a three-year-old son with my husband.

A little while after Steve and I got married, a single friend of mine had a birthday. I couldn't figure out what to get her. I was wandering through the Hallmark store when I saw him, a stuffed frog. I decided to pass on the frog prince to my friend. I figured that if it worked for me, it might work for her. On her birthday, I gave her the stuffed frog and told her the story. The frog sat on her bed for a couple of years, but last year she met someone.

I could tell from how she talked about him that this was someone special. She recently called me to tell me that they are engaged and will be getting married this summer. She asked if she should keep the frog. I told her that she should pass it on to whoever she felt was ready to open her life to love. Maybe there's something to this frog thing after all.

~Laurie Ozbolt

我愿意亲吻青蛙，即使青蛙不可能变成迷人的王子，因为我就是喜欢青蛙。

——卡梅隆·迪亚兹

　　我想告诉所有期待王子的单身女孩，你的梦想可以实现。你所需要的只是一只青蛙。说真的，几乎任何类型的青蛙都管用。让我告诉你，我是如何在青蛙的带领下，找到自己的王子的。

　　一个周六清晨，我到自己最喜爱的花园商店购物。独自徘徊在摆满花园雕像的区域，我为自己感到难过，已经很长时间没有任何约会了。

三十多岁的我，急切地希望遇到梦想中的男人，和他组建家庭。但目前为止，我没看到任何希望。

正当我转身离开的时候，我看到了身形矮小、半蹲体态、头戴王冠的它——我的青蛙王子。对，就是它，一座头戴王冠的青蛙雕像。我伸手拿起了它，忍不住咯咯地笑了起来。我心想，难道上帝在和我开玩笑吗？它就是我的白马王子吗？不知何故，这座青蛙王子雕像让我感到心情愉悦。于是，我决定买下它作为一个提醒。提醒自己轻松一点，达观地看待生活。

它被安放在一个花坛中，每次经过看到它的时候，我都会笑一下，对自己说："总有一天，我会找到自己的白马王子。"这座青蛙雕像成了我的小秘密，满载着我对未来的期望。后来，我遇到了一个人，我们开始约会。我问自己："他是我的王子吗？"最终，我意识到他不是我要等的人。于是，新一轮的搜索重新开始。与此同时，我开始收藏各式各样的青蛙。我也和家人分享了青蛙王子的秘密，很快，在我生日和圣诞节的时候就收到母亲送来的青蛙。她也对我寄予厚望。

一段时间后，我觉得自己需要加倍努力寻找白马王子，所以将个人信息上传到交友网站。

此后，我参加了很多约会，这其间也亲吻过几只青蛙。虽然王子还未出现，但我从未放弃找到他的希望。

圣诞节的时候，哥哥和他的未婚妻送给我一份特别的饰品——一只头戴王冠、小巧而华丽的青蛙。因为圣诞节当天才拿到礼物，而且已经到了快将圣诞树收起来的时候，所以我没有把它挂在那年的圣诞树上。第二年，像往常一样，感恩节过后，我在家里摆上了圣诞树。也就是那天，我在交友网上更新了个人资料，换上了新的照片。周日晚上，我突然想起去年哥哥和嫂子送我的青蛙饰品，把它挂在了圣诞树顶端的星星下面。

第二天，我上网核实资料的时候，发现有人留言。他看起来还蛮有趣的。接下来的事，大家都猜到了。两个月后，我们订了婚。不，妈妈，我没有怀孕。我们只是知道，我们注定会在一起。现在，我们已经结婚五年了，有三个了不起的继子女，还有一个三岁的儿子。

史蒂夫和我结婚后没过多久，就赶上我一位单身朋友的生日。我不知道送她什么礼物合适。在商店徘徊的时候，我忽然看到一个毛绒青蛙。我决定把青蛙王子的好运传递给朋友。我想，如果这对我有用的话，没准儿也能帮到她。她生日那天，我把毛绒青蛙送给她，也向她讲述了青蛙王子的故事。那只青蛙在她床边陪伴了她好久。去年，她遇到了合适的人。

从她的描述中，我知道这个人就是她的王子。前些天，她打电话给我，告诉我订婚的消息，婚礼就定在今年夏天。她问我是否应该继续保留那只毛绒青蛙。我告诉她，或许她应该把青蛙送给那些已经准备好迎接爱情的人。也许青蛙王子的说法真的有道理呢。

——劳里·奥兹波特

第三部分 恋爱篇

Chapter 3
Meant to Be

True love stories never have endings.

~Richard Bach

真正的爱情故事从来不会结束。

——理查德 · 巴赫（德国作曲家）

布朗利先生

There is no instinct like that of the heart.

~Lord Byron

One Friday night, my senior year in high school, my boyfriend was driving me home from the basketball game. I told him that I knew who I was going to marry. I felt him tense up.

I said, "Don't worry. It's not you, it's Mr. Brownlee. I had a dream last night and when I woke up I knew that Mr. Brownlee was going to be my husband!"

Dan almost wrecked the car laughing.

Mr. Brownlee was a young, good-looking, accounting teacher and basketball coach at our school. Nearly every girl in town had a crush on him. And he certainly wasn't interested in me.

Not only was Mr. Brownlee attractive, he had a very magnetic personality and carried himself with confidence. Many people thought he looked like Clark Kent from *Superman*. There weren't many men like him from our small farming town and the local women wanted to be his Lois Lane!

It wasn't long before my dream about marrying Mr. Brownlee became a joke among my friends and their parents.

I went to college, got a job, and married a man who I met at work. We divorced after five years of marriage and one child.

After three years of being a single parent, I booked a trip to California for my son's Christmas present. The day after Christmas, Nicholas and I flew to Orange County and enjoyed a nice vacation.

Then, on New Year's Eve we headed back to Dayton, Ohio. Our flight was from Orange County to Pittsburgh and, after a two-hour layover, from there to Dayton.

In Pittsburgh, we waited for our flight at the gate. I read and Nick played his handheld video game. Looking around, I saw Mr. Brownlee leaning against one of the columns! He still had that Clark Kent look! I sat paralyzed for a second. Then I decided to talk to him.

I approached him and said, "Excuse me, are you Mr. Brownlee?"

He looked at me and said, "Yes. Do I know you?"

Rather uncomfortably, I said, "I'm Sheryl Hafle."

He said, "Yes, I do remember you, because you were one of my first students. How have you been and what are you doing here?"

I said, "Come sit with me, meet my son, and I'll tell you."

I told him where we'd been and he said he was returning from playing golf in Florida.

He asked me if I was on the 5:35 flight and where was I sitting. I told him row 35, seats B and C. He showed me his ticket and he was assigned to row 35, seat A.

I felt a chill go down my spine.

We boarded the plane and talked all the way to Dayton. That's when I found out he wasn't married, engaged or dating anyone. He was teaching high school in a larger district and still involved in basketball and golf. The forty-five minute flight was way too short.

Once in Dayton, I handed Mr. Brownlee my business card. I told him that I worked for a radio station and got free tickets to events. If he was interested in something, he could call me and I'd see what I could do.

He looked at my card and said, "Okay, I might." He got his bags and hailed a taxi.

While we were talking, we realized that we had a mutual friend. A couple days later, I ran into her and relayed my story.

She said, "Rick will never call you, but you need to call him." She gave me his number.

I dialed Mr. Brownlee's number and he answered. I told him that I was wondering how much his cab fare was. He said, "Twenty-seven dollars and I left a three-dollar tip."

I said, "Wow, I never imagined it would be that much in Dayton."

He said, "Don't you think it's weird that we were seated by each other?"

I said, "Yes."

Then he said, "I'm watching the game and I need to go."

We hung up and I felt like I'd made a fool of myself.

Our mutual friend called me a few days later and asked what happened. When I told her she said that I'd have to call him again.

After much persuasion, I called Mr. Brownlee again. I told him that I had free concert tickets and asked if he'd like to go. He told me he wasn't interested.

I was embarrassed and said that I had to go. He asked me if he could call me sometime and all I said was "Whatever".

152_

A couple of days later, Mr. Brownlee left a voicemail on my work phone asking for my home number.

That evening we talked for over two hours about everything. We realized that we had a lot in common. We spoke nightly for two weeks and he never asked me out. Finally, one evening, I asked him to a Dayton Flyers basketball game. He gave me some lame excuse. That's when I decided that I was too old to continue talking to my high school teacher who wasn't interested in me. I said, "I have no idea what is going on here, but I'm thirty-three and you're forty-one and I'm not participating anymore. I'm hanging up and ending this game."

Mr. Brownlee said, "Wait, so that's what's going on here? I wasn't sure! Actually, I'd like you to go to Friday night's basketball game with me."

Mr. Brownlee picked me up Friday night; we went to the game and had a great time. After the game and dinner he said to me, "Look, I'm not into dating, so if you're not working towards marriage then I think I should just drop you off and forget it."

I realized then why a great man like Mr. Brownlee wasn't married.

We dated a week. Then he told me that he loved me and said, "Tomorrow let's go to the Justice of the Peace and become Mr. and Mrs. Brownlee."

I said that I'd always loved him, but that we should date a while.

Six months later Rick Brownlee and I got married on the porch of the Island House on Mackinaw Island, Michigan.

~Sheryl Brownlee

唯有心的直觉指引着你。

——拜伦

高三那年的一个周五晚上，刚打完篮球的男朋友开车送我回家。我告诉他，我知道自己将来会嫁给谁。我觉得他一下子紧张起来。

"别担心，不是你，是布朗利先生。昨晚，我做了一个梦，等我醒来的时候，我就知道我将来的丈夫一定是布朗利先生！"

听完了我的话，丹气得几乎开不好车。

布朗利先生年轻英俊，是我们学校的会计老师和足球教练。几乎镇上的每个女孩儿都暗恋他。当然，他对我不感兴趣。

除了英俊的外表，布朗利先生还有着迷人的性格，他总是自信满满。很多人都觉得他很像《超人》里的克拉克·肯特。在我们那个以农业为主的小镇没有多少男人像他那么有魅力，当地的女士都想成为他的"露易丝·兰恩"。

没过多久，我嫁给布朗利先生的梦想就成了朋友和他们父母之间的笑话。

后来，我上了大学，找了工作，嫁给一个工作时认识的男人。结婚五年后，我们离婚了，有了一个孩子。

单身三年后，我预定作一次加州之旅，想陪儿子过个快乐的圣诞节。圣诞过后第二天，我带着儿子尼古拉斯登上飞往奥兰治县的航班。我们在那儿度过了愉快的假期。

新年前夕，我们决定返回俄亥俄州代顿市。要先搭乘从奥兰治飞往匹兹堡的航班，中途停留两小时之后，再从匹兹堡飞往代顿。到达匹兹堡机场之后，我们坐在登机口旁，尼克玩着他的掌上游戏机，而我在一旁看书。我抬起头的瞬间，忽然看到布朗利先生。他斜靠着一个圆柱，看起来仍然像极了克拉克·肯特。那一瞬间，我仿佛瘫痪一般。等回过神来，我决定走过去和他打招呼。

我走到他身边，问："打扰了，请问你是布朗利先生吗？"

他看了看我，回答说："是的，我们认识吗？"

我感到十分尴尬，但仍介绍说："我是雪莉·哈福。"

"哦，我记得你，你是我的第一批学生。你最近好吗？为什么过来这边？"他说道。

"到那边坐吧，先认识一下我儿子，之后我再告诉你。"我回答说。

我告诉他我们游览了哪些地方，也知道了他刚从佛罗里达打高尔夫回来。

他问我是不是在等5：35那趟航班，我的座位号是几号。我告诉他，我和儿子坐在35排B座和C座。他拿出自己的机票给我看，上面标着35排A座。我不由自主地哆嗦了一下。

登上飞往代顿的航班后，我们一路畅谈。也就在这时，我得知了布朗利先生从未结婚，从未订婚，也没同任何人约会。他在比我们镇规模稍大些的地方教高中，仍然喜欢打篮球和高尔夫。45分钟的航班实在是太短暂。

回到代顿之后，我把自己的名片递给布朗利先生，告诉他，我在广播电台工作，可以拿到免费的门票。如果他有感兴趣的比赛，可以直接打电话给我，我会尽量帮忙。

他看了我的名片，回答说："好的，我可能会打给你。"之后，他带上自己的行李，拦了一辆出租车离开了。

和布朗利先生聊天的时候，我发现我们有一位共同好友。几天后，我偶然碰到了那位共同好友，并向她讲述了自己和布朗利先生的故事。

她告诉我说："里克不会主动打电话的，你要打给他。"之后，她给了我布朗利先生的电话号码。

我拨通了他的电话。我告诉他，我很好奇他那天的车费是多少。他回答说："27 美元，再加 3 美元的小费。"

"哇，我从未想过在代顿打车会这么贵。"我说。

他问："你不觉得，我们的座位挨在一起，很神奇吗？"

"确实很神奇。"我回答。

然后他说："我正在看比赛，需要回去了。"

之后，我们结束了通话。我觉得自己就像个傻子。

几天后，我们的共同好友打来电话，问事情发展得怎样。听完我的诉说，她建议我再次打给布朗利先生。

在她苦口婆心的劝说下，我又一次拨通了布朗利先生的电话。我告诉他，自己有两张免费的音乐会门票，问他愿不愿意一起去。他的回答是不感兴趣。

我十分尴尬，随便找了个借口要挂断电话。他问我，能不能给我打电话。我的回答是"随便"。

几天之后，我的工作电话上收到了布朗利先生的语音留言，问我家里的电话是多少。

那天晚上，我们谈天说地，聊了大概两小时。我们发现我们有很多共同点。接下来的两周，我们每晚都会通电话，但他从来没有约我出去。终于在某天晚上，我约他一起看代顿飞人队篮球赛，他却编一些蹩脚的理由推三阻四，我爆发了。我意识到自己已经不小了，不该再继续和一个不喜欢自己的高中老师调情。我说："我不知道会发展到什么地步，但我已经33岁了，你也41岁了，我不想再耗下去了。我要挂断电话并结束这场游戏了。"

布朗利先生着急地解释："等等，等等，发展到什么地步是指什么？我不明白！事实上，我想约你一起去看周五晚上的篮球赛。"

周五晚上，布朗利先生过来接我。我们一起观看比赛，度过了愉快的时光。在比赛和晚餐结束后，他对我说："要知道，我并不喜欢约会。如果你不打算结婚的话，我想我应该放手，并忘了这一切。"

这时，我才明白，为什么布朗利先生这么优秀的人却一直没有结婚。

在我们约会一周之后，他说他爱我："我们明天到治安审理所，成为布朗利先生和夫人吧。"

我告诉他，我也深爱着他，但是去治安审理所之前，我们应该再约会一段时间。

半年后，里克·布朗利和我在密歇根州麦基诺海岛大厦的走廊上完了婚。

——雪莉·布朗利

Somehow I Knew

我就是知道

Nothing in life is to be feared. It is only to be understood.
~Marie Curie

The yellow cab was stopped at a red light. Sitting in the back seat on a second date with a man named Ted, I was checking my calendar. He had asked me when I was next free. I opened my date book to the week of July 7th and skimmed the days. "First anniversary" was written in big blue letters on Saturday, July 12th. Silently I cursed. Ted had seen it too.

"What's the anniversary?" he asked.

My mind fought for a quick, appropriate answer. It failed.

"You know what?" I said. "I'll tell you about that later."

Ted and I had met the week before on a blind date. Set up by Julia, a co-worker of mine, she had met Ted backstage after a play. The lead in the play was Julia's roommate and a friend of Ted's from

158_

high school.

For the first date we met near Ted's office in Tribeca, a hip area in New York City. He worked long hours and he had a short break for our dinner date.

I wore black Capri pants, flats, a white short-sleeved oxford shirt, and a jean jacket. I wanted my personality to be rated before my breasts and hips. Ted wore a gray shirt, which matched his pallor, and an ugly tie. The man was clearly single. But it didn't take me long to realize that he was funny and smart—my top two requirements. Dinner was fast and fun.

Our second date was the Marathon Date. We had each passed the other's first inspection, and we wanted to spend time getting to know each other. The date was on a Friday night, and we were meeting at the Metropolitan Museum of Art to see a Winslow Homer exhibit. After the Met we were going to have dinner at the Yale Club, where he belonged. And after that, if all continued to go well, we would head down to Alphabet City to see my friend perform in an improvisational comedy theater group.

On the second date I decided to highlight a physical attribute or two. I wore a yellow sundress that cut a little low on the neckline and pinched in at my waist. As I walked up the steps at the entrance to the Met—a perfect five minutes late—I saw Ted on the top step in an ocean blue shirt that matched his eyes, looking at me, smiling a great big smile.

We toured the busy exhibit, and every time I looked for him, I found him looking at me. It was clear that neither of us was taking in any of the art. Soon we headed south on the subway. We ate burgers at the Yale Club and enjoyed effortless dialogue. I had never met a man filled with such kindness and gentleness who was able to be strong and confident at the same time. He was smart without being cocky and somehow made me laugh without having to say anything mean or negative.

It was in the taxi ride to the comedy show that Ted asked about the next

Chicken Soup for the Soul 心灵鸡汤 最初的你，最后的爱 True Love I

date, raising the dreadful anniversary question. What I didn't want to tell him was that on July 12th a year before I had been raped. The trial that put my attacker behind bars had ended in April, just a few months before our first date. I knew that this was information Ted might need to know at some point, but I didn't know how he'd react, and I feared its effect.

After I avoided answering his question, the date chugged along. We discussed our plans for the weekend. Ted was going to crew on a friend's sailboat in a two-day race on Long Island Sound, and my college roommate was flying in from Boston for a visit. We laughed a lot during my friend's show, and everything was as easy and comfortable as it had been from the beginning—five-and-a-half hours and counting.

At twelve-thirty, in yet another yellow cab, this time pausing in front of my building to let me out, I leaned over to give Ted a kiss. It seemed like the right thing to do. I aimed for his lips, made it quick, and fled the taxi—ending a date was never my forte.

The next day I woke up to the news that Hurricane Bertha was going to hit New York. Her winds were high, her rain would be fierce, and all flights in and out of the city were cancelled. My friend called to say she couldn't make it in. My thoughts jumped to Ted's sailboat race. I considered calling him, but too nervous, I decided to grab a bagel and coffee around the corner instead. Walking home I decided that I would call him. Why not? When I opened my front door I saw my answering machine's message light blinking. I knew he had beaten me to it.

We took a wet walk through Central Park and he tried to impress me with his knowledge of tree varieties. I grinned often since many of the trees were labeled, and his data and the labels often disagreed.

We went back to my apartment, where I made my famous black bean soup for lunch—by opening the can, heating it, and serving it. Seeing that he was perfectly happy with my offering, I decided that now was the time. If this guy was going to have a problem with my history, I needed to know. If he was going to run because I was dirty and used, I didn't want to keep feeling the way I was feeling.

I spoke as I passed him his cup of black bean soup.

"I want to tell you about the anniversary that you noticed in my date book," I said.

Along with a punch of nausea, I could feel anxiety creeping up my neck. I took a deep breath. Although I saw his soft eyes steadily watch my face, I couldn't look back.

"The anniversary that you saw on July 12th is the day I was raped." I waited a moment for it to sink in. "Last year a man came into my apartment and raped me." I couldn't control the tears that fell. "I didn't know if I should tell you, but I think it's important that you know."

"I am so sorry," he said. He put down his cup of soup and spoke slowly. "Will you come here so I can I give you a hug?"

I walked to him and he folded me into his arms, holding tight. Finally he released me and looked right into my blotchy, tear-stained face.

"Somehow I knew," he said. "I knew right away that you were raped, Jen. I knew when you said you couldn't tell me. I don't know why, but I did."

Today, Ted is my husband. We've been married only ten years, but we'll be together for a long time.

Somehow I know.

~Jennifer Quasha

生活中没有什么可怕的东西，只有需要理解的东西。

——居里夫人

　　红灯亮起，黄色的出租车停了下来。泰德和我一起坐在车后排。这是我们第二次约会。我正在翻看记事本，因为他刚才问我什么时候有空。我翻到了 7 月 7 日，继续往后快速浏览。"一周年"三个蓝色大字赫然出现在 7 月 12 日周六那天。我心里暗自叫苦，因为泰德也看到了。

　　"关于什么的一周年？"他问道。

　　我脑子飞快地转着，想给出一个恰当的答案。但是失败了。

　　"你知道吗？"我说，"我以后会告诉你的。"

　　一周前，泰德和我在茱莉亚安排的相亲会上遇到。茱莉亚是我的同事，她在剧院后台遇到泰德。因为这部戏剧的主演是茱莉亚的室友，也是泰德的高中同学。

　　泰德所在的公司位于纽约的时尚地区——翠贝卡，我们第一次约会选在了这附近。他的时间很紧，只能趁短暂的休息时间吃顿晚饭。

　　我穿着黑色七分裤和平跟鞋，上身是带有牛津大学标志的白色短袖 T 恤和牛仔外套。我希

162_

望对方看重的是我的性格，而不是身材。泰德穿了件很配他苍白脸色的灰色衬衫，但系了条难看的领带。很明显，他是个单身汉。但没过多久，我就发现他既聪明又风趣——这两点也正是我看重的。晚餐时间不长，但很愉快。

我们第二次约会的安排，长得就像一场马拉松比赛。因为都通过了对方的初审，所以我们需要花些时间加深了解。约会安排在周五晚上，我们计划先去大都会艺术博物馆看温斯洛·荷马的画展。之后，到耶鲁大学俱乐部吃晚餐，泰德是那儿的会员。在此之后，如果一切顺利的话，我们会到字母城看我朋友即兴喜剧小组的演出。

第二次约会的时候，我决定要在身材上展现一两个亮点。我选了一件低领口黄色背心裙，贴身的剪裁正好衬出玲珑的腰线。当我走上大都会入口的台阶——故意晚了不多不少的五分钟——我看到身穿蓝衬衫的泰德，正站在最高的台阶上等着我，脸上带着灿烂的笑容。顺便说一句，他的蓝眼睛在蓝色衬衣的映衬下，越发动人。

我们参观了人头攒动的画展。每次我看他的时候，都发现他也正望着我。很显然，我们谁也没有认真欣赏艺术。很快，我们往南走，进入地铁，去往耶鲁大学俱乐部。在那儿，我们享受了美味的汉堡，并且轻松地交谈。我从来没有遇到过既坚强自信又这么善良温柔的人。他聪明但不自大，也不用说些刻薄话就能把我逗乐。

正是我们搭出租车去看喜剧表演途中，泰德问我什么时间有空，这才引出了那个可怕的周年问题。我不想告诉他的是一年前的7月12日，我被强奸。今年4月，罪犯的审判刚刚结束，就在我和泰德初次见面的几个月前。我知道，交往以后，泰德需要知道这些。但是，我不知道他会如何反应，我害怕这件事带来的影响。

　　绕开他的问题后，约会继续进行着。我们分享了各自的周末安排。泰德会和朋友一起参加在长岛海峡举行的帆船比赛。我的大学舍友从波士顿飞来看我。朋友的喜剧表演很有意思，我们整场都很开心。五个半小时的约会轻松又愉快。

　　夜里12：30，另一辆黄色出租车停在了我家门前。我侧身靠近泰德，准备给他一个吻。我觉得自己应该这么做。我吻了他的唇，然后飞快地打开车门逃了出去——我不擅长结束约会。

　　第二天早上醒来，电视上正播报着飓风柏莎袭击纽约的新闻。受恶劣天气影响，纽约所有航班都被取消。朋友打电话说来不了了。我忽然想到了泰德的帆船比赛，考虑要不要打电话给他。但我实在太紧张了，最后决定到转角的商店买个百吉饼和咖啡。回家的路上，我下定决心要打电话给他。为什么不呢？当我打开前门走进去的时候，我看到电话答录机上的留言灯闪烁不停。我知道泰德早我一步，打电话过来了。

　　我们沿着中央公园散步，地面湿漉漉的，泰德一路上都试图展示自己丰富的林木知识。我被逗得咯咯直笑，因为很多树上都有标签，他给出的名字往往和这不同。

　　回到公寓后，我做了拿手的黑豆粥——打开罐头，加热，然后端出去。看到泰德满意的样子，我觉得是时候告诉他我被强奸的事了。如果他对我的过去有意见，我需要知道这点。如果他觉得我很脏或者是二手货，我也不想再爱他。

　　递给他黑豆粥的时候，我开口了。

　　"我想告诉你有关一周年的事，就是你在记事本上看到的那个。"我说。

　　想到这些，我的心里一阵恶心，就像被人打了一拳。我觉得脖子后面凉飕飕的。深深地吸了口气，我知道泰德此时正温柔而坚定地望着我，但我没有勇气抬头。

"你看到的周年纪念 7 月 12 日是我被强奸的日子，"我顿了一下，等泰德慢慢接受，"去年，一个男人闯进我家，强奸了我。"我的眼泪止不住地流，"我不知道该不该告诉你，但我觉得你知道这些很重要。"

"真的很抱歉，"他放下杯子慢慢地说，"你愿意到这儿来吗？让我抱抱你。"

我向他走去，他把我紧紧地搂在怀中。最后，他放开我，看着我满是泪痕的脸。

他说："不知为什么，我只是'知道'。当你说不能告诉我的时候，我立刻就想到了。我不知道为什么会这样，但的确如此。"

现在，泰德是我的丈夫。虽然结婚仅仅 10 年，但我们会永远在一起。

不知为什么，我就是知道。

——詹妮弗·秋莎

Destiny on Two Wheels
车轮上的爱情

> Every man has his own destiny: the only imperative is to follow it, to accept it, no matter where it leads him.
> ~Henry Miller

There was a time when hitchhiking was considered a safe mode of transportation. In fact, in the 1970s, Vancouver, BC's bus drivers were on strike and the government actually encouraged pedestrians to hitchhike and drivers to give them rides.

But I had stuck out my thumb because the insurance on my car had run out and, being a student at the time, the money for it needed to be spent elsewhere. I knew that King Edward Avenue was a notoriously difficult road on which to hitch, but I was scheduled to write a French exam and there was no option.

Few cars passed and the drivers in those that did, ignored me. I was enjoying the sunny, warm day in late September, but getting concerned that I might end up missing my test.

Finally, a Volkswagen began to pull over and I sighed my relief. The next thing I knew, a motorcyclist cut the Volksie off and encouraged the driver to be on his way. As the latter left, shaking his head, I found myself getting very angry. Thinking that the motorcyclist was simply parking I couldn't believe that he'd done so by getting rid of the only ride I could get!

The motorcyclist reached behind him and grabbed a helmet. "Ever been on a bike before?"

Squinting, I took in the scene: he was a tall man with a white, full-coverage helmet sporting a dark flat shield, hiding the face but allowing a beard to show below; a black leather jacket, black gauntlets, black pants and black boots. As any young woman of that era would do, I replied, "Are you kidding? I used to own a bike!"

"Great! Hop on."

Later, I'd discovered that he had ridden the hour and a half to the town of Hope for breakfast and was heading home when he saw me on the other side of the boulevard. He'd rushed home to retrieve his spare helmet and came back, in hopes that I'd still be there. He wasn't about to let that Volkswagen pick me up.

He drove me to my destination, and we talked briefly before I went in for my test. We didn't even exchange names as we parted ways. That night he went to a party and told his good friend, Laurie, about the girl he'd picked up. "Did you get her phone number?"

"No."

Laurie, always trying to set him up, chastised, "You idiot!"

"Don't worry," he said. "I'll see her again."

The next day I needed another ride. My mom, who supervised the daycare center at a local college, and I had planned on meeting for lunch. So I walked up to the main crossroad and again, extended my thumb. I couldn't believe it when I saw the motorcyclist riding my way. But he was intent on turning left into the service station and didn't see me. "I bet he'll give me a ride," I thought as I crossed the road.

He was in conversation with the attendant, an old friend, as I came up from behind. But, as he turned around and our eyes met, it was as if the attendant had transferred to another dimension. The latter quickly left as he became aware that he had no part in whatever was now taking place. "Hi!" the motorcyclist said.

Of course he'd give me a ride! It was another banner day and the ride was wonderful. We discovered each other's names, Harry and Diane, that we'd gone to the same, large high school (two years apart) and that he knew my older brother.

Once at the college, Harry asked me for a date, took off his gauntlet and wrote my name and number inside.

Within five weeks (it took four weeks to find a place that would allow all my animals) we'd moved in together and a year later we were married.

Our lives have been filled with many joys, including two living sons, and many sorrows, including twin sons who died shortly after birth. But we've weathered the storms, celebrated the calms, have maintained and grown our extraordinary love for each other, and continue to share all aspects of our individual lives, together.

And Harry, a sentimentalist at heart, still keeps the gauntlet...

~Diane C. Nicholson

每个人都有自己的命运：最重要的是要遵循命运、接受命运，无论它将你引向何方。

——亨利·米勒

曾经有一段时间，搭车被看成是一种很安全的交通方式。事实上，20 世纪 70 年代，温哥华巴士司机罢工，政府鼓励行人搭便车。

但我不得不伸出大拇指搭便车是因为汽车保险到期。作为一名学生，这笔钱要用到别处。虽然知道爱德华国王大道是出了名的难搭车，但要参加法语考试的我别无选择。

有几辆车经过，但那些司机像人们所说的那样，不理睬我。尽管 9 月下旬阳光明媚温暖，我却越来越担心可能错过法语考试。

终于，一辆"大众"开始靠过来，我长舒了一口气。但接下来发生的一幕让我目瞪口呆，一辆摩托车挡在了"大众"和我中间，他还鼓励汽车司机继续开。"大众"车主摇摇头，开车离去的时候，我异常气愤。想到摩托车手不过停车而已，他竟然毁了我唯一的搭车机会。

车手转到身后，抓起了一个头盔："以前坐过摩托吗？"

我迎着阳光，眯缝着眼，一个高大的男人站在我面前。他戴着白色头盔，黑色面罩掩住了脸，只能看到些许胡子。他一身黑，黑色皮夹克、黑色手套、黑色裤子，还有黑色靴子。这种情况下，那个年代的女生大概都会像我一样反问："开什么玩笑？我有过自己的摩托车。"

"很好，跳上来吧！"

后来，我知道他骑了一个半小时到希望镇吃早餐，回来的路上，看到了等在路边的我。他飞快地赶回家，取来备用头盔，然后急忙返回，希望我还在那儿。他可不希望让那辆"大众"把我带走。

开车送我到目的地之后，我们只是简单地聊了两句。之后，我就进去考试。分别的时候，我们并没有互通姓名和交换电话。那晚，他去参加派对的时候，告诉了好友劳丽自己遇到了一个搭便车的女孩。劳丽问："你留了她的手机号吗？"

"没有。"

总想帮他找女朋友的劳丽责怪他："你这个白痴！"

"别担心，"他回答，"我还会再遇到她的。"

第二天，我又需要搭便车。母亲负责当地一所大学的日托中心，我们计划到那儿碰面，一起吃午餐。所以，我再次走到主道的十字路口，伸出拇指拦车。我简直不敢相信又看到了那个摩托车手。但他好像要去左边的服务站，并没看到我。"我打赌他一定会送我的。"这么想着，我穿过马路走到另一边。

当我走到他身后的时候，他正在和服务员交谈，看起来他们是老朋友了。但他转身，我们目光相遇的那一刻，服务员好像不存在了。这种情况下，服务员知趣地走开了。"嗨！"摩托车手和我打招呼。

当然，他又载了我一次。这是个值得庆贺的日子。不仅搭车很愉快，而且我们互通了姓名——哈利和黛安。我们还发现我们念同一所高中（他高我两级），而且他认识我哥哥。

到达母亲所在的学校后，哈利问我愿不愿意同他约会。他摘下手套，将我的名字和电话写在手心。

不到五周（四周的时间都在找一个能容下我所有宠物的房子），我们搬到了一起。一年之后，我们结婚了。

我们的生活有很多乐趣，包括两个活泼可爱的儿子。也有很多悲伤，包括出生不久就夭折的双胞胎儿子。但我们同甘共苦，一同呵护我们非凡的爱情，也分享彼此生活的方方面面。

内心深处仍是个性情中人的哈利，现在还保存着那顶头盔……

——黛安·C.尼科尔森

Change of Address
地址的变更

> There is no such thing as chance; and what seem to us merest accident springs from the deepest source of destiny.
> ~Johann Friedrich Von Schiller

After being "on the bench" and not dating for quite some time, with the exception of one disaster, I decided that marriage wasn't for me. As I drove home from work one evening, I suddenly found myself briefly looking towards the sky through my windshield and telling God, "Lord, I'm not getting married." Afterwards, I felt a huge sense of peace and continued making my way home down Los Angeles' 101 freeway, feeling sorry for all those other women in their forties who were practically howling at the moon every night because they wanted a husband so badly.

Two years later, my life had changed quite significantly. I was making less money and had just moved to an apartment in Burbank after selling the beloved condo I had lived in for nine years. I simply couldn't afford it any more. If that weren't enough, the oldest of my three cats, Risqué, had just been put to sleep. She had cancer and I didn't even know it. I was exhausted from all of the crying. I missed her so much. And, as if my heart wasn't already broken enough, it would break a little more every time I saw my two remaining cats, Esther and Joseph, looking for their sister.

After I had unpacked the last of the boxes, it dawned on me that while I had notified all of the appropriate parties regarding my change of address, I had yet to notify Bed Bath & Beyond. I needed some stuff for my new place and didn't want to miss getting any coupons they would be sending out in the near future. I called and was greeted by a very friendly voice. "Thank you for calling 1-800-GO-BEYOND. This is Jason. How may I help you?"

Jason proceeded to assist me with my change of address, but couldn't hold back his response when he heard the name of the street I was now living on. "Screenland Drive? Sounds like you live near a bunch of movie theaters," he said.

I quickly responded, "Oh, actually, I live by all the studios, like Disney, Warner Bros. and NBC."

"Well," he said. "I work here during the day, but I'm actually a musician. Would you like to see my website?"

I seized the opportunity to drum up some business for myself. "Sure! I'm a freelance writer, but I work a full-time day job for steady income, so I completely understand where you're coming from. As a matter of fact, if you're a musician, I can help you with your bio. Would you like to see my website?" Jason and I exchanged our website information and he completed my change of address request.

When I got home that night, I had completely forgotten about my promise to check out Jason's website. That is, until I logged into my e-mail and found a message from him. "Ah!" I thought to myself, "I forgot to check out that dude's website." I typed the URL into the address bar. Alright, so he was handsome and I noticed. The photo I was looking at was the cover of his latest CD. I then proceeded to read the page, which by the way, was written very poorly.

I could see that Jason was based in New Jersey and as it turns out, is a vibraphonist who was mentored by Lionel Hampton. I was familiar with his music. Jason also had a couple of Grammy ballot nominations under his belt. Quite impressive, but the guy really did need some help in the writing department. His website was a mess.

I responded to Jason's e-mail and complimented him on his accomplishments. I then closed my message in a businesslike manner, stating that I was looking forward to possibly serving his writing needs in the future.

The next night, there was another e-mail from Jason waiting for me. This time, he asked me if I was married with children. I started typing a response. "If you read my bio then you saw that I am studying to become a licensed minister, which is something I take very seriously. So, if these e-mails become inappropriate, I will let you know! I am not a desperate woman." My keyboard was practically smoking! Then my phone rang.

"Hello, Anji. This is Jason Taylor. I just sent you an e-mail, but I thought I would go ahead and give you a call. I know you know the Lord. That's why I wanted to talk to you. I know we were discussing you doing some writing work for me and I still intend on having you do that, but there is something else I want to talk to you about." I couldn't imagine anything this guy would need to talk with me about besides writing. So, I braced myself, ready to hang up, if necessary. He began to speak. "I don't know how to say this, so I'm just going to say it. I went to your website last night, and after reading your bio, I do believe you're the woman I've been praying for." Jason then began to speak in a language he knew I would understand—scripture. "Don't limit God, Anji. Because with God, nothing is impossible." Those words immediately warmed my heart and in spite of the way I felt about marriage, I was willing to listen to what he had to say.

After a few conversations with Jason, he and I decided to give a long distance relationship a try. Because of the distance, he jumped through a lot of hoops and met a lot of people who were interested in my wellbeing. We all needed to make sure he was the gentleman he presented himself to be. After we got married, I moved to the East Coast, making it necessary for me to change my address again.

~Anji Limón Taylor

没有什么是偶然的，对我们来说，决定人一生命运的往往就在一瞬间。

——弗里德里希·席勒

一次失败的恋爱，加上坐多了"冷板凳"，我已经很长时间没有约会了，也觉得自己不适合结婚。一天晚上下班回家，我透过挡风玻璃望着天空，暗自祈祷："主啊，我不想结婚。"之后，我感到非常平和，继续沿洛杉矶 101 高速公路开车回家，对那些四十多岁迫切希望找到丈夫的女人充满同情。

两年后，我的生活发生了巨大的变化。收入减少后，因为负担不起，我卖掉住了九年的心爱公寓，搬到了伯班克。如果这还不够悲惨，我养的三只猫中最大的那只——瑞可去世了。我一点也没意识到它得了癌症。我那么想念它，哭得肝肠寸断。每当看到另外两只猫咪艾斯特和约瑟夫寻找姐姐，我就忍不住伤心落泪。

打开最后一个箱子的时候，我突然想起来忘记通知万能卫浴寝具批发商城了。新家可能还要添置一些家具，我可不想错过他们以后可能赠送的优惠券。于是，我打电话过去，听到了亲切的问候："谢谢您致电1800——万能卫浴。我是贾森。能为您做些什么？"

贾森开始帮我办理地址变更手续。当听到我现在居住地点的时候，他激动地叫道："电影街？听起来好像你家周围有一堆影院。"

我解释说："呵呵，其实，我家周围有很多工作室，像迪士尼、华纳兄弟，还有全美广播公司。"

"真棒！"他回答，"我白天在这儿工作，但实际上，我是个音乐人，你想看看我的网站吗？"

我抓紧时间为自己争取一些业务。"当然愿意，我是名自由撰稿人。为了稳定的收入，我也有一份全职工作，所以完全理解你。实际上，如果你是名音乐人，我想我可以帮你完善你的简介。你愿意看一下我的个人网站吗？"于是，我和贾森互换了网址，他也帮我完成了地址的更改。

当天晚上回家，我已经完全忘记了看他页面的承诺。直到登录邮箱，看到贾森的邮件时，我才突然想起来："啊！忘了看他的网站。"于是，我在地址栏输入网址。好吧，我注意到他很英俊。我看到的照片是他新发专辑的封面。之后，我开始阅读他的介绍资料。顺便说一句，写得实在很差劲。

我注意到贾森主要在新泽西发展，师从李昂纳·汉普顿，是一名颤音琴演奏家。我对李昂纳·汉普顿的音乐非常熟悉。贾森也获得过几次格莱美选票提名，非常了不起。但在写作推广上，他的确需要一些帮助。

他的网站实在是一团糟。

我回复了贾森的电子邮件，恭贺了他所取得的成就，以一种商务方式结束了我的回信，信中写道，如果他有写作需求，很期待能同他合作。

第二天晚上，我再次收到贾森的邮件。这次，他问我，是否已经结婚，有没有孩子。我开始打字回复："如果你读了我的介绍，那么你应该知道我正在努力学习，争取成为合格的牧师，这是我非常关注的事。所以，如果这些邮件不合适，我会告诉你。我不是一个绝望的女人。"键盘被我敲得都快冒烟了。之后，电话铃响了。

"你好，安吉，我是贾森·泰勒。我刚给你发了封邮件，但我觉得应该提前给你打个电话。我知道你相信上帝，这也是我想和你谈谈的原因。我知道，我们正讨论你是否能为我做些文字工作。事实上，我也想让你来做。但我还想和你谈谈其他方面的事情。"我不知道这个家伙除了写作，还能和我谈什么。我打起精神，心想如果必要的话，就挂断电话。他开始说："我不知道该怎么表达，所以就干脆直接说了。昨晚，我看了你的网站，读了你的介绍后，我相信你就是我一直祈盼的女人。"之后，贾森用了《圣经》上的话，因为他知道我一定明白。尽管我对婚姻抱有成见，但他的一番话还是立刻温暖了我的心，我开始认真倾听他接下来的话。

在和贾森交谈过几次之后，我们决定给这次异地恋一次机会。由于距离的关系，他接受了层层考验，同很多关心我幸福的人见面。我们都需要确定，他是否真的是位绅士。很快，我又要变更地址，因为结婚后，我搬到了东海岸。

——安吉·利蒙·泰勒

Searching for a Soulmate
灵魂伴侣

There are two kinds of sparks, the one that goes off with a hitch, but burns out quickly. The other is the kind that needs time, but when the flame strikes... it's eternal, don't forget that.

~Timothy Oliveira

My husband and I met in driver's training class when we were fifteen. We've been best friends ever since. How corny is that?

Friendship doesn't always lead to romance, however, and for us that leap didn't come until years after we'd declared our best-friendship.

During the time after we met, but before we started dating, we helped each other out in the romance department. I set him up with my friends. He provided comfort when an unbelievably stupid boyfriend broke up with me. I often criticized his choice in women; he hardly ever liked the guys I went out with.

Each year, on our birthdays, we'd go out on a "date". And on New Year's Eve, if neither of us was in a relationship, it was agreed that we'd celebrate the night together. You know, sort of like best friends would do.

All the while I was in search of Mr. Right—my soulmate. The mere thought of him made me sigh with anticipation. I knew he was out there—somewhere—the guy who was born just for me, and I him.

Trouble was, this soulmate of mine wasn't making himself easy to find. He had no distinguishing characteristics that I knew of. I couldn't tell him from a hole in the wall, or a best friend.

A funny thing happened on my search for a soulmate. One summer, my best friend and I began to see each other in a new light. The air around us changed and was charged with an energy we couldn't ignore.

By this time, we'd been friends for so long that we already knew almost everything about one another. A romance like that is brief. We were engaged after just weeks and married within the year.

I'd been searching for my soulmate and he'd been right there beside me the whole time! Or so I thought.

It wasn't long after our honeymoon, when I looked at him lovingly and posed the hypothetical question: "Do you think we're soulmates?"

His answer was not what I expected. "What's a soulmate?" he asked with the innocence of a newlywed.

I was stunned. How could he be my soulmate if he didn't even know what it was?

Thing is though, I was in love with the guy. Soulmate or not, I was committed to him for better or worse. So for us, life went on—together. I tried to quit worrying about silly ideals like soulmates.

Through the years we've learned that in many ways we are more different than alike. I am a bargain hunter; my husband is an impulse shopper. I read poetry; he scans the front page. He hunts; I knit. He prefers spicy hot barbecue;

I'm a cool ranch fan. I believe in soulmates; he doesn't know what they are.

But as different as we seem to be, we've managed to keep each other interested (and at times entertained) for more than twenty years. Despite the fact that I tend to hog the covers and he (occasionally) snores, we've found a weird sort of rhythm that works for us. There is a happy cadence to our days.

Each night, I get the coffee maker ready for the next day. And each morning, he brings me my first cup, poured just the way I like it with the right amount of cream. One evening, I was tired, and said, "It's late. I don't think I'll make the coffee tonight."

His answer wasn't what I expected. "But then I won't be able to bring you your cup in the morning," he said. "And that's what I do." His words had a certain tenderness that can only be earned after years together.

Needless to say I made the coffee that night.

I haven't forgotten about finding my soulmate, except my definition has changed. I no longer think a soulmate is someone born for me. I realize that would be way too easy. A soulmate is someone you grow with and into over time until the day comes that something as simple as cup of coffee illustrates feelings so deep that they bring tears to your eyes.

That is what my soulmate—and best friend—does for me.

~Jill Pertler

火花有两种：一种一点就着，但很快熄灭；另一种需要时间，但当火焰燃烧……不要忘记，它将永不熄灭。

——蒂莫西·奥利维拉

我和丈夫是在驾校培训课上认识的，那年，

我们只有 15 岁。从那以后，我们成了要好的朋友。听起来很老土吧？

友情并不总能发展为爱情。但是，在那么多年的友谊后，我们实现了这一步的跨越。

在相遇之后到约会之前的那段时间里，我们总为对方出谋划策。我会把自己的朋友介绍给他。而他会在一个愚蠢至极的男友和我分手后，安慰我。我常常批评他对女人的选择，他也很少赞同我的约会对象。

每年，我们生日的时候，都会一起出去"约会"。新年前夕，如果两人都没有伴的话，我们也会一起庆祝。你知道，就是那种好朋友会一起做的事。

我一直在寻找真命天子——我的灵魂伴侣。一想到他，虽然怀有期待，我还是会忍不住叹气。我知道他一定就在某处，那个我为他而生，他为我而存在的人。

麻烦的是，这个同我心心相印的人却不容易找到。我不知道他有什么明显的特点，也无法从墙壁的小孔或者最好朋友的身上看出来。

在我寻找灵魂伴侣的过程中，发生了一件有意思的事。有一年夏天，我和最好的朋友忽然用崭新的眼光审视对方。我们之间的气氛变了，空气中充满了不容忽视的能量。

到此时为止，我们已经做了那么多年的朋友，早已熟悉了彼此的一切。这样的恋情是简单的。数周后，我们订婚了。不到一年，我们举办了婚礼。

我一直在寻找灵魂伴侣，却没意识到这么久以来他一直陪在我身边。至少我是这么想的。

蜜月过后没多久，我含情脉脉地看着他，提出了那个假设："你觉得我们是灵魂伴侣吗？"

他的回答同我的预期不符。"什么是灵魂伴侣？"他带着一脸新婚的天真问道。

　　我惊呆了。如果他连这是什么都不知道，他怎么会是我的灵魂伴侣？但事实上，我爱这个男人。不论他是不是我的灵魂伴侣，我都已经承诺无论好坏都要和他厮守一生。所以，生活还得继续，我们也将一同面对。我试着摆脱灵魂伴侣之类的愚蠢想法。

　　多年的相处让我们意识到，在很多方面，我们异大于同。我热衷讲价，他冲动购物；我读诗歌，他只看新闻；他打猎，我编织；他喜欢热辣的烧烤，我喜欢凉爽的牧场；我相信灵魂伴侣，他连那是什么都不知道。

　　尽管有那么多差异，这二十多年来，我们还是和谐地相处（偶尔，也会逗乐彼此）。尽管我总是拱被子，他（偶尔）打呼噜，我们还是找到了彼此都适应的节奏，快乐生活的节奏。

　　每天晚上，我都会把第二天要用的咖啡壶准备好。而他会在次日清晨，为我端上第一杯带着适量的奶油的咖啡，是我喜欢的那种。一天晚上，我非常疲倦，告诉他说："太晚了，今晚我不想准备做咖啡的东西了。"

　　他没有给我预期的回答。相反，他说："那么，我明天就不能为你做咖啡了。那是我的责任。"他的话中带着只有经过多年相处才能获得的柔情。

　　不用说，那天晚上，我准备了煮咖啡所需的材料。

　　我没有忘记寻找灵魂伴侣，只不过对它的定义已经改变。我不再认为灵魂伴侣是一个生来就同你各方面都很合适的人，那样的话，灵魂伴侣太容易。灵魂伴侣应该是和你一同成长的人，随着时间推移，你们之间的感情深刻到就连一杯简单的咖啡，也能证明你们的深情，也能让人感动得热泪盈眶。

　　那就是我的灵魂伴侣以及我最好的朋友可以为我做的。

　　　　　　　　　　　　　　　　　　　　　——吉尔·佩特勒

Chapter 3 Meant to Be
第三部分　恋爱篇

When You Wish Upon A Star
当你对着星星许愿

We were written in the stars, my love, all that separated us, was time, the time it took to read the map which was placed within our hearts, to find our way back to one another.

~Source Unknown

I was a fourth grader in love. Our families were friends and our moms thought it "cute" that I had such a crush on the neighbor's son, who was five years older and entering high school. But, to me, it was real love from the first moment when he gently smiled and looked at me with his soft hazel eyes.

Each night as I lay in bed, I quietly half sang and half recited, "When you wish upon a star, makes no difference who you are... anything your heart desires will come to you." I was sure that Walt Disney had gotten it right. Did it really matter that I was in my awkward stage, with buck teeth, and that he was in high school and didn't know my name? Not really, I decided, because somehow marrying my fourth grade crush was going to happen.

As the years slowly passed, I still "wished upon my star," yet reality was slowly creeping in. He was in college, had a serious girlfriend, and life beyond college would be starting soon. I reluctantly tried to move on, but each young man I dated unknowingly shared some similarity with the boy that I "wished upon a star" for—the hazel eyes, soft smile, tall and slender frame, or a gentle and kind heart. Yet no one I dated was him—not even close. In my heart, as strange as it seemed, I couldn't let go. Was it because I had fallen hard for my first crush, or did I really know something? Such a simple question, but one that I truly couldn't answer. Maybe one day my heart's question would be answered honestly.

The summer I graduated college was the summer my brother got married. It was a small and intimate wedding with just family and close friends. "He's probably not coming," said my mom, when I asked if my crush would be there. He was moving and his life had become busy with work and weekend plans. "His parents will be there though," she added. It would be nice to see them and find out what had happened to the boy I had once known. I quietly "wished upon a star" as my heart fluttered. Maybe he would come after all.

A few days before the wedding, my mom found out that he in fact would be coming. It was one of the few weekends that he had free to come home to spend time with his family. And, since there was a wedding of a longtime friend, this weekend seemed like the perfect time. As excited as I was to hear this, it only complicated things though as I had refused to go to my brother's wedding alone. A college friend had accepted my invitation as my date and it was obvious that he hoped for a more serious relationship despite my desire to only be friends.

My heart skipped a beat as I entered the church in front of my soon to be sister-in-law. I scanned the backs of the guests as I walked down the aisle. I spotted him almost instantly—and he was just as I had remembered him. As I led the wedding procession past his pew, he looked at me with astonishment. Goodbye to the pigtails, braces, and buck teeth. I was no longer "Jeff's sister" as he finally noticed me for who I was. As our eyes met, his head gently nodded towards me and he smiled the tender smile that I had loved for so long.

It was the longest twenty-minute wedding I had ever attended. "Where is he?" I asked when the service was over. "I don't know," said my mom as she greeted every guest with hugs. "He'll be at the house, I'm sure," she added. My heart continued to leap, skip, and jump. Even though I was a college graduate heading off to a new life in two weeks, I tingled while thinking of reuniting with my fourth grade crush at the reception.

"Why did I ever invite a date?" I wondered. Conversations I hoped to have with my crush were definitely going to get complicated. As the reception began, I found myself sitting between my date and my crush. My crush was just as anxious to get to know me as I was to see if this was a crush or if this could be true love. We snuck in moments away from the wedding guests and my date to quietly catch up on the years that had separated us. The wedding reception quickly became a blur; an instant friendship, gentle love, and admiration for each other quietly began that day.

Two weeks was all we had before summer ended and I moved to Maryland for my dream job. The summer was ending too quickly and I found myself wishing I could stay at home, but I had no choice. We constantly dated yet I always found myself wondering if I was living out my girlhood dream or if it was true love.

On one of our last dates, he gently took me in his arms as we stared up at the stars in the night sky. "Susan, would you ever consider marrying me—if I asked at some point?" He had taken my breath away again. "Yes, I think that could be very possible," I quietly replied. My heart was leaping as I realized that it was true love that we shared. It had taken awhile for us to find each other, but all my wishes had come true.

Three months later, during one of his visits to Maryland, we headed to the Eastern shore. Soft breezes, seagulls, and the gentle lapping sounds of the waves relaxed us as we quietly sat down to a picnic on the beach. Nestled in his arms, I watched a couple walk by hand in hand and I smiled, knowing that I had also found such happiness, friendship, and love. As I turned my head to look up at him, my dream became real. "Susan," he began, "will you marry me?" My heart's question was finally answered as he slipped the ring on my finger.

After almost seventeen years of marriage and children, my husband is still the boy I fell in love with thirty years ago, but even better. Yet one thing remains the same—my heart still skips a beat every time I know he's coming home. The star that I wished upon so many years ago is brighter than ever.

~Susan Staunton

我们的爱情写在星辰上，我的爱人。真正让我们分开的是时间。时间让我们看清心中地图，重回爱之路。

——逸名

四年级的时候，我爱上了隔壁邻居家的小男生。他大我五岁，即将升入初中。我们两家是朋友。两位母亲觉得我的行为非常"可爱"。但是，当他对我淡淡微笑，用淡褐色的眼睛温柔地望着我的那一刻，爱情来临了。

每天晚上，我躺在床上半哼半唱："当你对着星星许愿，你是谁并没有区别……你真心期望的一切，都会来到你身边。"我相信迪士尼是正确的。尽管我处在尴尬的阶段，长着龅牙，而读初中的他连我名字也不知道。但这些都不重要。我相信有一天，我的梦想会实现。

时间渐渐过去，我仍然"对着星星许愿"。然而，现实却慢慢彰显。他在念大学，有认真交往的女友，也即将毕业步入社会。无奈之下，我也试图摆脱过去，继续前行。但不知不觉中，我交往过的每个男生都带着他的某些特质——淡褐色眼睛，温柔的笑容，身材高挑细长，还有一颗善良温柔的心。但是，我交往过的每个人都不是他——差得很远。尽管听起来很奇怪，但我感觉自己无法放手。是因为第一次暗恋陷得太深，还是我真的知道些什么？这么简单的问题，我却无法回答。或许，有一天我内心的疑惑会得到诚实的解答。

大学毕业的那年夏天，我的哥哥结婚，计划举行一场只有家人和亲近朋友参加的小型婚礼。问到我的暗恋对象会不会出席的时候，妈妈回答："他可能不过来了。"他刚刚搬家，繁忙的工作和周末计划填满了他的生活。"但是他父母会过来。"母亲补充说。能够见到他们，了解一下我曾暗恋过的人的近况，这也不错。内心激动的我悄悄地"对着星星许愿"，希望他也能来。

婚礼前几天，母亲发现，实际上他会参加婚礼。这是他有空回家陪伴家人的几个周末之一。加上是位老朋友的婚礼，所以这时候回来最合适不过。听到他能来的消息，我非常激动，但同时又担心事情变得复杂。之前，因为不想一个人参加哥哥的婚礼，就邀请了一位大学同学。尽管我只想和他做普通朋友，他却期待能有更进一步的发展。

当我走进教堂，来到未来的嫂子面前时，我怦然心动。走下过道的我，打量着来宾的背影，几乎一眼就认出了他——他仍是我记忆中的样子。当我带着婚礼队列走过他座位前的时候，他吃惊地看着我。告别了辫子、吊带背心和龅牙的我，对他来说不再仅仅是"杰夫的妹妹"，他终于注意到我了。目光相遇的时候，他对我微微点了点头，脸上带着我爱了那么久的招牌式微笑。

我觉得这 21 分钟的婚礼是有史以来最长的一次。"他在哪儿？"仪式结束后，我问母亲。"我不知道。"母亲正同每位来宾拥抱问候。"他应该在房子里，我确定。"母亲补充说。我的心怦怦地跳个不停。作为一个大学毕业生，还有两周我就将步入社会。但此时，一想到和四年级的暗恋对象在婚宴上重聚，我的心里就激动不已。

"我为什么要邀请大学同学做我的伴儿呢？"我问自己。这样一来，同暗恋对象的谈话一定会变得复杂。婚宴开始的时候，我发现自己正好坐在大学同学和他之间。我急于想弄清楚对他的感情究竟是一时冲动还是真爱。他也和我一样，想更多地了解我。我们偷偷地离开婚礼宾客和大学同学，找了个安静的地方叙旧。那天婚宴的情形已经模糊，我只记得瞬间的认同。温柔的爱慕在我们两人间悄悄蔓延。

我们只有两周时间。暑假结束后，为了心仪的工作我搬到马里兰州。暑假过得太快，真希望自己能待在家里，但我别无选择。我们不断地约会，但我总怀疑这一切是否仅是我少女时代的幻想，这是不是真正的爱情？

夜空中繁星点点，他轻轻揽我入怀。"苏珊，你会考虑嫁给我吗？如果我某天问你的话。"他再次让我无法呼吸，"会的，我认为那是很有可能的。"我静静地回答。意识到此时拥有了真爱，我的心跳跃着。尽管过了很长时间，我们才找到对方，但是我的梦想实现了。

三个月后，在他到马里兰出差期间，我们一起到东海岸游玩。我们安详地坐在沙滩上野餐，享受着轻拂的海风，成群的海鸥，还有海浪轻拍的声音。这一切让人感到惬意放松。我依偎在他怀里，看着一对夫妇手牵手从我们面前经过。我笑了，知道自己也找到了这样的幸福、友谊和爱情。转头看向他时，我的愿望变成了现实。"苏珊，嫁给我好吗？"他为我戴上戒指的那一刻，我内心的疑惑终于得到了解答。

虽已结婚 17 年，也有了孩子，我的丈夫仍然是我 30 年前恋上的那个男生，只不过比当时更优秀。但有一点始终没有改变——他每次下班回家的时候，我都会心跳加速。多年前，我许愿的那颗星星比以往任何时候都要明亮。

——苏珊·士丹顿

One Little Word
一个字

Sometimes new love comes between old friends. Sometimes the best love was the one that was always there.

I am not one of those people. You know the ones who have houses full of "treasures". The people who cannot get rid of anything. A napkin, a ticket stub, a crumpled up old leaf. Some people call it junk, but to the person who owns it, it holds value because of the memory attached to it. I admit I do have one of those items. It is small and simple but oh so important to me. It measures only two inches by three inches and contains one little three-letter word. It's not a romantic word, and anyone reading it would surely wonder what it meant. What is the word? Well I think I should start at the beginning...

I grew up like many other little girls dreaming of my big wedding day with visions of my Prince Charming dancing in my head. I even wrote one of those lists. Oh, admit it; you know the list. The list

Chapter 3 Meant to Be
第三部分 恋爱篇

of all the traits of that wonderful person you would surely one day meet. A sense of humor, romantic, blue eyes. I've always been a sucker for blue eyes. But somehow in my twenties that list was forgotten. The guys I dated were promising, but then the real frog would emerge and it would become evident they were certainly not my Prince Charming. And so I began what would be a long journey of disappointment in love.

By the time I reached my thirties, still single, I wrote off those dreams as the whimsical ponderings of a little girl. I chose a different route and decided to become self-sufficient so no man would be required. It would just be easier. I would often be heard saying things like, "It is so great to be single and do whatever I want" or "I just don't have time to date with my busy schedule." I wonder if I ever actually convinced anyone.

So men became my friends. It seemed perfect. And guess what? I found out guys could be really great friends when I wasn't expecting anything from them. I became really good friends with one man. A fellow single thirty-something-year-old. We talked and laughed and swapped dating disaster stories. It put a lot in perspective! It was a perfect friendship. But then the evitable happened when a single man and woman are friends. We've all analyzed the *When Harry Met Sally* movie and know the risks. And so it happened to us.

It was a lovely day in May and we were out golfing together. We were doing the usual talking and laughing but then it changed. The teasing took on a new tone and sounded more like flirting. The casual hugs lingered a bit longer. It was a magical out-of-control day. The unwritten rules were being seriously disobeyed. But we could've cared less. Or so I thought.

When I got home that night and was alone the freak-out set in. I was an expert on freaking out because I spent most of my adult life doing that. Over-analyzing every conversation with every man I ever dated. I would ask my girlfriends, "What do you think he meant when he said I'll call you later?"

"Do you think he was trying to make me jealous?" "Do you think I should call him?" And on it would go.

But this time it was different because I really knew this man. This wasn't some guy I could just ignore and eventually he'd go away. This was my dear friend. And he really knew me too. The real me. Then insecurity decided to pay a visit with its comments. "You were imagining it. He doesn't really want you that way." Maybe I was making something out of nothing. I was so, so scared of falling in love and getting hurt again. And he knew that. Why is it all so complicated? I went to bed with this whirlwind of emotion in my head and heart.

The next day at work I went to open my e-mail with a good solid mix of excitement and fear. What would he say? Would he suggest getting together for "the talk?" I went to my inbox and cautiously hit enter and… Empty. Great. Now what?

Within an hour, I had a delivery of beautiful flowers. In the envelope was a small piece of paper. It had one little word on it. My heart melted and every insecure thought and fear fled. With just one word this man knew me well enough to express to me his love and understanding. His understanding of my fear of love. He won my heart and everything became crystal clear with that one silly word: "BOO!"

The rest of our story is magically simple. I fell in love with him with no fear. There were no hurts or disappointments. I found out how love should be. It was so easy. It was just meant to be.

We have been married almost six years now. I still adore this man. Our love is simple and pure and good. It is so much more than that little girl could have ever imagined. Oh yes, and by the way, he does have beautiful blue eyes…

~Linda Baskin

有时候，朋友间也会擦出爱情火花。有时候，最深最真的爱情原来一直都在。

——逸名

　　我不是那种房间里堆满各种"宝藏"、什么都不扔的人。一张纸巾、一份票根或者一片皱巴巴的树叶，有些人称之为垃圾，但对持有者来说，这些是承载着他们过去美好回忆的宝贝。我承认自己也有一件这样的物品。它小而简单，约5厘米x7厘米大小，上面写着一个由三个字母组成的单词。不，这不是一个浪漫的字眼，任何人刚看到它的时候都不明所以。那么，上面到底写了什么呢？还是让我从故事的最初讲起吧。

　　小时候的我，同其他女孩儿一样，幻想着某天自己能身穿白纱，在盛大的婚礼上同白马王子优雅共舞。我甚至列了一张单子。哦，承认吧，你肯定也写过，就是那种列出对未来伴侣所有期望的单子。幽默、浪漫、蓝眼睛，这就是我的要求，我一直觉得蓝色眼睛非常迷人。但是，不知为何，二十多岁的我已经完全忘了这张单子。那些交往过的人一开始也很不错，但是慢慢地我会看到他们身上的一些缺点，他们不是我的王子。

爱情之旅中，这种失望持续了很长时间。

　　30 岁依然单身的我，决定放弃那些小女孩儿的胡思乱想。我选择了不同的道路，决定成为自力更生的女人。别人问到的时候，我的回答常常是"单身很好啊，可以随心所欲做任何想做的事"或者"工作太忙了，实在是没有时间约会"。但我猜，大概没人会相信。

　　同男人，我只做朋友，不交往。看起来似乎很不错。你猜怎样？我发现，当自己不对男人抱有期待的时候，他们真的是很棒的朋友。我同其中的一位关系非常好。他是个三十多岁的单身汉。我们常常聊天，也分享彼此的约会糗事。他的友谊带给我很多快乐，还有看问题的新角度。但一个单身男人遇到一个单身女人，并且成为好友时，不可避免的事情发生了。我们曾经分析过《当哈利遇上莎莉》，也知道单身男女做朋友的风险，相同的故事在我们身上也发生了。

　　5 月，阳光灿烂的一天，我和他一起打高尔夫。我们同平常一样有说有笑，气氛却不经意间变了。平日的戏弄忽然有了新的基调，听起来更像是调情。以前的随意拥抱，现在延长了一些。这是神奇失控的一天。不成文的规则被严重违反了，但我们不在乎。至少当时，我是这么想的。

　　当晚回到家，独自一人的时候，我开始胡思乱想。我可是这方面的专家，因为我大部分的成年生活都在这样做，过度分析每个约会对象的每一句话。我会问自己的女性朋友："他说之后联系我，你觉得这是什么意思？""他是想让我嫉妒吗？""我该给他打电话吗？"诸如此类。

　　但这次不同，因为我真正了解这个男人。他不是那些我可以简单忽略、直到他自动放手的人。他是我亲近的朋友，同我了解他一样了解我。但不安全感还是从中作梗，"这是你自己的幻想，他根本不爱你。"或许，是我自己多想了。我不想再次为爱受伤。他也知道这点。为什么这么复杂呢？我躺下了，脑海中一直萦绕着这样的思绪。

　　第二天上班的时候，我带着既兴奋又恐惧的心情，打开电子邮箱。他会说些什么呢？他会建议我们坐下来"谈谈"吗？我登录邮箱，小心翼翼地点击"进入"，打开来，里面是空的，并没有新邮件。很好，那么现在该怎么办呢？

　　没过一小时，我收到了一束鲜花。上面的信封中装着一个小纸条。纸条上只有一个字。看到那个字的时候，我的心都融化了，再也没有任何的恐惧和不安。仅这一个字就足以说明他对我的理解和爱慕。他了解我对爱情的恐惧。这个字帮他赢得了我的心，一切都明朗了，这个字就是"嘘（BOO）"！

　　接下来的故事非常简单。我们相爱了，没有恐惧，没有失望，没有伤害。我明白了什么是爱情。它是那么简单，那样命中注定。

　　现在，我们结婚已将近六年时间，但是我仍然崇拜着这个男人。我们的爱情简单、纯洁而美好，比任何一个女孩儿的梦想都要完美。哦，顺便说一下，他的确有迷人的蓝眼睛。

——琳达·巴斯金

Amore
我的爱人

A man is not where he lives, but where he loves.

~Latin Proverb

I was born and raised in Canada, by parents who both emigrated from Italy. A typical Italo-Canadian, I grew up with Italian ideals but lived a Canadian lifestyle. I am ashamed to say I didn't even speak Italian when I was young. Nevertheless, I made my first venture to see our glorious mother country with my family when I was ten years old. A shy, reserved child hiding behind bulky glasses and a bad haircut (which I still regret), I had no idea what I would find there.

In the piazza of my mom's town, Mignano di Monte Lungo, was the most gorgeous, confident thirteen-year-old boy I had ever seen. His name was Ludovico. He cruised around on his bike, suave and sweet with a genuine smile that lit up his whole face. He seemed like such a man. One day he bought me gelato (with his own money!). My heart raced every

Chapter 3 Meant to Be
第三部分 恋爱篇

time he came near. I could barely look at Ludovico, so great was my crush. Of course, I could tell no one of my feelings—not my mom, not even my cousin! It was too embarrassing…besides, I didn't understand a word he said (but it sure sounded good to my ears). I left Italy after a month, sad to leave behind the new world I had discovered, and the boy who made my heart beat fast.

Time passed, and I didn't think much about Mignano during my teenage years, but for some reason, I wanted to learn Italian. I took a few courses at school and spoke horribly, but was able to spit out a few words in the beautiful language… which prepared me for my next adventure.

When I graduated from high school, my mom and I planned an extensive trip to Europe that would include a return to Italy. On the plane ride there, I thought of the people I hadn't seen in years. The cousins, relatives… him. I felt a tingle in my stomach at the thought of Ludovico. Would he find me pretty now that I had grown up?

I still remember the exact moment he pulled up behind me on his motorcycle on our return visit. I was wearing a denim miniskirt, overwhelmed by the midday August heat. My mother and I had been exploring the streets of her hometown. Everyone who lived there was resting, it seemed, hiding from the blazing sun. Except for him. I turned around to see him straddling his bike on the edge of the road, grinning behind his sunglasses.

"Do you remember this young man?" my mother smiled.

Of course! I wanted to scream… he was still SOOOOO BEAUTIFUL.

I felt like I had been struck by lightning. Thankfully, this time around, he felt something, too, because he mysteriously showed up everywhere I went in the next few days.

Finally, Ludovico and I had an opportunity to be alone. He took me on a breathtaking tour with his motorcycle, introduced me to all his friends, and ultimately, told me how he felt…that he was in love with me and wanted me to return quickly to Mignano. I said, of course, that I would and that I loved him, too!

We enjoyed that feeling for another day and then, regretfully, I had to leave. I felt like my heart was being ripped from my chest. To make things worse, my mom had clued into what was happening, and tried to discourage this long distance affair…it was torture! I told him I would be back soon, and he said that he would wait for me.

I cried so hard when I got back to Canada. My parents kept trying to console me.

"If it's meant for you, it won't go by you!" they would tell me. A silly cliché meant to calm me down. I don't think they really believed those words as they do now.

Ten years passed and I was twenty-eight years old when it happened again. I'd had my share of relationships, but never quite found the man I wanted to marry.

One day my mother announced casually that Ludovico from her town was coming to Canada for two weeks to confirm his nephew and that we should have everyone over for dinner in this Italian's honour. I was stunned.

"I don't want to see him," I told her adamantly.

"Why not?" She was shocked. Did she forget what had happened?

I tried to tell her how I felt. "I am way too embarrassed…the last time I saw him, we said we would wait for each other, and now ten years has passed… how humiliating."

What I really felt, however, was that somehow my life would change. That he would awaken something deep inside. I didn't want to feel such immense sadness again, the pain that came from loving someone so far away.

Some things are unavoidable. The moment we laid eyes on each other, it was as if not a day had passed since our last encounter. In my mind I was eighteen again, he twenty-one, the feelings as strong as ever and we were both a little shocked at the enormity of it. Suddenly he had to leave again, and this time he said, "I don't want to wait another ten years, this time we will be together."

And, after many sacrifices, tears, trials and tribulations, he moved here to marry me the following year…proof that dreams do come true, and that we can never escape our true destiny!

~Sylvia Suriano-Diodati

置身何处不重要，重要的是爱在何方。

——拉丁谚语

　　我在加拿大出生并长大，但父母均为意大利人。作为典型的意籍加拿大人，我采用加拿大人的生活方式，却怀抱着意大利人的理想。说来惭愧，小时候的我甚至不会讲意大利语。不过，10岁那年，我随父母一同回到家乡，回去看望我光荣伟大的祖国。当时的我羞涩拘谨，戴着厚厚的眼镜，留着糟糕的发型（我到现在还很后悔），我完全不知道这趟意大利之旅会发生什么。

　　在母亲家乡米格纳诺市的广场上，我遇到了平生所见最英俊最自信的 13 岁男孩儿卢多维克。我看到他的时候，他正骑着自行车，在广场上转圈，脸上带着甜美温柔的笑容。他看起来很有男子汉气概。某天，他用自己的钱，给我买了支冰激凌。每次他靠近的时候，我都会心跳加速。我那么喜欢他，甚至不好意思抬头看他。当然，我没有告诉任何人，包括母亲，还有表哥。太尴尬了。此外，我一点也听不懂他在说什么（但是我觉得很动听）。一个月后，我离开意大利，离开了那个新世界，还有让我心跳加速的意大利男孩儿。

时光流逝，青春期的我并没有经常想起米格纳诺。但是，出于某种原因，我想学习意大利语。于是，我选修了学校的一些课程。虽然讲得很糟糕，但是也能用这种优美的语言讲出几句话来。这些为我下次冒险打好了基础。

高中毕业后，母亲和我计划到欧洲游览，意大利也是目的地之一。在飞往意大利的航班上，我想起了多年未见的亲人、堂兄弟，还有他。想到卢多维克的时候，我心里一阵激动。他会觉得长大了的我很漂亮吗？

我仍然记得他将摩托车停在我们身后的那一刻。8月的中午，烈日炎炎，我穿着牛仔短裙，同母亲在故乡的街道上散步。为了避暑，大家似乎都在休息，除了他。我转身，看到道路尽头他戴着太阳镜跨坐在摩托车上，冲我们笑。

"还记得这个年轻人吗？"母亲笑着问。

当然，我想大声尖叫，他还是那么英俊帅气。

太震惊了！但值得庆幸的是，他好像也对我有感觉。因为接下来的几天，无论我们去哪儿，他都会露面。

终于，我和卢多维克有了单独相处的机会。他开着摩托，带我领略了一次惊险之旅，也介绍他的朋友给我认识。最后，他告诉我他的感受，他爱上了我，希望我能尽快回到米格纳诺。我向他保证，会尽快回来，而且我也爱他。

之后，我们一直沉浸在恋爱的喜悦中。遗憾的是，我不得不离开。我的心似乎都被撕裂了。更糟糕的是，母亲知道了这些，她并不支持我们的远距离恋爱。这一切都是折磨！我告诉他我会很快回来，他也答应一定等我。

回加拿大的路上，我哭得悲恸欲绝。父母一直试着安慰我。

"属于你的，无论什么人或事也抢不走。"他们这么告诉我，试图用一句陈词滥调劝我冷静下来。我不认为当时的他们会像现在一样，相信这句话。

十年过去了，我再次遇到卢多维克的时候，已经28岁。这其间，我也交过男友，却一直没有遇到合适的结婚对象。

一天，母亲随意地说，来自家乡的卢多维克要来加拿大待两周，看望他的侄子。按照意大利人的传统，我们会邀请他们共进晚餐。听到这个消息，我整个人都惊呆了。

"我不想见他。"我坚决地告诉母亲。

"为什么？"母亲吃惊地问。难道她忘记以前的事了吗？

我试着告诉母亲我的感受："太尴尬了，上次见面的时候，我们都信誓旦旦地保证会等待对方，现在十多年过去了……多尴尬。"

但我真实的感受是，见到他后，我的生活会改变。他会唤醒我内心深处的感情。我不想再次感受这种巨大的悲伤，爱上远在异国的他。

有些事情是无法避免的。眼神交汇的那一刻，这十多年的分离好像从未发生。我仿佛重新回到18岁，而他21岁。我们的感情和以往一样强烈。但是这份爱情的艰巨，还是让我们稍稍吃了一惊。转眼间，又到了离别时刻，这次他说："我不想再等一个十年，这次我们会在一起。"

经过许多牺牲、眼泪、考验和磨难之后，次年他搬来加拿大同我结婚。事实证明，美梦的确可以成真，而且我们永远无法摆脱真正的命运！

——西尔维娅·苏芮纳诺－迪奥答提

Unforgettable
难以忘怀

Never, never give up.
~Winston Churchill

Divorced and living the life of an empty nester in Dallas, I wasn't interested in marriage, and I had given up on finding a good man to date. The best relationship I could recall was with Gary, my college sweetheart thirty years earlier. He traveled from Massachusetts to school in Texas because of a football scholarship. Like many love-struck college students, we talked of marriage.

However, a back injury forced Gary to return to Massachusetts for surgery, and he lost his scholarship in Texas. Without low airfares, continuing our relationship seemed impossible. His whole future was in question since he wanted to get his teaching degree and coach the sport he loved. Our world was turned upside down, and in great emotional pain, I ended the relationship before Gary left. We talked on the phone once after he returned to Massachusetts, but the 1,750 miles between us was too big a hurdle to conquer—at least in my shortsighted vision.

Over the next three decades, I thought of Gary periodically and looked through my scrapbook that held newspaper clippings of his athletic achievements. I always wondered what became of him. He was tall, handsome, and had a terrific sense of humor bolstered by his Boston accent. My mother loved him too, and she was sorry when I ended our relationship. My dad, on the other hand, feared Gary would take me far away to New England. Consequently, my father painted a bleak picture of life in the cold Northeast. I later realized Dad's comments were self-serving, but at such a young age, I might not have undertaken a big move to Massachusetts even without his cautionary statements.

Once my own daughter left for college, random circumstances brought Gary to mind more frequently. Whenever I heard Barry Manilow's song "Weekend in New England," thoughts of Gary drifted my way. When I switched to country stations, Reba McEntire belted out "Whoever's in New England." Recurring questions rambled through my head. Had Gary's surgery been successful...so much so that he was drafted and sent to Vietnam to die like so many men of our generation? Or did he graduate from college and became the coach he talked of being? If so, I assumed he was married with a large family like the one in which he was raised.

One weekend in March, I went to dinner with a neighbor, and we met a man from New Hampshire. Gary came to mind. The next night, I came home and turned on a televised Bee Gees concert just as they sang "Massachusetts", which was popular when we dated. On this night, the Bee Gees song hit me like a ton of bricks, and I raised my hands to the heavens saying, "Okay...enough. I'll try to talk to him."

I knew when Gary left Texas, he felt I didn't care about him, and I had a long-overdue need to explain my actions. I also needed to know how things had turned out for him. I wanted to find him alive and well.

I dialed Directory Assistance, and the operator relayed the only listing she had in the Boston area for a Gary Bogart. As his phone rang, I wondered what in the world I was going to say. What if his recorder answered? Should I leave a message? What words were appropriate after thirty years? What if a wife answered?

I didn't know why thoughts about calling Gary had been hounding me. All I wanted to tell him was why I ended our relationship when he was struggling to keep his world together. My father had colored my thinking to a great degree back then, and I just didn't see how we could achieve our dream of being together with all those miles between us. After all, neither of us had any money.

After a few rings, I heard a routine "Hello" from a man's voice.

"May I speak to Gary Bogart?" I asked.

As one might guess, he responded, "This is he."

I muttered, "Is this the Gary Bogart who attended college in Texas?"

He later told me that, at that moment, he knew the voice was mine. I hadn't realized the time was after 10:00 P.M. on the East Coast. Thankfully, Gary was home alone sleeping, and he told me he sat up like he'd been hit by a bolt of lightning when he recognized the voice on the phone. He had been divorced for eight years.

I finally had the chance to explain the thoughts that led me to end our relationship in 1968. He said my call healed something inside him, because he never understood why I turned away from someone I proclaimed to love. He always suspected there was another guy in my life—possibly an old boyfriend—and nothing could have been further from the truth. He had never forgotten how much we meant to one another, and he also wondered where life might have taken us if we had stayed together.

We talked for forty-five minutes before I said I had to hang up. I had achieved my purpose in calling, and I was elated to have been able to answer the decades-old questions that lingered in his mind. For the second time in my life, he asked for my number. After six weeks and many long phone conversations, we met in Florida. It was surreal, as if three decades had suddenly disappeared. I worked for an airline, which allowed us to spend lots of time together that year.

Dozens of flights and nine months later, Gary and I married on the beach at Sanibel Island, Florida. The sun was setting as we became husband and wife, and the onlookers included two dolphins that swam unusually close to shore. One passer-by proclaimed the dolphins' presence to be a spiritual blessing. That may have been so, but all we knew for sure was we were ready to fulfill the dream that fate had suspended for us.

Two nights after we married, we attended a Bee Gees concert where Barry Gibb made a surprising announcement before they sang "Massachusetts". My best friend had let them know about their role in our rekindled romance, and Barry dedicated that song to "Gary and Betty" before beginning its enchanting melody.

I finally made that once-foreboding move to Lynn, Massachusetts, where we lived for several years before relocating to Florida. As we celebrate ten years of marriage, we are grateful we can be together at this point in our lives.

~Betty Bogart

永远，永远不要放弃。

——温斯顿·丘吉尔

　　刚经历离婚，独自一人居住在达拉斯的我对婚姻没有任何期待，并且已经放弃找寻合适伴侣的希望。能回忆起来的幸福时光，便是 30 年前同大学时期男友格雷交往的那段日子。为了赢取一项橄榄球奖学金，他从马萨诸塞州来到得克萨斯州的一所学校。同许多痴情的大学恋人一样，我们也谈论婚姻，计划两人的未来。

　　然而，由于背部受伤，格雷不得不回马萨诸塞州进行手术治疗。他也因此丢掉了得克萨斯州的奖金。格雷的未来似乎一片黑暗，受伤使他不能获得执教资格，从而粉碎了他做橄榄球教练的梦想。高昂的机票价格，给我们这段异地恋增加了很大的阻碍。我们的生活发生了翻天覆地的变化。格雷离开之前，我狠下心，决定同他分手。他回到马萨诸塞州以后，我们又通过一次电话。但约 2816 公里的距离，在我看来实在是无法克服的障碍。至少当时的我是这么想的。

　　接下来的 30 年里，我总会时不时地想起格雷，偶尔也翻翻贴满了关于他报道的剪贴簿。我总会想象现在的他会是怎样。记忆中的他高大英俊，浓重的波士顿口音更增添了他的幽默。母亲也非常喜欢他。因此，知道我们分手后，她感到非常遗憾。但另一方面，父亲却担心格雷会将我带到遥远的新英格兰地区。因此，父亲口中寒冷东北部的生活总是凄苦惨淡。后来，我意识到父亲的评论只是出于自身的考虑。但即便没有父亲的那番话，当时年纪尚轻的我，也没有勇气搬到遥远的马萨诸塞州去。

女儿离家上大学之后，我对格雷的思念更加深切，一些琐碎的小事也能让我想到他。听到巴瑞·曼尼洛的歌曲《新英格兰的周末》，我会想起他。转到乡村音乐电台，听到瑞芭·麦肯泰尔的《无论谁在新英格兰陪你》，我也会想起他。脑海中总有些问题挥之不去，他会像我们这代的大多数人一样参加越战，不幸牺牲吗？他大学毕业了吗，有没有当上一直渴望的教练？如果真是这样的话，我想他一定已经结婚了，并且有很多孩子，就像他成长的大家庭一样。

3月的一个周末，我同邻居一同吃饭的时候遇到了一位来自新罕布什尔州的男士。我立刻想到了格雷。次日晚上，当我回家打开电视，上面正播放着比吉斯乐队的《马萨诸塞州》，这首歌在我们约会的那个年代非常流行。那天晚上，比吉斯乐队的歌曲给了我很大震撼，我对天宣誓："好了，够了。我会试着联系他。"

我知道格雷离开得克萨斯州的时候，他一定认为我不在乎他。我一直欠他一个解释。与此同时，我也想知道这些年来他过得怎么样。我希望他一切都好。

我拨通了查号台的电话，接线员凭着唯一的线索——波士顿地区的格雷·博加特，帮我转接。等待接通的这段时间，我一直在想自己究竟该说些什么。如果是答录机的话该怎么办，我该留言吗？事隔30年，该说些什么呢？接电话的如果是他妻子，又该怎么办？

我不明白为什么给格雷打电话会让我这么烦恼。我只是想告诉他，为什么我会在他最失意的时候选择离开。那时，父亲的话很大程度上影响了我，而且我不知道该如何继续我们的远距离恋爱。毕竟，当时我们都没什么钱。

铃响了几声之后，电话那头传来了一个男性的声音："你好。"

"我找格雷·博加特。"我说。

同大家所想的一样，他回答说："我就是。"

我喃喃地问："是在得克萨斯州念大学的格雷·博加特吗？"

后来他告诉我，就是在那一刻，他听出了我的声音。打电话的时候，我没有意识到当时已经是东部时间晚上 10 点。值得庆幸的是，格雷一个人在家睡觉。他告诉我，当意识到是我的时候，他像被雷击中一样，霍地从床上坐起来。他已经离婚八年了。

我终于有机会解释 1968 年决定分手的原因了。他告诉我说，我的这些话治愈了他内心的一些创伤，因为他一直不明白为什么口口声声说爱他的我，会选择在他最无助的时候离开。他一直怀疑是第三者插足，或许还是个老男人，总之都是些无妄猜测。他一刻也未忘记我们的感情，偶尔他也会想，假如当初我们在一起，现在会是怎样。

挂电话前，我们一共谈了 45 分钟。我已经实现了打电话的初衷，也为能解开缠绕他三十多年的谜团而感到高兴。在我一生中，这是他第二次向我要电话号码。此后，我们频繁打电话联系。六周后，我们在佛罗里达会面。这次见面是不同寻常的，仿佛从未有过三十年的隔阂。那年我在一家航空公司工作，所以我们能够常常见面。

九个月后，经历了几十次航班往返，格雷和我在佛罗里达州桑尼贝尔岛的海滩举行了婚礼。落日余晖，在路人以及两只海豚的见证下，我们结为夫妻。一位行人称不常上岸的海豚能出现在我们的婚礼上，这是上帝对我们的祝福。或许是这样吧，但有一点可以确定：我们已经准备好弥补过去的缺憾。

两天后，我们参加了比吉斯乐队的演唱会。演唱《马萨诸塞州》之前，巴里·吉布做了一个惊人的举动，将这首歌献给"格雷和贝蒂"。因为之前，好友向他们讲述了这首歌对于我和格雷的意义。

后来，我终于搬到了位于马萨诸塞州的林恩市。在那儿生活了几年之后，我们搬到了佛罗里达州。结婚十周年纪念日的今天，我们仍为能再次相聚感到幸运。

——贝蒂·博加特

We'll Manage
我们会有办法的

Live the life you've dreamed.

~Henry David Thoreau

As the young bride and groom walked slowly down the stairs, their faces displayed a solemn expression that belied the joyous spring to their steps. They took this momentous occasion in their young lives very seriously.

The bride wore a simple dress buttoned up to her slender throat. White ankle socks accentuated a pair of her mother's black high-heeled shoes. A lace window curtain was on her head, the "train" flowing several feet behind her.

The groom wore starched jeans, a Roy Rogers T-shirt, and a pair of brown cowboy boots. He held her closely, supporting her down each step, as she placed one foot unsteadily before the other. Her arm was wrapped around his and their hands were clasped tightly together as he looked down at his bride with pride in his eyes and love in his heart.

They didn't care that there was no wedding party, no flowers, nor even the traditional Wedding March, but both were humming the tune softly together. It was a simple ceremony because the groom was six years old and the bride was four.

It was Valentine's day of 1945.

Lynne's mother met us at the bottom of the stairs. She was my mom's best friend. Her eyebrows rose questioningly and the beginning of a smile formed upon her lips.

She turned toward the kitchen. "Viv, look at this," she called.

When my mother saw Lynne and me, her hand flew to her mouth in an evident effort to suppress her laughter.

Letting go of Lynne's hand, I hesitantly approached her mother, looked into her eyes and said, "Em, when Lynne and I get old enough, can we get married?"

Em knelt in front of me, placed both hands on my shoulders, then looked steadily into my eyes. "Gary, when you're old enough and have a good job, if you still love each other, then the answer will be yes. And I'll buy you a set of dishes as a wedding present."

Lynne and I then went happily into the kitchen for some Jell-O topped with whipped cream.

A couple of years later my parents and I moved away.

I had been several years in the army, stationed overseas, when my mother wrote that Lynne was very sick with mononucleosis. That Valentine's Day of 1945 was far in the past, and I'd almost forgotten about her. Nevertheless we began writing regularly, getting to know each other all over again, and soon we exchanged pictures. It was the first time I'd seen her face since I was ten years old. Looking back at me was a now beautiful young woman of nineteen with the bluest eyes I'd ever seen. I was in love all over again.

As we wrote, the time passed very slowly. I couldn't wait to see her, and over the months our letters had become more intimate and it was as though the passing years were inconsequential. Two years later I came home on leave and flew to Portland to see her. She was standing on the tarmac as I approached the top of the ramp. We stood looking at each other silently for long moments until a cough behind me got me moving. I bolted down the steps, took both of her hands in mine, looked into those gorgeous blue eyes, then took her in my arms and kissed her. We were soon engaged. It was Christmas, 1962.

On Valentine's Day of 1963 I was at Fort Bragg, North Carolina getting ready to undergo Airborne training with a small group of candidates. At one in the afternoon I was called into the orderly room and handed a telegram.

"Arriving at 3:00 P.M., February 14 at Piedmont Airport, Fayetteville. Can hardly wait. Love Lynne."

I had no idea she would be coming this soon. We had agreed that we would wait until my training was complete. She told me later that it was my letters and phone calls telling her I missed her so much that convinced her to come early. Besides our mothers thought it would be a wonderful Valentine's present for us both.

In those frantic two hours, I rented a small trailer and bought what we would need at a local pawnshop. The only things new were the linens. With twenty-five dollars left and payday two weeks away I'd forgotten about food.

Luckily a general and his aide had to be taken to the airport and, because of Lynne's pending arrival, I was allowed to replace the regular driver for that trip.

At 2:45 we pulled up in front of Piedmont Airport. I took the general's bags to the ticket counter and was dismissed. I was just in time to greet Lynne at the arrival gate and soon she was in my arms. What a wonderful Valentine's Day! The hassle of the past several hours made it all worthwhile.

Lynne saw the unfurled flag on the staff car waiting at VIP parking. "Wow!" She smiled.

"We're lucky to have this car, Lynne. But this is just for today. The only transportation we're going to have is what I can borrow. And," I said sadly, "I have to report to jump school at Fort Benning in a little over a week."

I could see disappointment on her face but then she said something that was to be the hallmark of her outlook whenever difficulty arose in our lives together. She placed her hand on my arm and smiled bravely. "We'll manage."

One week later, on February 21st, we were married in Post Chapel 21. Like our earlier "marriage" it was an informal affair and we wanted it that way. My best man and I were the only ones in dress green uniforms. The rest of the unit, some forty men together with the chaplain, were in the duty uniform of the day (fatigues). My commanding officer gave her away.

One of our wedding presents was the set of dishes Lynne's mother promised us so many years ago.

Our marriage has occasionally been difficult for Lynne, especially since I made the military my career. There have been assignments in underdeveloped countries where she had to soak vegetables in water and bleach to avoid intestinal parasites and diseases. Many times our only transportation was a horse and cart in Africa or a smoke-belching motorized pedicab in Thailand. She endured martial law in Turkey and witnessed the bombing of a neighbor's apartment that narrowly missed killing our friend and her three-year-old child. In spite of it all, Lynne looked upon each setback as a challenge. And each and every time, Lynne's response was like the first time. "We'll manage."

One day we came across a picture of us that her mother had taken on that long ago day when I first asked for Lynne's hand. We were amazed that the dress she was wearing was almost an exact duplicate of the one she wore at our wedding all those years ago.

Now some forty-six years later we're still just as much in love as that six-year-old boy and four-year-old little girl in 1945.

And through it all, "we've managed."

~Gary B. Luerding

过梦想之生活。

——亨利·大卫·梭罗

　　年轻的新郎和新娘慢慢走下台阶，脸上庄重严肃的神情却掩饰不住脚下轻快雀跃的步伐。年轻的他们非常重视这一时刻。

　　新娘的礼服简单大方，前襟的扣子一直延续到纤细的颈项。脚上的白袜更突显了母亲的黑色高跟皮鞋。蕾丝窗帘被用作头纱，身后披落着几米长的尾摆。

　　新郎穿着印有罗伊·罗杰斯头像的 T 恤，笔挺的牛仔裤和一双棕色牛仔靴。他细心地扶着因为穿高跟鞋而走路摇摇晃晃的新娘子。她也紧紧挽着他，他们的双手紧紧地握在一起。每当望向他的新娘，新郎眼里都充满了骄傲和爱意。

　　他们不在意没有仪式，没有鲜花，甚至没有传统的婚礼进行曲。他们轻声地哼着，温柔地和着。这是一个简单的婚礼，因为新郎只有 6 岁，新娘 4 岁。当时是 1945 年的情人节。

Chapter 3 Meant to Be
第三部分　恋爱篇

琳恩的母亲同我母亲是要好的朋友，她在楼梯底部看到了这一幕。她的眉毛因为诧异而微微上挑，但随后便化成了嘴边的微笑。

她转身朝厨房喊道："薇薇，快过来看。"

母亲看到琳恩和我的时候，连忙用手捂住嘴，想止住停不下来的笑。

松开琳恩的手，我迟疑地走向她母亲，抬头望着她问："艾慕，等琳恩和我长大后，我们可以结婚吗？"

艾慕屈膝蹲下，双手放在我的肩膀上，坚定地望着我的眼睛说："加里，等你足够大，有一份好工作的时候。如果那时你们依然相爱，我会答应的。到时候，我会送一套餐具作为你们的新婚礼物。"

之后，我和琳恩愉快地走进厨房，吃了些淋上奶油的果冻。

几年后，我随同父母搬到了别处。

当母亲写信告诉我，琳恩得了单核细胞增多症，病得非常严重时，我正在军队服役，驻扎海外。这时距1945年的情人节已经非常遥远，我几乎忘记了琳恩。不过，我们开始定期通信，重新了解对方。不久，我们交换了照片。这是我自10岁以后第一次看到她，一个有着我所见过的最迷人的蓝眼睛的19岁女子。我再次坠入爱河。

在我们通信的那段时间里，时间似乎格外漫长。我总是迫不及待地想要见到她。信中的内容也变得更加亲密，就仿佛流逝的岁月根本无关紧要。两年后，我回家探亲，特意飞往波特兰见她。我一下飞机就看到了等在停机坪的她。我们默默地注视了对方许久，直到身后响起咳嗽声，我才想起来继续往前。我飞速地走下台阶，握着她的手，看着那双迷人的蓝眼睛，情不自禁地把她抱在怀里，吻了她。很快，在1962年的圣诞节，我们订婚了。

1963年的情人节，我在北卡罗来纳州的布拉格堡军事基地，同其他候选人一起，接受空降训练。某天下午，我被通知到中队办公室取一封电报。

"2 月 14 日下午 3 点，到达费耶特维尔的皮埃蒙特机场。不能再等，爱你的琳恩。"

我没想到她会这么快过来。因为之前已经说好，要等到我训练结束的时候再见面。她后来告诉我说，我的电话和信件让她了解到我是如此思念她，所以她终于决定提前过来。此外，母亲们也认为，这对我们两人都是份不错的情人节礼物。

在这仓促的两小时，我租了一辆汽车，到当地的一家典当行买了些可能用到的物品，唯有床单是崭新的。口袋里仅剩 25 美元，而领薪水要等到两周以后，不得已，我只好放弃购买食品的打算。

幸运的是，一位将军和他的助手要赶往皮埃蒙特机场。因为琳恩要来，部队破例允许我代替原来的司机。下午 2:45，我们赶到皮埃蒙特机场。把将军的行李送到售票柜台后，我可以离开了。正好赶上了从出口走出的琳恩，我紧紧地拥抱了她。我们度过了一个异常美妙的情人节。过去几小时的麻烦也变得值得。

当琳恩看到停在贵宾区插着国旗的军车时，她开心地惊呼："哇哦！"

"我们很幸运能用这辆车，琳恩，但只有今天一天。"我伤心地说，"而且，我只有一个多星期时间，之后就要到本宁堡的跳伞学校报到。"

我可以看出她脸上的失望，但很快她拍了拍我的胳膊，勇敢地微笑着说："我们会有办法的。"每当生活中面临困难，她都会这么说。

一个星期后，也就是 2 月 21 日，我和琳恩在 21 号邮政教堂举行了婚礼。同我们早前的"婚礼"一样，这次的婚礼虽不十分正式，却是我们希望的样子。婚礼上，只有我和伴郎穿着绿色军装，其他 40 名男士同牧师一样，穿着当天的迷彩军装。我的指挥官代替琳恩父亲把她交给了我。

我们收到的结婚礼物之一，便是多年前琳恩母亲答应送给我们的餐具。

有时候，我们的婚姻会给琳恩带来很大困难，尤其是我的军旅生涯。在不发达国家执行任务的时候，她不得不把蔬菜浸泡在撒有漂白粉的水中，用来防止寄生虫和疾病。很多时候，我们不得不忍受糟糕的交通工具，比如非洲的马车或者泰国冒着浓烟的机动三轮车。在土耳其，琳恩必须遵循当地的军事管制，她曾亲眼目睹一场轰炸，我们的朋友以及她3岁的孩子险些丧生。尽管经历了这么多不幸，琳恩仍把每次苦难看做人生的一次挑战。每一次，她都会像第一次一样告诉我："我们会有办法的。"

某天，我们看到了她母亲很久前拍的一张照片。那是我第一次向琳恩求婚的时候，我们惊奇地发现，照片上她的衣服几乎同婚礼当天的礼服一模一样。

结婚46年的我们，仍像1945年那个6岁男孩和4岁女孩一样相爱。

经历了这么多——"我们找到了办法。"

——加里·B.努尔丁

"I still love you as much as I did back then. I always had good taste ... and style!"

"我仍像当年一样爱你。我总是很有品味，而且风度翩翩。"

Hello Again
电话情缘

The more faithfully you listen to the voice within you, the better you hear what is sounding outside of you.

~Dag Hammerskjold

Eight years after I'd placed the scrap of paper into an old address book, it was still there. I smoothed it across my thigh to get the tiny wrinkles out and, thankfully, I could still read his phone number. At least it had been his number in Chicago almost a decade ago. Now there would be no more hesitating. No more driving myself crazy that perhaps I had cavalierly tossed aside something worthwhile.

My mind worked furiously, preparing for all sorts of contingencies. If I called the number and if it was disconnected, I would resign myself to never really knowing what happened to him. If it was no longer his number, I would apologize, hang up, and be done with it. If a woman answered, I'd silently hang up and, with my Dallas phone number, she'd suspect nothing. Believing I'd covered all scenarios, I dialed the phone with a shaky hand.

"Hello?" It was a male's voice.

OmiGod! In all my planning, I hadn't even thought of what to say if he answered. We'd known each other fifteen years, but fueled by my romantic wanderlust, we hadn't spoken for the last eight of those years.

For a second I thought about hanging up. Coward! Instead I swallowed and croaked, "Hi, Greg."

He responded as if we'd just spoken yesterday. "Hi, Carole."

My eyebrows shot up. "You don't sound surprised."

"I knew I'd hear from you again someday," he explained, as if an old flame calling out-of-the-blue was a natural occurrence.

We chatted for a few minutes. He sounded welcoming and relaxed. I was perspiring.

"Carole, I'd like to talk more, but I was just going out."

I didn't even think about it being Saturday when I called. He had a date. I didn't.

I giggled nervously, "Oh, I'm sorry. I didn't realize…" My voice trailed off, hoping I didn't sound like a dateless loser.

But he rescued me. "Can I call you tomorrow?"

Yes! I forced my voice down an octave. "That'd be fine." I gave him my number and hung up, feeling like a strand of spaghetti left to boil way too long.

The next day, I told my friends what I had done.

"How exciting!" Cindi, my kind friend exclaimed.

Dora, my worldly, cynical pal, didn't say a word at first. But I knew by her scowl, she disapproved. "Men are never as good as we remember them. You should have let sleeping memories lie."

I shrugged, refusing to let her doubts become mine.

He kept his promise and called that evening. The conversation flowed smoothly. Then he asked me the question I hadn't the courage to ask him.

"So…are you seeing anyone?"

Be coy. "Oh I'm dating several guys." I swallowed hard and forced my voice to stay level. "What about you?"

He was seeing someone.

My heart sank. I knew he wouldn't be pining for me. But at least he wasn't engaged.

He called once more and then without warning, stopped. I was disappointed and my fingers itched to dial his number, but I refused to scratch.

"At least I tried," I explained to Dora and Cindi. "Anyway, he's still in Chicago. I'm in Dallas."

Dora harrumphed. Cindi looked at me with such pity you'd have thought I'd lost both arms in one single, tragic accident.

A few months later, Greg left me a message, apologizing for disappearing and asking me to call.

I smiled from ear to ear, but decided not to call him that night. He could wait, as I had. But the next evening, I dialed his number, hoping my excitement wouldn't travel across phone lines. This marked the first of many calls. They were a bright spot and during them, my road-warrior job stress melted away.

On in-office work days, my travel planner, Jay, and I talked about my phone relationship. He asked when Greg and I planned to get together.

I answered vaguely, "Someday." I was comfortable with the phone relationship. Even though I'd initiated the contact, I didn't want to face the possibility that Dora was right. Memories were pliable and were often better than reality.

Soon after, though, Jay slapped the tickets for my next business trip on my desk and with a wicked grin told me, "They're non-refundable."

The flight itinerary included an eight-hour layover. In Chicago. Before I could say anything, this office Cupid folded his arms and insisted, "Call that man and tell him to meet you."

I called Greg, trying not to sound like a prepubescent girl with a crush as I told him about my trip. To my relief, he laughed and told me to thank Jay for him.

Then I blurted out, "I'm blond now, and I've put on a few pounds."

He snickered. "That's fine. I look about the same except I've got less hair."

"Okay, neither of us will be surprised." But I knew that descriptions never quite matched reality.

Thankfully, I was very busy and it wasn't difficult to put our meeting out of my mind. Until I stepped on the plane to Chicago. I boarded with an extra carry-on—butterflies in my stomach.

My legs shook as I waited to deplane, and I berated myself for letting this happen. I was going to kill Jay for setting this up.

In those pre-9-11 days, Greg stood waiting at the gate. Our eyes locked as we instantly sized each other up. We both smiled broadly.

He planned the whole day. It was great, but the best was when he took my hand in his as we walked. After dinner, he leaned back in his chair and asked, "Should we give this another try?"

My cheeks ached from grinning. "Definitely."

I'm not sure why, but things were different this time around. As far back as I could remember I was attracted to men who were opposites of me. However, I discovered that these differences made the relationships ultimately impossible. Before, it had irritated me that Greg and I were so similar, Now, I was thrilled to be with someone who understood and liked me for being me. When we were together, I felt cocooned in a warm, familiar place. I didn't think it could get any better. But it did, that July 4th.

I had flown in early that morning and I was tired, so begged off seeing the fireworks that night.

"Come on, you'll miss the best part of the day."

With a soft moan, I gave in and we lugged two lawn chairs up the hill to watch.

As soon as the first glare burst in the sky, I knew he'd been right. The display was spectacular, with its greens, reds, and silvers. I squeezed his hand. "Thanks for talking me into this. I really love fireworks."

He leaned close. "We could have fireworks the rest of our lives if you'll marry me."

The fireworks in the sky dimmed as the stars in my eyes grew brighter.

We've been married for eight years now, and I've learned that sometimes, making new memories is a lot better than polishing old ones. The trick is: you've got to try.

~Carole Fowkes

越坚定不移地聆听内心的声音，就越能听到外在的声音。

——达格哈马

8 年前，我曾将一张纸条夹在一本旧地址簿中，现在它还在那儿。我把它拿出来，铺在大腿上，抚平了上面细小的褶皱。幸运的是，他的电话依稀可辨。至少，这是 10 年前，他在芝加哥的电话号码。现在的我不再犹豫，再不担心因错过一段美好姻缘而把自己逼疯。

脑子飞速地转着，想象着该怎样应对各种突

发状况。如果电话没有接通，我不会再责怪自己没有试着联系他。如果电话换了，我会道歉，然后挂断电话，再不去想。如果接电话的是一个女人，我会默默地挂断，我的达拉斯号码，不会让她感到怀疑。确信自己已经想好了各种应对方法，我微微发抖地拨通了他的电话。

"你好。"电话那头传来一位男性的声音。

天哪！在我所有的设想和计划中，唯独遗漏了他接电话的可能性。我们认识已有15年时间，但是因为我富于幻想的旅行癖，我们已经有8年时间没有联系。

在那一秒钟，我有种想挂掉电话的冲动。懦夫！但是我还是顿了顿，用低哑的声音说："你好，格雷格。"

他平静得就好像我们昨天刚通过电话一样："你好，卡罗尔。"

我的眉毛扬了扬："你的语气一点也不惊讶。"

"我知道总有一天你会打电话给我。"他解释道，就好像昔日恋人突然打电话过来是再平常不过的事情。

我们聊了几分钟。他听起来既愉快又轻松，而我则紧张得满脸是汗。

"卡罗尔，真希望和你多聊会儿，但我正准备出去。"

我完全没意识到打电话的这天是周末。他有约会，我却没有。

我尴尬地回答："哦，对不起，我没想到……"我的声音渐渐弱了下来，不希望自己听起来像个没有约会的失败者。

但他帮我解了围："明天可以给你打电话吗？"

当然！我努力让自己的嗓音低了八度，故作平静地回答："好的。"留下电话号码之后，我挂断电话，感觉自己就像煮久了的意大利面一样。

第二天，我向朋友讲述了发生的一切。

"太刺激了！"我善良的好友辛迪惊呼。

多拉有点愤世嫉俗，可是她一开始并没有发表评论。但从她阴郁的表情，我知道她并不赞同："男人永远不像我们认为的那么好。你不该没事找事儿。"

我耸耸肩，不想被她的愁绪影响。

他信守诺言，果然在当天晚上打来电话。谈话进行得很顺利，然后他提出了那个我没有勇气问他的问题。

"所以……你现在有在交往的人吗？"

我有些支支吾吾："哦，我在同几个家伙约会。"我使劲儿地咽了下口水，努力让声音保持平静："你呢？"

他曾经同别人约会。

我的心猛然一沉。我知道他不会为我痴狂，但至少他还没有订婚。

后来，他又打了一次电话。之后，在没有任何提示的情况下，再也没有打来。我感到失望，虽然很想主动打给他，但是我拒绝这么卑微。

"至少我试过了，"我向辛迪和多拉解释说，"不管怎样，他还在芝加哥，而我在达拉斯。"

多拉不屑地哼了一声。辛迪则满是同情地看着我，那神情就像是我刚刚在事故中失去双臂。

几个月后，我收到了格雷格的留言。他为自己的突然消失向我道歉，希望我能再次打电话给他。

听到留言的我笑得合不拢嘴，但我决定当晚不给他打电话。也该让他尝尝等待的滋味。第二天晚上，我拨通了他的电话，希望自己的兴奋之情不要在电话中表露得过于明显。这次通话是之后频繁通话的开始。这些通话成了我生活中的一大亮点，商务工作的压力也不知不觉地烟消云散。

某天，在办公室工作的时候，我的旅行策划师杰伊同我聊起了这段电话情缘。他问我，打算什么时候同格雷格见面。

我含糊地回答："某天吧。"我对目前的电话联系非常满意。尽管是我主动联系格雷格的，但我并不想面对多拉所说的"记忆往往比现实更加美好"这个事实。

不过，没过多久，杰伊就把下次的商务旅行机票拍在了我桌子上，脸上带着坏坏的表情，告诉我："是不能退签的哦。"

飞行路线包括在芝加哥 8 小时的临时停留。没等我开口，杰伊这个办公室的丘比特怀抱双臂，坚持说道："打电话给他，约他见面。"

我给格雷格打了电话，告诉他我的行程安排。我努力保持镇静，避免自己听起来像个怀抱爱慕的青春期少女。让我宽慰的是，他笑了，并让我替他谢谢杰伊。

然后，我脱口而出："我现在是金色头发，比以前也胖了几磅。"

他窃笑："很好。我和以前差不多，就是头发少了点儿。"

"这就好，我们谁也不会惊讶。"但我知道描述从来和现实不符。

幸运的是，这其间我一直非常忙碌。这让我没有时间担心同格雷格的会面。登上飞往芝加哥航班的我比平日多带了一件行李，那就是心里怦怦乱撞的小鹿。

等待下飞机的那一刻，我的双腿忍不住颤抖。我一方面狠狠责骂自己不争气，另一方面真想杀了安排这一切的杰伊。

"9·11"之前的这天，格雷格站在出口处等我。人群中，我们立刻看到了对方，眼神久久不能分开，脸上都露出了灿烂的笑容。

他安排了整整一天的精彩活动。但是最精彩的部分是我们并肩散步的时候，他牵起了我的手。晚餐后，他斜靠在椅背上，问我："卡罗尔，我们是不是该再试一次？"

我笑得脸颊都疼了："当然。"

不知道为什么，但是这次同以前不一样。以前的我总是被一些性格截然相反的人吸引，但这些不同会让两人关系的维持变得异常艰难。在此之前，格雷格同我如此相似这点，总让我感到恼火。现在，我特别开心能找到一个理解我欣赏我的人。和格雷格在一起的时候，任何地方都变成了温暖又熟悉的场所。我没想到这一切还能更加美好。但是它发生了。7月4日这天，乘飞机清晨到达的我非常疲惫，央求他能不能不去看晚上的烟花表演。

"来吧，要不你会错过今天最精彩的部分。"

温柔地抱怨了一声，我决定让步，搬了两张户外椅坐在山顶上观赏烟花。

当天空出现了第一道炫彩，我就知道格雷格的选择是正确的。红、蓝、银，各色美丽烟花在天空中绽放。我紧紧地握住他的手："谢谢你说服我过来。我真的很喜欢烟花。"

他凑近身来："如果你答应嫁给我的话，我会一辈子给你放烟花。"

天空中的烟花模糊了，我眼中的星却越发明亮。

现在，我和格雷格已经结婚8年。我明白了体验新经历比沉湎于过去的回忆更加美好。诀窍就是：你必须去尝试。

——卡罗尔·福克斯

第四部分 求婚篇

Chapter 4
The Proposal

We love because it is the only true adventure.

~Nikki Giovanni

相爱是人生永恒的历险。

——乔瓦尼

Understanding the Rules of Engagement
求婚条件

It was so much fun, we proposed to each other all day long.

~Melissa Errico

It was a warm May afternoon in Buffalo Grove, Illinois, and my girlfriend Joanna carefully opened the presents that were on her lap. All eyes were on her…after all, it was *her* birthday party. Unfortunately, I wasn't able to be with her on this day because I was deployed to Afghanistan with the United States Army. But even though I wasn't present, many other loved ones were, including Joanna's best friend who flew in from Arizona and my best friend, Matt. In fact, it was Matt who had really orchestrated the gathering: months ago, he suggested that the group should throw Joanna a birthday party this year to cheer her up; to let her know that even though I wasn't with her, she wasn't forgotten. And thus came about Joanna's birthday.

Joanna finished opening the last present and got ready to thank everyone for the gifts, but not before

Matt approached her with a card in his hand. He offered it to Joanna, explaining that I had sent it to him to give to Joanna at her birthday party. Intrigued, Joanna opened the card.

Joanna, I know I already gave you presents for your birthday, but I didn't want to leave you empty-handed at your party... which is why you need to report directly to the secret hiding spot. Love, the Boy Toy

Joanna knew exactly what hiding spot my card was referring to. There was a spot in her house where I had hidden countless presents before: it was a small closet on the top floor in her house, just across from the guest bedroom. So, Joanna marched herself upstairs to see what the closet held.

In the closet, Joanna found a DVD waiting for her. It had implicit instructions to be immediately viewed, so Joanna popped in the DVD for everyone to see.

The DVD was a short video: the setting was the chapel in Gardez, Afghanistan, which was the chapel that I worked in as a chaplain assistant. Just a few seconds into the video, there was footage of me walking through the chapel door and strolling up to the camera to hold up a sign.

You have a surprise waiting for you in the spot we first met. Go get it before someone walks off with it! Bring everyone along.

Joanna knew instantly the "spot" that the video was referring to: it was the playground of Joyce Kilmer Elementary School. Not only is that where we first met in the sense that we went to kindergarten together there, it was also the spot that we decided to officially meet each other as adults in February 2006 when we were reunited by a series of very unusual events.

Within minutes, everyone found a car to jump into, and a convoy was headed to Joyce Kilmer for whatever it had in store for Joanna.

Everyone parked in the school parking lot and started speculating: "Isn't today a school day?" "What could be hiding on the playground?" "What if we misunderstood the DVD?" "What do you think this could be about?"

Within moments, these questions were answered for everyone. As Joanna walked up to the playground, she immediately saw and recognized what the surprise was for her on that warm day. On one of the playground's slides was the bright silhouette of a uniformed soldier.

In disbelief, Joanna neared the slide as my silhouette began to move. I slid down the slide, as I had done with Joanna so many years ago on that same playground when we were children. I emerged at the base of the slide and walked up to give a hug to a very weepy Joanna.

Joanna didn't say a word and simply dug her fingers into my side and cried her tears on my shoulder. I gently whispered in her ear, "I love you."

Shock began to set in for everyone else. They were personally witnessing the presence of a deployed soldier hugging his girlfriend on the playground, and yet it seemed all too surreal to be authentic. All of a sudden, I was no longer in the middle of a war; instead, I was in the flesh and blood right before them. It seemed a fantasy—a fairy tale too good to be true.

I gave a round of teary-eyed hugs and then began to explain the circumstances of the day: I had been given fifteen days of mid-tour leave, which is how I found myself before my loved ones on this day. Slowly, things began to make sense for those still seeking clarification of the situation.

To even further enhance the surprise for Joanna and me, our old elementary school faculty members emerged from the school to witness the event. They were our original teachers and principal who had guided us so many years ago, and now they were gathered again to see us through on such a joyous event.

But that wasn't all. I began to reason aloud that I had originally thought this opportunity would be a great time to formally propose to Joanna, but I had instead made a promise to her a long time ago that I would only propose after two conditions had been met: one, I had to be physically present for the proposal (which, in this rare case, was a standard that was met), and two, I would have asked my future father-in-law, Chuck, for his blessing of the marriage.

At that moment, when I announced the stipulations for such a proposal, Chuck knew something that the others didn't: I *had* already gotten his blessing last Thanksgiving, during a four-day pass home just before I deployed. And so, it came as no surprise to Chuck when I looked into Joanna's eyes, got on one knee directly before her, and pulled a diamond ring out of my pocket and uttered the words, "Will you marry me?"

Joanna's eyes swelled with tears, barely able to muster a "Yes." And in the sight of our loving family and loyal friends, in the sight of our first teachers and beloved principal, and, most importantly, in the sight of God, we became a couple engaged to be married in the near future to live a life of love and joyfulness.

I slipped the engagement ring onto the finger of my fiancée, and then the two of us began hugging each other once again, holding onto each other for dear life as if this would be the last time we'd ever see each other again. But in fact, this was only the beginning of a life in which we would be with each other forever more.

Only, unlike every other moment up to this point where we saw each other as boyfriend/girlfriend, we would soon be seeing each other as husband/wife.

~Sgt. Nate Danger Geist

真有趣，我们一整天都在向对方求婚。

——梅丽莎·埃里克

　　一个温暖的五月下午，伊利诺伊州的布法罗市，女友乔安娜正小心翼翼地拆开膝盖上的礼物。所有人的目光都聚集在她身上……毕竟，这是她的生日派对。不幸的是，我被派往阿富汗随美军驻扎，没办法陪她。虽然我不在场，但有很多关心乔安娜的人来参加她的生日派对，其中包括从亚利桑那州特意飞来的乔安娜的好友，还有我最好的朋友马特。事实上，正是马特提议并策划了这次派对。几个月前，马特建议为乔安娜办一个生日派对，让她高兴起来。让她了解到，即便我不在，还有其他人关心着她。所以才有了这个派对。

　　正当乔安娜拆开最后一份礼物，准备感谢大家时，马特递给了她一张卡片，并解释说，这是我临走之前特意让他转交的。出于好奇，乔安娜打开了卡片。

　　乔安娜，我知道已经送过你生日礼物，但我不想让你在生日派对上两手空空……这就是为什么你需要立刻赶到藏宝地点。爱你的，内特。

　　乔安娜知道我所说的藏宝地点，那是我之前藏过无数礼物的地方。就是她家顶楼的一个小衣柜，就在客房对面。乔安娜依照指示上楼，看衣柜里藏了什么。

一盘 DVD 在等着她，上面含蓄地建议立即打开。所以，乔安娜把它放进了播放机，和大家一起观看。

DVD 是一个简短的视频：场景是阿富汗东部城市加德兹的一个教堂，我在这里做牧师助理。视频只有短短几十秒，我穿过教堂，来到镜头前，举起一个标志，上面写着：

在我们初次相遇的地方有一个惊喜在等着你。在别人拿走之前赶快过去吧，记得带上大家！

乔安娜知道"相遇地点"指的是乔伊斯·基尔默小学的操场。那儿不仅是我们上幼儿园的地方，也是我们 2006 年 2 月决定正式交往的地方。当时的我们被一系列不寻常的事情带到了一起。

几分钟内，每个人都跳上车，浩浩荡荡地开往乔伊斯·基尔默小学，期待着我为乔安娜准备的惊喜。

车在学校停车场停好后，大家忍不住猜测：今天不是教学日吗？操场上能藏什么呢？我们是不是误解了 DVD 的意思？你觉得会是什么？

别着急，答案马上揭晓。当乔安娜来到操场，她立刻认出了那份惊喜。温暖的天气里，操场滑梯旁是穿制服的士兵塑像。

心里正在打鼓的乔安娜慢慢走近，此时塑像开始移动。我从滑梯上滑下来，就像我和乔安娜小时候玩的那样。这时候，乔安娜已经眼泪汪汪。我从滑梯上站起，走过去给了她一个拥抱。

乔安娜没说话，只是靠在我身边，默默流泪。我在她耳边轻声低语："我爱你。"

在场的每个人都感到震惊。他们都看到了一个原本该在阿富汗的士兵，现在却在操场上拥抱女友。一瞬间，我从战火纷飞的前线来到他们面前。太超现实主义了，简直难以置信。这似乎像个幻想，像个太美好而让人难以相信的童话。

我拥抱了在场的每一个人。之后，我开始解释这一切：我在这月中旬有一个 15 天的休假，这也是我能来到乔安娜身边的原因。慢慢的，迷惑不解的他们开始明白这究竟是怎么一回事。

更让我和乔安娜惊讶的是，小学的全体教职工都出来见证这一幕的发生。他们是多年前教过我们的校长和老师。现在，他们再次聚在一起，见证我和乔安娜的爱情。

但是这还不是全部。我本来想在这样的场合向乔安娜求婚是再合适不过了。但是，我在很久之前曾经答应她，只有在满足以下两个条件时才会正式向她求婚：第一，我本人要在场（这次难得符合）。第二，我要得到未来岳父大人查克的祝福。

当我向大家讲述求婚规则的时候，查克知道一些别人不晓得的事：上个感恩节，在我被派遣之前的 4 天假期里，我已经得到了他对婚姻的祝福。所以，当我望着乔安娜，单膝下跪，从口袋里拿出一枚钻戒，问："你愿意嫁给我吗？"查克并不惊讶。

乔安娜眼中盈满了泪水，只能含糊地说着"我愿意"。在亲爱的家人、忠实的朋友，还有曾经的教师、尊敬的校长，最重要的是，在上帝的见证下，我和乔安娜订婚了。不久的将来，我们会结婚，过着幸福美满的生活。

我将订婚戒指戴在未婚妻手上。我们再次紧紧相拥，仿佛这是我们最后一次见到对方。但事实上，这只是我们共同生活的开端。

和以前不同的是，我们不再将对方看做男女朋友，而是未来的丈夫和妻子。

——内特·丹哲·盖斯特中士

"I'd marry you even if you were a mirage!"

"我会娶你的，即便你只是一个幻影！"

Love or Success?

爱情还是成功?

The loving are the daring.

~Bayard Taylor

Buenos Aires is famous for its magnificent European architecture, its exceptional Malbec wines, and its status as the birthplace of the tango. But the city's most distinctive characteristic is its people, who have an unrivaled passion for living life to the fullest, evident in their spirited three-hour conversations over dinner, the nightlife that starts at 2:00 A.M., and the couples sharing a kiss on any street corner or park bench.

It was on a humid April evening in this Latin capital that I first laid eyes on Natalia, a tall, olive-skinned brunette whose appetite for life was exceptional, even by Buenos Aires standards. When I saw her across the dance floor, she hypnotized me with her brown eyes, silky shoulder-length hair, and full lips framing the most lovely smile I'd ever seen. She glanced my way and our eyes made contact, just

---

for a brief, intense moment. She had a confident air that both drew me to her and gave me butterflies in my stomach.

Overcoming my natural shyness, I approached her and we talked. Despite my limited Spanish, she patiently conversed with me as if I spoke fluently. I explained that I was an American studying abroad and she said she was a student at the local university. We talked and danced well into early morning.

Our conversation continued the next day, and the day after that. And within a week, I was hopelessly falling for her. We spent every waking moment together, exploring the city and losing ourselves in conversation, often finding ourselves sharing a kiss, as the Argentine tradition goes, wherever the urge arose.

Then, one afternoon, Natalia broached the taboo topic we had avoided discussing for two months. My time in Argentina was almost up, and I had to return to college in the U.S.

"What do you want to do about us?" she asked, looking me in the eyes and trying to see the answer in my face. "Since you're going back to your country in a few days, do you think it's worth it to stay together?"

"Of course," I said without hesitation. "We'll make it work." I took her hands in mine. "It's too early to give up on us. I'm too in love with you. I'm not ready to say goodbye. If it is meant to be, it will work out, no matter how far apart we are."

Despite my confident words, I was just as scared and uncertain as she was. I didn't know when or if I'd ever return to Argentina. But we were young and in love, and we listened to our hearts. We decided to go for it. And we sealed the deal with a kiss.

Over the next several months, we spoke every day on the telephone. Weeks flew by, then months. Each afternoon, I called to share my day with her, and she called every evening to say "buenas noches". Her sweet voice put a smile on my face every time she answered the phone. Aside from the 7,000 miles between us, we had a pretty enviable relationship.

But after a year and a half, the separation was wearing us down. We were both tired of the lack of intimacy, the dinners alone, the increasing questions from our concerned friends and families.

"When will we be together?" Natalia began asking with increasing frequency. "I don't know how much longer I can wait..."

For the first time, I felt I might lose her. The "I love you" and "I miss you" that had been so frequent in earlier conversations became "How much longer?" and "When will I see you?"

As a result, I found myself faced with one of the most difficult decisions of my life.

It was my senior year of college, still seven months from graduation, and I was determined to get into law school. I had sacrificed for years in pursuit of that goal. While my classmates socialized, I studied. And my sacrifice had paid off; I carried a 4.0 grade point average. At that point, I was just two weeks away from my next final exams, which would be crucial to my law school applications.

But I could feel Natalia and I slipping apart. I knew if I didn't see her immediately, our love would fizzle out. And I could lose her forever.

While studying one evening, I asked myself whether I should stay and study, or whether I should go to Natalia. Success or love? If I stayed, I could finish up another perfect semester. If I left, I might save our relationship and have a chance to build a future with Natalia.

The answer was easy. I dropped the textbook I had been reading and hurried to my computer. Within five minutes, I had purchased a ticket to Buenos Aires.

Two days later, unbeknownst to Natalia, I made the twenty-hour trip to Buenos Aires. When I arrived, Natalia was at work. I asked Deby, a friend of

Natalia's, to help me organize an unforgettable evening for Natalia, and she agreed.

That evening, Deby and some other girlfriends took Natalia to a Mexican restaurant where she and I had shared a romantic evening. I waited outside the restaurant, nervously rehearsing what I would say. My heart raced and I was shaking, a million thoughts running through my head. After so much time, would it be like before? What if she had changed? What if I had changed? It had been a year and a half, and I had just come halfway around the world to surprise her. Was I crazy?

After a few minutes, as planned, mariachis approached Natalia and began serenading her with a famous ballad that says "señorita, I'll give my heart to you…" but they replaced the word "señorita" with "Natalia." Hearing her name caught her off guard, and she looked up at the mariachis, wondering if it had been her imagination. Then they sang the chorus again, "Natalia, I'll give my heart to you…" Natalia couldn't believe her ears. She looked at Deby, searching for a clue as to what was going on.

At that moment, I walked over to her with a dozen red roses, handing them to her as she looked at me wide-eyed and speechless. I took her left hand in mine and got down on one knee. "Natalia, you are the love of my life," I told her. "My feelings for you have grown stronger every day we've been apart. I'm tired of missing you and I want to spend the rest of my life with you. Will you marry me?"

She took a deep breath, her eyes tearing, her hand trembling slightly. And with one word, she erased the doubt, the fears, and the questions, she closed the distance between us and made the eternity we'd spent apart a distant memory.

She said "yes".

~Wes Henricksen

Editor's note: Although Mr. Henricksen's grades dropped slightly and he lost his 4.0 GPA on account of his spontaneous flight to Argentina, he was nonetheless accepted to law school and is today a practicing attorney in southern California. He and Natalia are very happily married.

敢爱的人最勇敢。

——贝亚德·泰勒

布宜诺斯艾利斯以宏伟的欧式建筑、独特的马尔贝克葡萄酒，以及探戈的发源地闻名于世。但是这个城市最大的特点在于这里的居民。对生活，他们总抱有无与伦比的热情：晚餐结束后能兴致勃勃地谈论三小时；凌晨两点之后夜生活才算真正开始；街角或者公园长椅上随处可见热烈拥吻的恋人。

四月一个闷热的傍晚，在这个有着浓郁拉丁风情的城市，我第一次遇到纳塔利娅——身材高挑、有着橄榄色皮肤的黑发女子。即便用布宜诺斯艾利斯的标准衡量，她也显得格外出色。棕色眼睛，齐肩顺滑的头发，饱满的双唇绽放着世上最动人的微笑，她穿过舞池的样子，让我深深迷醉。她朝这边看了一眼，只短短的一瞬，我们的目光相遇。我被她的自信深深吸引，心在怦怦乱跳。

害羞的我鼓起勇气走到她身边，同她交谈。

尽管我的西班牙语非常蹩脚,但她还是耐心地同我交谈。我告诉她我是到这边留学的美国学生,她回答说她也在当地一所大学读书。我们愉快地跳舞、聊天,直到次日清晨。

之后几天,我们一直保持联系。不到一周时间,我发现自己已经无可救药地爱上了她。我们一起度过醒来的每一个时刻,在城市里散步,入神地聊天,像阿根廷传统一样不分时间、地点和场合,情不自禁地亲吻。

然后,某个下午,纳塔利娅提出了这两个月来我们一直回避的问题。因为我在阿根廷的学习基本结束,必须返回美国的学校。

"你对我们的未来是怎么打算的?"她望着我的眼睛,希望从中找到答案,"再过几天,你就回美国了,我们以后会在一起吗?"

"当然会,"我毫不犹豫地回答,"我们会走到最后的。"我紧紧握住她的手:"现在放弃我们的感情还太早。我那么爱你,不打算和你说再见。如果我们注定是彼此的另一半,那么无论相隔多远,我们都会在一起。"

尽管听起来信心十足,但实际上,我和纳塔利娅一样感到害怕和不确定。我不知道何时能重返阿根廷,甚至怀疑以后再没有机会过来。但那时候年轻的我们沉浸在爱河中,我们决定听从自己的心意,用一个吻订立誓言。

接下来的几个月,我们每天通电话。几周过去了,几个月过去了。每天下午,我都会给纳塔利娅打电话,同她分享我的一天。每天晚上,她也会打给我,用西班牙语对我说"晚安"。每次听到她甜美的声音,我的脸上总会绽放笑容。尽管我们相隔一万多公里,但我们的感情却甜蜜得让人羡慕。

一年半以后,这种分离让我们疲惫不堪。纳塔利娅和我已经厌倦了亲密缺失、独自晚餐,还有父母和朋友越来越多的质疑。

"我们什么时候能在一起？"纳塔利娅问，类似问题出现的次数越来越多，"我不知道自己还可以等多久。"

我第一次觉得有可能失去她。以前对话中频繁出现的"我爱你""思念你"变成了"还要多久？""什么时候可以见到你？"

因此，我发现自己正面临着人生中最重要的抉择——成功还是爱情？

大四的我，距离毕业还有7个月时间。我的目标是进入法学院继续深造。多年来，我一直为此努力。同学出去玩的时候，我坚持学习。我的牺牲没有白费，拿到了4.0的平均绩点。所以，两周后最后一次期末考试对我法学院的申请至关重要。

但我能感觉到我和纳塔利娅渐行渐远。如果不立刻见她，我很可能会永远失去她。

一天晚上，在学习的时候，我问自己是应该继续留在这儿学习呢，还是应该去见纳塔利娅？选成功，还是爱情呢？如果留在这儿，我会完成另一个完美的学期。如果离开，则可能挽救我们的爱情，或许能和纳塔利娅走到最后。

答案很简单。我丢下正在看的教科书，跑到电脑前。用不到5分钟的时间，订好了一张飞往布宜诺斯艾利斯的机票。

两天后，在没有告诉纳塔利娅的情况下，我坐了20小时的飞机赶到布宜诺斯艾利斯。那时，纳塔利娅正在工作。我请求她的好友黛比帮我为纳塔利娅策划一个难忘的夜晚。黛比答应了。

当天晚上，黛比和其他一些女性朋友带着纳塔利娅来到一家墨西哥餐厅。我和纳塔利娅曾在这里度过了一个浪漫的夜晚。在餐厅门外等待的我，紧张地排练着一会儿要说的话。我浑身发抖，心怦怦乱跳，脑子里闪过无数个念头。这么长时间没见，我们还能像以前一样吗？如果她变了呢？如果我变了呢？一年半以后，我突然飞越了大半个地球只为给她一个惊喜，我疯了吗？

几分钟后，按原定计划，墨西哥流浪乐队来到纳塔利娅身边，为她唱响那首著名的小夜曲："迷人的小姐，我愿将自己的心献给你……"但是他们将歌词换成了"纳塔利娅，我愿将自己的心献给你……"猝不及防地听到自己的名字，纳塔利娅抬起头看着流浪乐队，想确定是不是自己的幻觉。然后，大合唱再次响起："纳塔利娅，我愿将自己的心献给你……"纳塔利亚困惑地转向黛比，希望弄清楚到底发生了什么。

那一刻，我捧着12朵玫瑰走了进来。纳塔利娅睁大眼睛望着我，激动得说不出话。我握住她的左手，单膝跪下："纳塔利娅，我此生的挚爱，分离的那段时光更让我明白了自己对你的爱。我已经厌倦了无休止的思念，想同你共度一生。嫁给我，好吗？"

她深吸了一口气，眼泪止不住地滴落，双手微微颤抖。只一个字，她抹去了所有困惑、担心和怀疑，结束了我们之间的距离，让那段分离的日子成了遥远的回忆。

她回答说："好。"

——韦斯·亨里克森

编者注： 由于亨里克森突然飞往阿根廷，他的成绩有所下降，失去了4.0的平均绩点。但他还是成功地被一所法学院录取。现在，他是南加州的一名职业律师，同纳塔利娅幸福地生活在一起。

Perfect Timing
完美时刻

Love is the greatest refreshment in life.

~Pablo Picasso

I wriggled out of my underwear underneath my ankle-length skirt and slipped on my shorts. In one decisive move, I undid the knot that held the skirt wrapped around my waist, and let the long, hot fabric drop to the ground. My boyfriend and I had been cycling for nearly a month in Morocco, I usually kept my skin covered out of respect for the Muslim culture.

We had decided to take this detour to Africa halfway through our six-month bicycle trip in Europe. Now I wished we hadn't come here. Bob and I had been dating for five years, and we'd joked that we'd either come back from the trip engaged, or on separate planes. It didn't seem very funny any more.

Wearing just my running shorts and a T-shirt, I felt practically naked. All day, we'd been riding east along the Route des Kasbahs through a broad, flat valley bordered on our left by the Atlas Mountains. As we peddled through miles of empty desert, I thought about just one thing: ice-cold watermelon. It was my birthday, and since we were in the middle of the desert, I knew there would be no fancy dinner and no celebratory alcoholic beverages. But there could be watermelon.

I told Bob my fantasy. As I set up our tent in the garden at the youth hostel in Goulmima, Bob had walked to the market down the street to get a watermelon. A group of men sat in the shade in front of the hostel, talking and drinking sweet mint tea. I had wanted to sit in the garden under the apricot and pomegranate trees, split the watermelon in half, and eat until all that was left was the empty, green bowl of the rind.

Bob had returned, cradling a large watermelon like a baby. In a friendly gesture, he had offered to share the watermelon with the men at the hostel. I, however, wasn't going to budge. As Bob walked back to the men, he promised to bring me a slice of watermelon. I sat in the garden, fuming. Bob didn't come back. Finally, I walked over to the house and saw the men eating watermelon. My watermelon.

"Thanks for bringing me some watermelon," I had snapped at Bob. I was so angry I was shaking. Bob looked at me, startled. This wasn't like me.

I'd been struggling with how to maintain my sense of identity on our trip. The clothing was just the beginning. My relationship with Bob had changed. Public displays of affection—holding hands and kissing, but also the casual touch on the arm—were taboo, and after trying so hard to remember these new rules all day, at night when we were alone in our tent, we forgot to fall back into our old, affectionate habits. But mostly, I hated that we had to call each other husband and wife to appear proper, because I wasn't his wife. And I wanted to be, more than anything.

Suddenly, I felt trapped in the walled compound of the youth hostel. If I couldn't have my watermelon, I was going to give myself something I'd wanted for a long time. And that was when I stripped down to my running shorts.

"I'm going for a run. Alone." I told Bob.

"Be careful!" he called as I turned to leave.

Outside the gate, I looked right, the direction we had come from, and turned left down the dusty street. I'd been a faithful runner for years, but had given it up after a painful marathon. As I started running, it felt like being reacquainted with a lover after a long absence—I remembered how good it used to be, but now it was just awkward. My stride was stiff, and I could feel pebbles through the worn-down soles of my shoes. The wind was blowing dust so thick that I closed my eyes and held my breath as I ran through a tunnel. On the other side, I opened my eyes to see people filling the narrow street.

"Ça va bien?" people called out to me.

Nodding, I replied tersely, "Oui, ça va bien." It's going very well.

It was true. My stride wasn't smooth, and I was breathing hard, but it felt good to run. My feet kicked up puffs of dust as I ran past boys playing soccer and girls filling plastic jugs at a well. Soon, my body took over and I found my rhythm. Running was as easy as breathing when everything's right in the world. As my pace slowed to a walk, I realized it had been a long time since I'd felt at peace with myself.

My anger about the watermelon had been hiding something else: a hurt that sat like a hard lump in my throat. I had thought Bob was waiting for the perfect opportunity to ask me to marry him. But maybe it wasn't about the perfect opportunity. The truth was, I probably wanted more from Bob than he might be able to give me.

I turned around and headed back to the hostel. I wanted to go back and tell Bob about the kasbah I ran past in town. Most evenings we'd sit outside our tent in the dark, drinking tea and talking. But after taking so many turns on my run through town, I wasn't sure how far it was back to the hostel. My mouth was chalky dry, and I regretted leaving my water bottle behind. At the edge of town, when I looked up to see Bob walking towards me, carrying a bottle of water, I almost didn't believe it could be him.

"I'm sorry," he said, and handed me the water. I took a long drink. "Here's your birthday present." He handed me a Picasso postcard from a museum in Madrid we'd been to more than a month ago. On the back of the postcard, he asked me to marry him.

"How did you find me?" I asked.

"I just knew," he said. "I walked out of the hostel and I asked myself which way you would go, and I knew that if I just kept going, I'd find you."

I looked down at the card. Bob always knew when to keep me company and when to let me go on my own, like when he helped me train for the London marathon, and then waited for three months for me to come back from Europe.

"You don't have to answer now, if you don't want," Bob told me.

It was the worst time for a proposal. We'd just had a fight and I was covered in dirt. There was no ring. Instead, he brought me a bottle of water because he knew I'd be thirsty. He followed his heart to find me, and I realized that's all I needed.

"Of course! Of course I'll marry you!" I told him. A group of twelve-year-old girls were watching us nearby, and to their delight, Bob gave me a brief hug. We held hands for a moment, and the girls covered their mouths and giggled as we walk side-by-side back to the hostel.

That night, we sat outside our tent, eating watermelon and spitting seeds into the garden. When you just know, you don't have to wait for the perfect time to ask.

~Jennifer Colvin

爱是生活最好的提神剂。

——毕加索

　　我扭动腰身，褪下及踝长裙里的内衣，换上了好穿的短裤。这一刻，我作出了一个重要决定，我解开了系在腰间的结，任由这身又热又长的袍子滑落地面。我和男友已经在摩洛哥骑车转了一个多月。为了尊重当地穆斯林的文化习俗，我尽量包裹得严严实实。

　　为期 6 个月的欧洲自行车之旅中，我们中途决定改道非洲。现在，我真希望我们没有那么做。鲍伯和我已经交往 5 年。我们曾开玩笑说，这次旅行结束后我们要么订婚，要么就各自搭飞机回来。旅程已经不像开始时那么有趣。

　　穿着 T 恤和运动短裤的我，感觉就像赤身裸体。阿特拉斯山脉右侧是广阔平坦的山谷，我们一整天都在沿着代斯卡斯巴路线骑行。穿过数英里空荡荡的沙漠后，我脑子里只有一件事：冰镇西瓜。今天是我的生日。因为在沙漠中，所以我不奢望华丽的晚宴、庆祝的酒水，但是西瓜应该可以。

　　我告诉鲍伯我的愿望。之后，他走到街角市

场买西瓜，我在古勒米迈一家青年旅馆的花园里搭帐篷。旅馆门前的树荫下，一些男人喝着清甜的薄荷茶，闲坐着聊天。而我则期待着一会儿坐在花园杏树、石榴树的凉荫下，剖开西瓜尽情地吃，直到只剩翠绿的瓜皮。

鲍伯回来了，怀里抱着一个婴儿般大小的西瓜。出于友好，他提议分些西瓜给旅馆的其他客人。我也不打算阻止他。朝那些男人走去的时候，鲍伯对我保证，会带块儿西瓜给我。但很久后，还不见鲍伯回来。我坐在园子里干生气。最后，终于决定出去找他。只见他们正酣畅淋漓地吃着西瓜，我的西瓜。

"谢谢你给我带的西瓜。"我气得浑身发抖，对鲍伯怒吼。他吃惊地看着我，这和平日的我太不一样。

旅行途中，我一直在努力寻找自己的定位。衣服只是个开始。我和鲍伯的关系也发生了改变。公开表露感情——牵手、亲吻，甚至偶尔的胳膊触碰，也成了禁忌。白天努力适应这些规则后，夜间独处的我们也忘记了往昔深情亲密的旧习惯。但最让我在意的是我们不得不以夫妇相称。因为只有这样，我们的关系才算合乎道德。但事实上，我并不是他的妻子，尽管再渴望不过。

突然间，我觉得自己仿佛被围困在青年旅馆的牢笼中。如果吃不到西瓜，我应该送自己一份渴望已久的礼物。这就有了我脱下长袍，换上运动短裤的那一幕。

"我要去跑步，一个人！"我告诉鲍伯。

"小心点儿！"他在我身后喊。

大门外，右边是我们来时的路，所以我沿着尘土飞扬的街道向左跑去。一直以来，我都是一名忠实的跑步爱好者。但一次痛苦的马拉松比

最初的你，最后的爱 True Love I

赛后，我不得不放弃了这项运动。刚开始跑步的感觉，像极了再次遇到旧日情人——过去那么美好，现在却只剩尴尬。我步伐僵硬，磨破的鞋底甚至能感受到路面上硌脚的石子儿。穿过隧道时，风扬起了厚重的沙尘，我不得不闭上眼睛，屏住呼吸。过去之后，我睁开眼睛，狭窄的街道上人头攒动。

"你好！"热情的人们用法语向我打招呼。

我冲他们点点头，简洁地回答："谢谢，很好。"我确实感觉不错。

尽管步伐僵硬，呼吸急促，但跑步的感觉真的很好。我经过踢足球的男孩儿，经过井边用塑料壶灌水的女孩儿，身后腾起一缕微尘。很快，身体适应了，我找到了自己的节奏。当一切正确时，跑步变得像呼吸一样简单。随着渐渐放慢的步伐，我找到了内心久违的平和。

我忽然意识到自己并不是因为西瓜生气：一直以来，我都认为鲍伯在等待一个完美的时刻向我求婚。但事实上，我的某些要求他做不到。这像个硬块一样哽在我的喉咙，让我异常难受。

我转身朝旅馆走去。我想回去告诉鲍伯这一路上的见闻。大多数的夜晚，我们都会坐在帐篷外，享受夜色，边喝茶边聊天。但是，在转过这么多弯后，我已经找不到回去的路。加上跑了这么久，我的嗓子干得冒烟，真后悔没带瓶水过来。忽然，在小镇边缘，我看到了鲍伯的身影，他手里拿着一瓶水朝我走来。那一刻，我简直不敢相信自己的眼睛。

他边递给我水，边向我道歉："对不起。"我大口地喝着水，缓解干渴。"这是你的生日礼物。"说着，他递给我一张几个月前我们在马德里一家博物馆买来的毕加索明信片，背面写着：嫁给我好吗？

"你是怎么找到我的？"我问。

"我只是知道，"他回答，"出来的时候，我问自己，要是我是你的话会去哪边。我知道只要我一直走，就一定能找到你。"

我低头看着明信片。鲍伯总知道什么时候该陪着我，什么时候该让我一个人静静，就像他陪我准备伦敦马拉松比赛，又耐心地等了 3 个月，等我从欧洲回来。

"如果你不愿意的话，可以先不回答。"鲍伯说。

这真不是求婚的好时候。我们刚刚吵过架，现在的我又是一身泥。也没有订婚戒指，相反，因为知道我会口渴，他给我带了一瓶水。但我知道，这正是我需要的。

"当然！我当然想嫁给你！"我连忙回答。一群 12 岁左右的女孩在旁边看着我们，为了满足她们，鲍伯给了我一个简单的拥抱。当我们手牵手朝旅馆走去的时候，她们在身后用手捂着嘴咯咯地笑。

那天晚上，我们坐在帐篷外，开心地吃着西瓜，吐着籽儿。当你意识到对方是合适人选的时候，你并不需要等待一个完美的时刻才能求婚。

——珍妮弗·科尔文

Who Are You?
你叫什么?

I would say, "Yes," if he asked.

I felt sure he would ask, but how long would I have to wait?

Steven was careful in every decision. He researched and planned. What plans was he or wasn't he making?

It wouldn't be the first marriage for either of us. In fact, both of our spouses had died from accidents in our sixteenth year of marriage when they were each thirty-six years old, and we both had two children just entering their teens when we became single parents. We discovered this extraordinary coincidence as we chatted after a concert at our church one Sunday night.

Now, it was a year later. We just left a citywide prayer service asking God to bless us with rain because the drought was becoming severe. Steven had asked me to share the sunset with him at our park.

We sat in the dark a while after the sunset, savoring the cool night air, enjoying the stars and each other.

Steven got up from the lawn chair. I wasn't sure if it was time to go. But then he knelt down on one knee, took out a tiny box, opened it and said, "Sheila Dianne, will you marry me?"

I was totally confused. Of course I wanted to marry him, but he used my middle name. I wanted to respond in the same way he asked me; I want to say Steven (whatever ???). I realized I didn't know his middle name. Why couldn't I remember it? How could I marry a man when I didn't even know the simplest thing about him like his middle name?

"Sheila? Will you marry me?" Now he sounded concerned. I had hesitated too long. It was not the time to admit I didn't know his full name. I would just have to figure it out somehow. I'd look at his driver's license or something.

"Yes, oh, yes. I will marry you Steven."

I threw my arms around him and we kissed. Then he slipped the simple but elegant ring on my finger. I was amazed it fit perfectly.

He told me, "I measured it against a ring I saw at your house. It was a choice between two rings but this one looks more like you—simple and beautiful."

We had just turned the corner to exit the park when I remembered. I did know his middle name. Of course, I knew his middle name! I couldn't suppress a giggle.

He looked over with the one eyebrow raised, "Are you going to share the fun?" he asked.

I was caught.

Now laughing full out I said, "I do know your middle name. I always knew your middle name. It's Steven. It's your first name I couldn't remember!

You are Frederic Steven Kale."

"Yeah?"

I explained why I hesitated when he asked me to marry him. We both laughed. Especially as he recounted, "One of the first times I talked with you I asked for your vote on whether I should go by my first name. Remember? I had just moved here. Since I moved to Fredericksburg, I wondered if I should be known as Frederic from Fredericksburg. You and almost everybody else agreed I didn't 'look' like a Frederic."

Steven loves to tease me about how I made him ask me twice.

Recently we laughed again with each other as we shared the story while getting acquainted with a new friend over dinner.

She looked stunned. "Two nights ago I had an awful fight with my fiancé because I thought he didn't care enough to remember my middle name." Looking down at the table, she said, "Maybe it isn't that big a deal. Maybe other things are a lot more important."

~Sheila Sattler Kale

茫茫人海中，你一定能辨别出心爱的王子。因为当你遇到他的那一刻，不仅脸上露出微笑，连心灵也会绽放出幸福。

——逸名

如果他向我求婚，我一定答应。

我知道他一定会向我求婚，只是究竟还要等多久呢？

史蒂文总是谨慎地决定每件事情。作决定前，他会先研究，先计划。他有没有不计划的计划

Chapter 4 The Proposal
第四部分 求婚篇

呢？呵呵。

我们之前都结过婚。更准确地说，他和我都在 36 岁，也是结婚第 16 个年头，意外地失去了配偶；都有两个孩子，在他们步入青春期的时候，他和我成了单身父母。一个周日晚上，教堂音乐会结束后，我和他在闲聊时，发现了上述的巧合。

现在，已经一年之后。因为干旱十分严重，有关人员组织了一场全市范围的祈祷，请求上帝赐福降雨。活动结束后，史蒂文要我陪他在花园里坐一会儿，欣赏日落。

日落后，我们又坐了一会儿，享受着美丽的夜色，清爽的夜风，闪烁的繁星，还有彼此的陪伴。

忽然，史蒂文从躺椅上起来。我还以为他打算离开。但随后，他却单膝跪了下来，从口袋里掏出一个小盒子，打开后问我说："希拉·戴安妮，你愿意嫁给我吗？"

刹那间，我整个人都蒙了。当然，我当然愿意嫁给他。但他用了我的中名，我也想用同样的方式回答他。我想回答说"什么什么史蒂文，我愿意嫁给你"，问题是我不知道他的中名。我怎么会忘记呢？若是连他名字都记不得的话，我怎么能嫁给他呢？

"希拉，你愿意嫁给我吗？"他听起来很急切。我犹豫了太长时间。但现在不是反思的时候，我以后会想办法弄明白的，比如看看他的驾照或者其他证件。

"哦，愿意，愿意，我愿意嫁给你，史蒂文。"

我抱住他，深情拥吻。之后，他帮我戴上了那枚简单却大方的戒指。我很惊讶，戒指不大不小，正好合适。

他告诉我，前些天，他比照着我的一个旧戒指量了一下。有两枚都很合适，但是这个看起来更适合我——简单而优雅。

正当我们转过弯，走出公园的时候，我想起来了。我的确知道他的中名。当然，我一直都知道。我忍不住咯咯地笑了。

他眉毛微挑，好奇地问："有什么趣事吗？"

被逮到了。

笑够了之后，我告诉他："我知道你的中名，我一直都知道。我忘的是你的名字！你叫弗雷德里克·史蒂文·卡尔。"

"这和你笑有什么关系？"

我向他解释了求婚时犹豫的原因。我们都笑了。他问我："你记不记得刚搬来的时候问过你，我是不是要用弗雷德里克这个名字，我是不是应该向别人介绍说，我是来自弗雷德里克镇的弗雷德里克。你，包括其他人都认为我看起来一点也不像弗雷德里克。"

史蒂文至今还拿这件事开玩笑。

前些天，在和一位新朋友共进晚餐的时候，我们向她讲述了这个故事。

她听了之后非常惊讶。她说："两天前，因为未婚夫不记得我的中名，我们刚刚大吵了一架。"她低着头，看着桌子，"可能，这没什么大不了。或许其他事情更加重要。"

——希拉·萨特勒·卡尔

Sweet Surprise
甜蜜的惊喜

Love must be as much a light, as it is a flame.
~Henry David Thoreau

"I'm sorry to leave you with all this, Mom," said my daughter, Jennifer, surveying the kitchen counters laden with cupcake tins, bowls, and ingredients that go with baking.

"That's okay, Honey. Your sister and I can survive without you for awhile."

She grinned and headed out the door.

Heather and I got busy baking six dozen cupcakes for the church youth charity fundraiser. That's seventy-two cupcakes! How did I get myself into these things?

"We're out of icing," Heather suddenly exclaimed, throwing off her apron, "I'll run down to the store for some." She grabbed her wallet and keys as she dashed out the front door.

I was puzzled as I checked the shelves in the pantry. I was sure I bought plenty but she was right.

Odd, I thought, and began to clean the kitchen as the cupcakes cooled.

She finally breezed in the door. "I'm back."

I heard a male voice. Who was that? There stood Jennifer's boyfriend, Bob, who was supposed to be 3,000 miles across the country, with a bunch of red roses in one hand and a tuxedo in the other.

My jaw dropped. "What are you doing here?"

He grinned. "I've come to propose to Jennifer."

"Now? You can't," I stammered. "Jennifer isn't here."

"I know. Heather arranged to keep Jen out of the house and then picked me up at the airport in time to set things up here."

"Heather? I thought you went for icing…" My voice faded as I slowly began to put it all together.

"I hid the icing, Mom. It's in the garage—sorry." Heather's dark eyes danced with excitement.

"You flew all the way from Boston tonight?" I asked Bob, bewildered. "Aren't you supposed to be here next weekend?"

"Yes, but it wouldn't be a surprise if I proposed then." He laid his tux on the back of a kitchen chair and propped the roses in the sink between bowls and tins before coming over to give me a hug. "Would it be possible to borrow twelve candles and candle holders? And is there some way to get music to the backyard?"

I nodded mutely and surveyed the kitchen. This is a disaster, I thought, not an elegant and beautiful place for Jennifer's proposal.

We knew this day would be coming since he had asked for our permission to marry her several weeks earlier, but this young Portuguese man was full of surprises.

I sighed and went to find candles while Heather ran upstairs for her boom box. She set it up on the patio table and popped in the CD soundtrack of *When*

Harry Met Sally, readying the scene for her sister. Then she turned to me and said, "We have to leave, Mom."

"But…but what about the cupcakes? And where do we go? I'm a mess…." I sputtered.

"We just have to get out of the house for awhile—we'll finish the cupcakes later."

I was banished from my house. My own house!

I should have gone next door and asked to watch the backyard happenings from their glass-enclosed balcony. But I didn't. I must have been in shock. I could think of only one place where I could show up at 10:00 at night and know they'd not be perplexed or annoyed. For the next hour I spent a nervous but excited time drinking tea with my friends, who lived twenty miles away. They were thrilled to be involved in this small way. "We feel like conspirators," they confided with big grins.

Finally the phone rang. It was Heather. "You can come home now, Mom."

I stepped into the house shortly after midnight and was greeted with ecstatic hugs from Jennifer. Then I pulled back and asked, "Well, tell me, did he get down on one knee?"

"Yes," she dragged out the word like it had six syllables.

"And?" I persisted. After all, I'd helped set up the event, now I wanted details.

"Oh, Mom, it was so romantic!" Her eyes sparkled. "The porch light wasn't on when I got home but there was a candle glowing and a red rose lying by it with a piece of paper. I picked it up with the rose and read, 'How do I love thee?'" She took a breath and smiled at her new fiancé, then continued.

"I immediately thought of Bob because that's 'our' sonnet, but I knew he wasn't here, so I figured Heather must be up to something. It was eerie as I cracked open the front door. The house was almost dark but I saw a second candle with another rose and slip of paper. 'Let me count the ways,' it read."

She glanced beyond me, remembering. "I could see candles glowing down the hall and out to the patio. Harry Connick, Jr. was singing "It Had to Be You" from somewhere. I still had no clue what was going on or why. Boy, am I naïve."

She then told me that she stopped at each candle, retrieved the red rose and the next line of the sonnet, and finally made it to the back door. "Then I saw him." Her voice rose in excitement. "He was dressed in a tuxedo and held out another rose." She paused, amused. "You won't believe this but the first thing I thought was that I was wearing about the worst clothes possible: jeans, flip-flops, even a headband. I felt so schleppy."

"Oh, Honey, it doesn't matter what you're wearing, you're always beautiful," I said.

"I need to call Dad," she interjected, flashing her new Marquise-cut diamond ring at me.

I found the out-of-town hotel number where my pilot husband was on a layover and handed it to her. While she dialed, I noticed the frosted cupcakes sat in boxes ready to deliver. I was surprised and grateful.

"Daddy, Bob's here," she squealed. "He proposed to me!"

"You didn't say yes, did you?" he responded.

"Yes, I did," she told him and, with a laugh, added, "quit teasing me."

Their wedding followed the next spring. Everyone received a ribbon-tied scroll with those special calligraphy-penned lines from "Sonnets from the Portuguese."

Now, some fifteen years and two children later, we watch him surprise her with flowers for no reason, sweet notes, and romantic getaways, as we "count the ways" he still shows how he loves her.

~Jean H. Stewart

爱是火焰，其亮似光。

——亨利·戴维·梭罗

"对不起，妈妈，让你应付这一切。"女儿珍妮弗看着厨房台面上堆满的蛋糕杯、碗，还有用于烘烤的原料。

"没关系，宝贝。希瑟和我还能再撑一会儿。"

珍妮弗冲我笑了笑，出了门。

我和希瑟正忙着为教会青年募捐活动烘烤 6 打纸杯蛋糕。足足 72 个！我干吗要揽这些事儿呢？

"糖衣不够了！"希瑟惊呼。她摘下围裙："我去商店买些。"之后，抓了钱包和钥匙，冲出前门。

我打开食品柜的架子，糖衣的确没有了。真奇怪，我明明记得买够了的。但也没再想，趁着纸杯蛋糕冷却的工夫，收拾了一下厨房。

终于，希瑟风似的回来了："我回来了。"

我怎么听到了男子的声音。珍妮弗的男朋友鲍伯站在希瑟旁边。原本应该在 4 千 8 百多公里外的他怎么来了，一只手里还捧着一束红玫瑰，另一只手里拿着燕尾服。

我目瞪口呆地问："你怎么会在这儿？"

他笑着回答："我是来向珍妮弗求婚的。"

"现在吗？不行，"我结结巴巴地说，"珍妮弗这会儿不在。"

"我知道。希瑟故意安排珍妮弗出门，好去机场接我过来准备。"

"希瑟，我还以为你出去买糖衣了呢……"我声音慢慢低了下来，我开始明白这是怎么一回事儿。

"对不起，妈妈，我把糖衣藏车库里了。"希瑟眼里满是兴奋。

"你是从波士顿过来的吗？不是下周才能过来吗？"我一脸茫然地问。

"是的，但那时求婚就没有惊喜了。"鲍伯脱下燕尾服，搭在厨房的椅背上，然后放好玫瑰，他给了我一个拥抱，"能不能找到12支蜡烛还有烛台？有没有办法在后院放些音乐？"

我默默地点点头，然后开始在厨房搜寻。真是糟糕，这里太乱了，我心里暗想，珍妮弗求婚的地方应该是美丽优雅的。

我们知道这天一定会来，因为几周前，他征得了我和珍妮弗父亲同意。但这个年轻的葡萄牙男子总是充满了惊喜。

我轻叹了口气，继续寻找蜡烛。希瑟则跑上楼，去拿她的音响。

希瑟把音响放在庭园的天井表上，播放着《当哈利遇到莎莉》的主题曲，为姐姐珍妮弗布置好场景。然后，希瑟转过身，对我说："妈妈，我们得离开一会儿。"

"可是，那些蛋糕怎么办？再说了，我们能去哪儿呢？我整个人乱糟糟的……"我结结巴巴地说。

"我们只是离开房子一小会儿，蛋糕待会儿再做。"

就这样，我被赶出了自己家。

我应该到隔壁邻居家去，从他们的玻璃阳台上，看看后院发生了什么。但当时没有想起来，我一定是太震惊了。我能想到的，在半夜十点钟突然出现，没人大惊小怪或者感到恼怒的地方只有一个。一小时后，我坐在大约 32 公里外的朋友家，兴奋地同他们喝茶聊天。他们很高兴以这种方式参与进来："感觉我们就像同谋。"

终于，电话响了，是希瑟打来的："你可以回来了，妈妈。"

不久，我便回到了家。一进门，就被珍妮弗欣喜若狂地抱住。过了一会儿，我松开她，退后一步望着她问："告诉我，他单膝跪下了吗？"

"是——的。"她拖着长音回答。

"然后呢？"我穷追不舍地问。毕竟，我也帮忙布置了的，现在我想知道细节。

"哦，妈妈，那么浪漫。"珍妮弗的眼睛闪闪发光，"我回来的时候，门灯没亮，但是看到有支点燃的蜡烛，一枝玫瑰，旁边还放了张字条。我拿起玫瑰和字条，上面写着'我是怎样地爱你？'"她深深吸了口气，看了下她的未婚夫，然后继续说。

"我马上想到了鲍伯，因为这是属于我们的十四行诗，但他不可能在这儿。所以，我猜肯定是希瑟在搞鬼。打开房门的时候，那情景真是毛骨悚然，屋子暗暗的，只有另一支点燃的蜡烛、玫瑰，还有字条，上面写着'让我逐一细数'。"

她目光飘向远方，回忆着刚才的情景："我随着蜡烛一直走到庭园，听到哈里·康尼克的那首《非你莫属》，但我还不明白怎么回事。天哪，我太天真了。"

后来，她告诉我，她捡起每支蜡烛旁边的玫瑰和写着下句诗文的字条，直到走进后院。"这时候，我看到了鲍伯。"她的声音显得很兴奋，"他穿着燕尾服，手里拿着另一枝玫瑰，"珍妮弗幸福地笑了，稍微顿了一下，"你不知道，当时我的第一反应就是后悔我今天的打扮——牛仔裤、拖鞋，还扎了头巾。真是太糟了。"

"哦，宝贝，无论你穿什么都不重要，你看起来总是那么美。"我安慰她说。

"我要打电话给父亲，告诉他这件事。"珍妮弗打断了我的话，一边让我看她的订婚戒指。

丈夫是飞行员，在短暂的飞行停留，他会住在镇外的一家旅馆。翻到电话后，我递给珍妮弗。她拨号的时候，我看到抹好糖衣的纸杯蛋糕已经整齐地摆放在盒子里，只等送出。我既惊讶，又感激。

"爸爸，鲍伯在这儿，"珍妮弗悄声说，那模样就像告密一般，"他向我求婚了。"

"你没答应吧？你答应了吗？"电话那头儿故作生气地问。

"当然，我答应了他。"珍妮弗忍不住咯咯地笑，"爸爸，别再逗我了。"

第二年春天，他们举行了婚礼。每位客人都收到了印有葡萄牙十四行诗、系着红丝带的卷轴请帖。

现在，结婚 15 年，即便是有了两个孩子以后，他仍然会毫无缘由地送花，给她写甜蜜的字条，策划浪漫出游，依然"逐一细数"他对她的爱。

——珍·希瑟·斯图尔特

"不知怎的，我觉得这些线索会引出一个快乐结局！"

The Counterproposal
反对意见

A man's wife has more power over him than the state has.
~Ralph Waldo Emerson

I never liked rings. I do not wear a high school ring; I do not wear a college ring, and I did not want to wear a wedding ring. This was not because I did not want people to know that I was married, but because I just did not feel comfortable with a ring on my finger.

After graduating from college I finally was about to "pop the question" to my high school sweetheart, Sharon Gail Weingarton, who was at my side continually after I was almost fatally injured during a robbery.

Sharon was the best—pretty, kind, sweet, and goodhearted. However, what would she say when I proposed and said that I did not want to wear a wedding ring? I practiced what I was going to say to her. I thought long and hard. I finally decided that there was no answer to my dilemma. I would simply tell her, and then wait five minutes for the explosion.

So that night I proposed, and afterwards I told Sharon that I was not going to wear a ring. I simply said: "I just don't like rings. I don't wear a high school ring..." I expected Sharon to become enraged: "WHAT DO YOU MEAN YOU'RE NOT GOING TO WEAR A WEDDING RING?"

However, instead, I merely heard silence. After what in my mind seemed like an eternity, Sharon calmly remarked: "Fine. If you don't want to wear a wedding ring, I won't change my name. I will not call myself Sharon Segal."

On our fifteenth anniversary, I remembered the first lesson of marriage that was taught to me by my wife Sharon Gail Segal as I looked down upon the ring on my ring finger—COMPROMISE.

~Michael Jordan Segal, MSW

对男人来说，妻子有时比国家更有威力。
——拉尔夫·瓦尔多·爱默生

我从来就不喜欢戴戒指。我高中时不戴戒指；大学时也没戴戒指；曾经一度还想结了婚也不戴戒指。我也不是不想让大家知道我结婚了，而是我就是觉得有个戒指戴在我手上感觉不舒服。

大学毕业以后，面对着高中就在一起的爱人——莎伦·盖尔·万嘉顿，在上次的抢劫中我受了重伤，她依然不离不弃，可我还是不得不提出这个问题。

莎伦虽然是世界上最好、最漂亮、最善良、

最甜美并且最好心的女孩，可是，当我去求婚然后说不想戴结婚戒指，她又会作何反应呢？在跟她说之前，我还进行了演练。我努力地想要得出一个答案，并且想了很久，最终我发现关于我的这个困境没有答案。我只要告诉她，然后五分钟后等待她的爆发。

所以，那天晚上我就去求婚了，并且告诉莎伦我不想戴戒指。我简单地说道："我只是不喜欢戴戒指，我高中的时候就不戴……"我等着莎伦发怒："你说你不想戴结婚戒指是什么意思？"

但是，相反，莎伦没说什么，感觉就跟静默了一个世纪一样，平静地说："好。你不戴戒指，我也不会更改我的姓氏，我的名字不会改成莎伦·西格尔。"

结婚十五周年的时候，看着手上戴的戒指，回想莎伦教给我的关于婚姻的第一课就是相互妥协。

——迈克尔·乔丹·西格尔

My Ninja
忍者

Love makes your soul crawl out from its hiding place.
~Zora Neale Hurston

A young girl drives home from a hard day's work. She pulls into the driveway and opens the garage. As the door rises, she sees a blue dress bag hanging. Puzzled, she gets out of the car to further inspect the item. She sees a note taped to the bag. It tells her that she has an hour to get dressed up (in the dress of course), get back in her car, and start driving—she'll know where to go. Surprised and excited, the girl runs inside the house.

The girl goes into the bathroom to get ready. Taped to her mirror is another message telling her to shower in order to get off the "kid-stink" she might be wearing from her day of working with the kiddies. She laughs and jumps in the shower. After getting out, she decides to put on some perfume. On one of her perfume bottles is another message, "Don't forget to wear my favorite perfume." Smiling, she puts on a few extra sprays.

She puts on the dress and is doing her hair and make-up when her phone starts sounding. A text message! It informs her that she has one minute to get to her car. She puts on her heels and runs out the door.

When she arrives at her car, she sees a rose inside. On the rose is a note. The note instructs her to go to a certain Starbucks downtown and to give the rose to a girl named Shay. The young girl is confused. Why would she get so dressed up to go to a coffee shop to give another girl a rose? Enjoying the adventure, she jumps in her car and starts the journey.

Twenty minutes later, the girl pulls into a parking spot in front of the Starbucks. She quickly puts some money in the meter and runs inside. Cautiously, she approaches the counter to find two girls smiling at her. "Does someone named Shay work here?" she meekly asks. "I'm Shay," says a nice girl. "And I have something for you." Shay hands the girl her favorite coffee drink. YUM. But wait! Another note is taped to the cup!

The note tells the girl that the coffee will serve as a pick-me-up from a long day at work. Then it instructs the girl to go check on her car. Excited, yet still confused, the girl tells the nice workers that it appears she must leave again. Before leaving, the girls tell her to come back and let them in on what this scavenger hunt is all about.

When the girl gets back to her car, she finds another rose in the front seat. Knowing she locked her door and was only in Starbucks for a maximum of five minutes, she is sure her beau is near. She stands on the corner and surveys the area…she sees no one. She gets back in her car to read the note.

The note starts to talk about all things French. Toward the end of the note, the writer laments having to be in Omaha instead of France. But then he remembers that Omaha has an arch near the Old Market that resembles the Arc de Triomphe. The note tells her to go there with her next rose.

The girl drives a few blocks and parks. She walks to the arch and stands underneath—ready for something or someone to pop out. Nothing happens. She decides to go look at the water—maybe there's been a glitch, and her beau is running late. She leans against a railing and stares at the water, sincerely wondering where this hunt is going. All of a sudden, she feels compelled to turn around.

The girl turns to find her beau, on bended knee, with a diamond ring. Before he can say anything, the girl embraces and kisses the young man… accepting his proposal immediately. "Yes! Yes! Yes!"

The young man takes her back to the Starbucks, where the girl finds out that everyone was in on the whole thing. Then he tells her he will take her to a romantic dinner for two at a nice restaurant. When the newly engaged couple is led to their table, the young girl is faced with yet another surprise—a room where she finds her mom, dad, grandma, family friends, and future in-laws waiting to congratulate them. The young girl is overjoyed.

How did the young man accomplish such ninja-like feats? He hid in the trunk of her car and allowed the young girl to transport him to every stop.

That young girl is me…and that young man is my fiancé, Brian.

~Jennifer Hofsommer

爱可以呼唤隐藏在深处的灵魂。

——佐拉·尼尔·赫斯顿

　　忙完一天的工作后，一位年轻的女孩开车回家了。她驶入车道，打开车库。库门升起的时候，她看到门上挂着一个蓝色的服装套袋。她感到很困惑，于是从车里出来，想走近点看看是个什么东西。她看到袋子上贴着一张字条，说她有一小时的时间来梳妆打扮（当然是穿袋子里的连衣裙），她回到车中，准备出发——她知道要去哪里。女孩跑进屋子里，感到又惊又喜。

女孩走进浴室准备换衣服。镜子上也贴了一张字条，让她洗个澡，洗掉在一整天的工作中和小孩儿们在一起时携带的"乳臭味儿"。她笑了笑，跳进浴池里。洗完后，她决定喷点香水。在她的一个香水瓶上也贴着一张字条："不要忘了喷上我最喜欢的香水。"她笑了笑，又多喷了几滴。

她穿上袋子里的连衣裙，整理着头发，化妆，这时她的手机响了。有一条新信息！通知她距离上车还有一分钟。她穿上高跟鞋，跑向门外。

当她跑到车子前面的时候，看到车里有一枝玫瑰。玫瑰上贴着一张字条，让她到市中心的某个星巴克咖啡厅里，然后把这枝玫瑰给一个叫夏侬的女孩。这个年轻的女孩感觉很困惑。她为什么要精心打扮去咖啡厅，然后把玫瑰给另一个女孩呢？喜欢冒险的她跳进车里，踏上了征途。

20 分钟后，女孩把车停在星巴克前面的一个停车场。她匆匆投了一些钱在停车计时器中，就跑了进去。她小心翼翼地走到柜台，发现两个女孩正对着她笑。她轻轻地问了一句："有没有一个叫夏侬的人在这里工作？""我就是夏侬，"一位可爱的女孩说道，"我有一件东西要给你。"夏侬递给女孩一杯她最喜欢的咖啡，味道好极了。但是别急！杯子上也贴着一张字条！对女孩说这杯咖啡是缓解一天漫长工作的提神饮料，然后让女孩去看看她的车。她感到十分兴奋，同时也很困惑，女孩告诉友善的服务员，看来她又得走了。离开前，服务员说她得回来告诉她们这次的寻宝游戏是为了什么。

女孩回到车里后发现前排坐椅上又放着一枝玫瑰。她知道自己锁住车门了，而且在星巴克里最多也就待了五分钟，她确信她的男朋友就在附近。她站在拐角处，观察着周围……但是一个人也没看见。她回到车里，看到一张字条。

字条上写的都是法语。在末尾，写字条的人为自己必须待在奥马哈而不是法国感到遗憾。但是他又回忆起在奥马哈的老集市区附近有一座拱桥，和凯旋门很像。字条写着让她带着第二枝玫瑰到那里去。

女孩开车穿过几条街和几个公园。走向拱桥，站在下面——作好准备等待某个东西或某个人突然出现。但是什么也没有。她决定去水边看看——也许是她的男朋友有点事来晚了。她靠在栏杆上，盯着水面，很好奇这次要寻找的宝贝究竟是什么。突然，她忍不住转过身。

女孩看到了她的男朋友拿着一枚钻戒，单膝跪地。不等他说一个字，女孩拥抱并亲吻着这个年轻小伙子……马上接受了他的求婚。"我愿意！我愿意！我愿意！"

年轻人带她返回星巴克，女孩发现每个人都参与了整个事件。然后他告诉她，他要带她去一个豪华餐厅里享用一顿浪漫的双人晚餐。当这对刚刚订婚的小两口被引导入座时，年轻的女孩又吃了一惊——她看到她的妈妈、爸爸、奶奶、亲朋好友和未来的公婆都在这个房间里向他们表示祝贺。这个年轻的女孩欣喜若狂。

年轻人究竟是如何完成这个忍者般的壮举呢？他藏在她汽车的后备厢里，这样年轻女孩就会把他送到每一站。

那个年轻女孩就是我，而那个年轻男孩就是我的未婚夫——布莱恩。

——珍妮弗·郝夫索莫

A Different Calling
另一种呼唤

The very first moment I beheld him, my heart was irrevocably gone.

~Jane Austen

He was twenty and tall, with blond hair and green eyes. His body was sleek with muscular curves, and his face gave my heart twinges.

I was eleven, short, and wore glasses. I had fuzzy hair and freckles, and the only curves on my body were affectionately referred to as "baby fat".

His name was Ken. He knew my name, but the only attention he really gave me was a sort of pat on the head as he went by. But even then, I loved him, and knew that one day, we'd be together.

I was teased and laughed at by everyone who knew my feelings. They told me to forget it, that he had plenty of women his age. Not a chance, they told me.

I ignored them.

Two years later, I asked Ken to sponsor me for my confirmation ceremony in our church. I was thrilled when he accepted. The year of instruction beforehand would require him to spend more time with me.

Two years after that, I learned that Ken was moving to France to become a monk! I tearfully begged him not to go, but he said it was best. He felt a calling to that life.

The day Ken left I took my dream and, folding it carefully, put it away in a small place in my heart, and tried to forget. But I couldn't. I knew my feelings for him were real, no matter what others said or thought. I knew in my heart that we were meant for each other.

Years passed slowly, and the letters we exchanged help the pain in my heart. Not much, but enough to get by. We maintained as close a relationship as we could.

Thirteen years after Ken left for France, I received a letter from him telling me that he was moving to the States to help start a priory in Oklahoma. I was delighted on so many levels that I could barely think. He was coming back to this continent. He would be living on the same chunk of land as I was (albeit in a different country). It would cost less to write him. It would take less time for our letters to arrive. And best of all, I could phone him.

I quickly discovered another benefit of his move: he could visit! His few visits home were times of rejoicing for me, even though his behaviour gave me no real hope. He seemed so distant. But I still loved him, and I still believed we were meant to be together.

Shortly after that, I received a very serious letter from him, which scared me even as it made my heart swell with pride for him. He was working with inmates on death row in Oklahoma, and one of them had asked him to be present at his execution. This request lay heavy on his mind, as he did not know what to do. I knew my response would impact him for the rest of his life, and thought very carefully before I sent my letter. In it I told him that, no matter what choice he made, he would wish he had done otherwise. But, as I pointed out, a needy man was asking him to be present at his last hour on earth. Could he really say no?

The next time I heard from Ken, he wrote that he would be present at the execution, and that he might not feel like writing again until it was over. I understood, and made sure he still heard from me regularly. He needed my support.

I called a few days after the execution took place, and sat listening to him cry. We did not use words, but our hearts were talking to each other, and it did not matter much what they were saying. He knew I was there, and that was what counted.

After the execution, I began to notice a change in Ken. It was so gradual that I doubted myself at first, but others in his community were also taking notice. It soon reached a point where he admitted to himself, and to me, that his life seemed stuck in a rut. As monastic life was supposed to be slow, his attitude bothered me a little. My concern grew as his letters showed him getting worse, and I finally decided it was time I went down there to shake him up a bit.

I had intended to travel down to see him after a visit to my uncle in Pennsylvania, but during my stay, I received word that I should forget about my trip to Oklahoma, as Ken was returning to British Columbia to attend his grandmother's funeral.

My family and I attended the funeral. Later that night, Ken and I had some time together. I had something to tell him. Taking him by his hands, I looked into his eyes, and told him that I did not want him to go back to Oklahoma. Then I bowed my head and, with a heavy heart, waited for the polite refusal that I knew was coming.

Instead, he said he didn't want to go back to Oklahoma. Then the dam broke, and it all came out at once. He had always loved me, but felt it truly was best for him to distance himself from me all those years ago because I was so young and there was gossip in our community. So he left and joined a monastery halfway across the world.

But because he still loved me all those years, his superiors would not let him make any final vows. A man cannot swear to a life of celibacy when his heart beats for a woman. So Ken lived with the community, taking part in their life, but remained free to leave at any time. When his grandmother passed away, he decided that, unless something had changed, he would go back to Oklahoma after the funeral, take the vows, and never leave again.

But something had changed. Or rather, something had remained the same. The heart of the eleven-year-old girl who loved him had grown into the heart of a thirty-six-year-old woman who still loved him. We had both been through trials that had left their scars, but the love was still there. So, when he knelt down and asked me to marry him, there was no doubt in either of our minds when I said yes.

~Sharon Graham

看到他的第一眼，我的心就无可救药了。

——简·奥斯丁

　　他 20 岁，个子高高的，金发碧眼。体形圆润，呈现出完美的肌肉曲线，他的脸更是让我的心感到刺痛。

　　我 11 岁，个子矮小，还戴着眼镜。头发凌乱，满脸雀斑，我身材唯一具有的曲线被大家亲切地称为"婴儿肥"。

他叫肯恩。他知道我的名字，但是他对我唯一的关注就是经过的时候，拍拍我的脑袋。但即使是这样，我也爱着他，而且我知道终有一天，我们会在一起的。

知道我对他的这种感情的人都戏弄嘲笑我，让我打消这个念头，说像他这个年龄会有很多女人。他们对我说门儿都没有。

我不顾他们的反对。

两年后，我让肯恩到教堂来主持我的坚信礼。他答应的时候我兴奋极了。这意味着坚信礼前的一年时间，他将花更多的时间和我在一起。

两年后，我了解到肯恩要去法国当修道士！我含着泪水央求他不要走，但是他说这是最好的选择。他觉得这是生命在呼唤他。

肯恩离开的那一天，我把自己的梦想小心地收藏起来，放在心中的一小块地方，试着忘记，但是我做不到。不管其他人怎么说或怎么想，我知道我对他的感觉是真的。我的内心明白我们心中是有对方的。

时间过得很慢，我们之间的通信抚慰了我内心的伤痛。尽管不多，但是勉强过得去。我们尽量维持着亲密的联系。

肯恩去法国 13 年后，我收到他的一封信，信上说他要回美国了，帮忙在俄克拉何马创办一个修道院。我高兴坏了，想都不敢想，他要回到这个大陆了。他将和我居住在同一片土地上（虽然是在另一个国家），这样给他写信就便宜多了，信到达的时间也会缩短。最重要的是，我可以给他打电话了。

很快我发现他这次回来的另一个好处：他会回家探亲！他少有的几次回家探亲是我最高兴的时候，尽管他的举动没有让我感到真正的希望。他看起来是那么的遥不可及。但是我仍然爱他，也仍坚信我们一定会在一起的。

　　不久后，我收到他一封很严肃的信，让我感到既害怕，同时又心潮澎湃，为他骄傲。他要和俄克拉何马监狱里的死刑犯一起工作，其中一个死刑犯想在执行的时候让肯恩到场。这个请求一直萦绕在他的心头，因为他不知道自己要怎么做才好。我知道我的回信将影响他的一生，所以在寄信之前我十分认真地思考。在回信中，我告诉他，不管他作了哪种选择，都会后悔没有选择其他。但是，就像我说的，一个急需帮助的人想让肯恩见证他在人世间的最后时光。他怎么能拒绝呢？

　　之后我收到肯恩的回信，他信上说执行时会到场，但是在事情结束之前，他不想再写信了。我很理解他，而且确保他仍能时不时收到我的信。他需要我的支持。

　　执行过后的几天，我给肯恩打了个电话，坐着听他哭着。我们不需要语言，但是我们的心在和对方对话，它们在说什么已无关紧要。他知道有我在他身边，这是最重要的。

　　在执行事件过后，我开始注意到肯恩的一个变化。这个变化的过程很慢，以至于起先我都怀疑自己了，但是他所在社区的其他人也都注意到了。很快他就向自己和我坦白了，他的生活似乎在原地踏步，停滞不前。因为修道士的生活节奏应该是很慢的，所以他的态度让我有点不安。当他的好几封信中说到他的情况越来越糟时，也加剧了我的担忧，最终，我决定是时候去让他振作起来了。

　　我本来打算在看望住在宾夕法尼亚的叔叔后就去看望他，但是在叔叔家逗留期间，我得到消息，我得取消俄克拉何马之旅了，因为肯恩要去不列颠哥伦比亚省参加他祖母的葬礼。

　　我和我的家人也参加了葬礼。那天晚上给了我和肯恩一点相处的时间。我想要告诉他一些事情。我抓起他的手，看着他的眼睛，我告诉他我不想让他再回俄克拉何马了。然后我低下了头，心情十分沉重，等待着早已预料到的委婉拒绝。

然而，他说他并不想回俄克拉何马。仿佛河水冲破了大坝，倾泄而下。他说他一直都爱着我，只是因为我还年轻，而且我们的社区里经常散播一些流言飞语，他觉得和我分开几年对他来说才是最好的选择。所以，他决定离开，横跨半个地球，去当修道士。

但是，因为这么多年来他仍然爱着我，他的上级没有让他发最后的誓言。因为如果一个男人的心还在为一个女人而忐忑不安，那么就不能向禁欲生活宣誓。所以，虽然肯恩住在社区，和大家一起生活，但是仍可以随时自由地离开。他的祖母去世的时候，他决定只要在葬礼后没有其他什么事，他就回俄克拉何马，然后发誓永远不再离开。

但是有些事的确变了。或者更确切地说，有些事一直没有变。那个深爱着他的11岁少女的心变成一颗仍然深爱着他的36岁老女孩的心。我们一起经历各种考验，虽然留下了伤疤，但是爱依旧未变。所以，当他跪下来让我嫁给他的时候，我毫不犹豫地对他说我愿意。

——莎伦·格雷厄

第五部分 婚礼篇

Chapter 5
The Wedding

Now join hands, and with your hands your hearts.
~William Shakespeare

现在把你们的手牵上，还有你们的心。

———威廉·莎士比亚

Secret Wedding
秘密婚礼

When love is not madness, it is not love.
~Pedro Calderon de la Barca

　　We were engaged—complete with a nice-sized ring—and our wedding date was set for October 5th. We wanted to get married ten years to the day from the first time we had verbally expressed our love. We had been high-school sweethearts. Already engaged and planning a wedding a year away, we moved into a place of our own. Then we decided we just needed to be married right away. We made it legal.

　　It was a small affair with immediate family members and a few friends. Our dearest friends let us get married in their living room. We borrowed some folding chairs from the church and our pastor did a brief ceremony. We exchanged platinum bands, repeated vows, kissed and voilà—we were married. The afternoon was made complete with coffee, two small cakes from the supermarket on the corner, and an arrangement of daisies that cost less than twelve dollars. My best friends wanted to make me a bouquet but I refused. They did, however, convince me to buy a new white blouse to wear with my khaki skirt.

We had the ceremony after church, and then did what we do every other Sunday afternoon—we relaxed with friends. We played spades well into the night and my new husband re-strung his guitar. Peculiar, I know. But in all sincerity we were so ready.

That was my wedding day, well really, my marriage day.

As I consider all these things, it seems so very un-romantic—all except for the fact that it was a secret wedding, because we were still planning our formal wedding for October 5th, my dream wedding in the rose garden with a white dress, a string quartet, and mini-quiches.

Is it weird that our marriage license has a different date than the day we celebrate our anniversary? That the minister who married us is not the same minister who conducted our wedding? That I still haven't told my grandparents? Are these things that will thoroughly confuse our children one day?

I admit that it sounds weird, but we have a "married" date and a "wedding" date. Even though I don't expect flowers on both occasions, I feel like this simply reaffirms the fact that I am high maintenance. I got two weddings to the same man.

~Stefani Chambers

当爱情不再疯狂的时候就不是爱情了。

——佩德罗·卡尔德隆·德·拉·巴尔卡

　　我们订婚了——一枚大小合适的戒指——我们婚礼的日期定在 10 月 5 日。我们想在第一次告白那天的十年后结婚。我们在高中就成为了情侣。现在我们已经订婚，策划一年后的婚礼，我们搬到一个属于我们自己的地方。然后我们决定，我们只需要立刻结婚。就这样我们成为合法夫妻。

　　婚礼很小，只邀请了直系亲属和几个朋友。我们最亲爱的朋友们让我们在他们的卧室举办婚礼。我们从教堂借了几把折叠椅，让牧师主持了一个简短的仪式。我们互换白金婚戒，说出誓言，亲吻对方，瞧——这样就算结婚了。下午我们只准备了咖啡，两块从街角超市买的小蛋糕和几束总共不到 12 美元的雏菊。我最好的朋友们想给我编一个花环，但是被我拒绝了。但他们还是说服我买了一件新的白衬衣来搭配我的卡其色裙子。

　　在做完礼拜后我们举行了仪式，然后做起了我们每两个周日的下午都会做的事——我们和朋友们一起聚聚，放松放松。我们玩纸牌一直玩到晚上，然后我的新婚丈夫给他的吉他上紧弦。我知道这很奇怪，但是我们都作好准备了。

这就是举行婚礼的日子，是我结婚的日子。

当我思考这些事的时候，一切都看似非常的不浪漫——只有一点除外，这是一个秘密婚礼，因为我们还策划了 10 月 5 日举行的正式婚礼，我梦想中的婚礼，在玫瑰花园中，穿着白色婚纱，听着弦乐四重奏，吃着迷你乳蛋饼。

我们结婚证上的日期和我们庆祝结婚周年纪念日的日期不同，为我们证婚的牧师也不是主持婚礼的那个牧师，我还没有告诉我的祖父祖母，终有一天这些事也会让我们的孩子彻底糊涂，是不是感到奇怪呢？

我承认这听起来很奇怪，我有一个"结婚"的日子和一个"举行婚礼"的日子。虽然我没有想到在这两个场合都会有花，但是这再次证明了我是个难伺候的人。两次婚礼上，我嫁的是同一个男人。

——史蒂芬妮·钱伯斯

My Purple Wedding
我的紫色婚礼

> When you love someone, all your saved-up wishes start coming out.
>
> ~Elizabeth Bowen

I remember little about the day my husband proposed. Del is a down-to-earth kind of guy, so there were no frills, no fancy romantic dinner or airplane message written in the sky. Just a simple, "Will you marry me?" Caught off guard and uneasy with such a serious moment, I responded, "Sure. If you'll buy me a horse." He said he would.

My dad gave his wholehearted approval when Del asked for my hand. My mother was another story. She withheld her blessing, and as wedding plans moved forward, conflicts arose.

The people Del and I chose to stand up with us did not meet with Mother's approval. The attendants I wanted failed her litmus test. Del's best friend and choice for his best man became a tug of war between me and Mother. He was black and I was informed that if he was in the wedding my dad would not walk me down the aisle. Never having been taught prejudice, I was shocked when it reared its ugly head. Forced to choose between my dad or my convictions of right and wrong, I wrestled with this injustice.

All the while feeling guilty, I chose Dad, whom I adored, and Del agreed to ask someone else. Because his friend knew nothing of Del's original plan, his feelings were spared. Ours were not. Our hearts were broken.

As plans continued it became evident this was not my wedding, but the wedding my mother never had. She chose the people. She chose her favorite colors. Regardless of inflation, the budget for my wedding was not to exceed that of my sister's, who had married nine years earlier. This meant I could have only one attendant, who Mother chose.

As conflicts escalated, Dad offered us money to elope, but we decided to go forward with a formal wedding. Weddings don't always turn out the way we envision them, but healing can come in time.

Our healing came after we had been married twenty-five years. God laid it on my heart to celebrate our anniversary by having the wedding we had always wanted. Giddy as a first time bride, I picked the colors, the people, the cake and even the location for our honeymoon.

When it came time to shop for a dress my goal was to find one in my favorite color—purple. Since shopping is not something I enjoy, Del prayed I would find a dress at the first store. His prayer was answered. From the moment I tried on a beautiful purple princess style, I knew it was my wedding dress, a dress fit for royalty.

We called the friends we originally wanted in our wedding party, including as many as possible. "Oh, Pam," my girlfriend from sixth grade said, "I couldn't believe it when I heard your message on my recorder. I sat down and cried."

We even asked for the marriage counseling, which we never received the first time around.

Del and I were both nervous the night of our celebration. With twenty-five years of marriage behind us, we knew the seriousness of the wedding vows we repeated. At one point in the ceremony, Del was almost overcome with emotion. I saw tears in his eyes, and knew something stirred deep down in his heart. The ceremony ended with a prayer of blessing and two hearts on the pathway to healing.

After wedding pictures, we proceeded to the reception. The original cake topper, with touches of purple now added to the pink, adorned a delicious cake with fruit filling and cream cheese icing. The room, decorated with a white lattice backdrop covered with purple flowers, silver ribbons and greenery, provided a perfect setting for our guests. We mingled with friends from many years and caught up on their lives and shared about ours.

When the evening ended, we loaded gifts into the car and I slipped in beside my beloved husband. With memories of the wedding I always desired tucked away in my mind, I was satisfied for the first time in years.

In those sweet precious moments, I realized not only had my wedding vows been renewed, my heart had been also. Like cream cheese frosting on a hot summer day, all the bitterness, hurt and resentment that had haunted me for all those years melted away. This time, I felt God had been in charge of my wedding. My mother had been a guest. With my heart softened toward her, I looked forward to God's healing and restoration in our relationship.

Del and I spent our honeymoon sightseeing in historical Philadelphia and a romantic getaway in the Poconos. The beautiful scenery and a heart-shaped tub was a perfect new beginning for two romantic hearts joined as one.

~Pamela Humphreys

当你坠入爱河时，所有深藏在内心的愿望都会慢慢绽放。

——伊丽莎白·鲍恩

　　丈夫求婚那天的情形我已经记不太清楚了。德尔是个老实人，不会甜言蜜语，没有花哨的浪漫晚餐，也没有悬挂在飞机上的字幅。只有简单的一句："你愿意嫁给我吗？"在这么一个严肃的时刻，让我猝不及防，不知所措，我回答道："当然愿意。只要你给我买匹马。"他说他会给我买的。

　　当德尔说想和我结婚的时候，我的父亲一口答应了。而母亲却不同，她拒绝给我们祝福，随着婚礼策划的推进，冲突也产生了。

　　德尔和我挑选的给我们当傧相的人没有通过母亲的批准。我想邀请的伴娘没有通过母亲的测试。德尔最好的朋友以及选择最佳人选成为母亲和我之间的激烈竞争。他是个黑人，母亲告诉我如果他来参加婚礼，父亲就不会陪我走婚礼通道。从来未被教过偏见的我第一次面对这种情形时，大吃一惊。当被迫在我的父亲和是非之间作出选择时，我努力想克服这种不公平感。

　　始终感觉内疚的我选择了我所崇拜的父亲，

而且德尔也同意找其他人。因为他的朋友还不知道德尔最初的安排，也就不必考虑他的感受了。但是我们的感受却不同。我们的心都碎了。

随着计划继续推进，这很明显已经不是我的婚礼了，而是变成母亲从来没有过的婚礼。她来挑选参加婚礼的人。她选择自己最喜爱的颜色。尽管通货膨胀了，我的婚礼预算都不应该超过早在 9 年前姐姐举办的婚礼的花销。这就意味着我只能有一个伴娘，也是母亲挑选的。

随着冲突升级，父亲给了我们一些钱，让我们私奔，但是我们决定继续进行正式婚礼。婚礼总是不能和我们想象中的一样，但是迟早会让我们如愿的。

在结婚 25 年后我们终于能够如愿以偿了。上帝于冥冥之中暗示我要举办一次我们一直渴望的婚礼来纪念结婚纪念日。头一次当新娘让我眼花缭乱，我亲自挑选颜色、参加婚礼的人、蛋糕，甚至还有我们度蜜月的地点。

购买婚纱的时候，我的目标就是找一个我最喜欢的颜色——紫色。因为我不是很爱逛街，所以德尔就祈祷我能在第一家店找到合适的婚纱。他的祈祷应验了。从我穿上那件美丽的公主式紫色婚纱的那一刻，我就知道这就是我想要的婚纱，适合皇室的婚纱。

我们给之前想邀请来参加我们婚礼的朋友打了电话，来的人越多越好。"哦，帕姆，"我上六年级时的女玩伴说，"我在电话录音机里听到这个消息的时候，简直难以置信。我居然坐下来哭了。"

我们甚至还咨询了婚姻顾问，我们在举行第一次婚礼的时候从来没有这样做。

庆祝仪式当晚，德尔和我都非常紧张。因为我们已经经历了 25 年的婚姻生活，我们都知道说出结婚誓词的重要性。

在举行仪式的某个时刻，德尔几乎不能控制自己的感情。我看到他眼中的泪水，知道他的内心无限感慨。仪式末尾是一个有关祝福的祈祷，甬道上的两颗心在渐渐愈合。

照完相后，我们继续接待来宾。之前结婚蛋糕的顶层有几抹紫色，现在掺了些粉红色，还用水果和奶油奶酪糖衣把蛋糕装饰得秀色可餐。房间里，白色格子背景幕上铺满了紫色鲜花，还有银色丝带和绿树，为我们的客人营造了一个最佳场景。我们和认识多年的朋友一起聊着他们的生活，同时也分享着我们的生活。

晚上仪式结束后，我们把礼物塞进车里，我突然滑了一跤，跌入我最爱的丈夫的怀里。我把自己一直梦寐以求的婚礼的种种记忆深深藏入心底，这么多年来我第一次感到心满意足。

在那些甜蜜而又宝贵的瞬间，我意识到不只是我的结婚誓词更新了，我的心也焕然一新。就像在炎热夏季里的奶油奶酪，困扰我多年的所有的苦楚、创伤和埋怨都融化了。这一次，我感觉到是上帝在主持我的婚礼。而我的母亲只是其中的一个客人。我对她的怒气已经消了，我希望上帝能愈合并修复我们之间的关系。

蜜月期间，我和德尔游览了历史名城费城和浪漫胜地波克诺山。美丽的风景和心形桶标志着两颗浪漫的心合二为一的开端。

——帕梅拉·汉弗莱斯

Decisions
决定

A wedding is a start of togetherness... of walks in the rain, basking in the sunshine, shared meals, caring for one another and sensing the love that a marriage carries.

~Author Unknown

The easiest decision my husband and I ever jointly made was to get married in the first place. It was agreeing on all the details of the wedding that almost nullified our union, before we had even properly tied the knot.

To begin with, I had always dreamed of a large and extravagant wedding, with me clad from head to toe in white lace, walking veiled and demure down the aisle on the arm of my proud papa. Nothing, but nothing was going to sway me from that vision, especially not my husband-to-be. Wasn't marriage all about compromise anyway? He on the other hand, a solid pragmatic engineer, had other thoughts on the matter.

"You know how much money we're going to have to plunk down for what is essentially a one-day party? Why not take the money we would have spent, and use it for a down payment on a house? Surely that would be a better use of our money."

The really annoying part was that in a way he was right. He still had student loans, I was paying off my car, and in a short while, we would acquire our first mortgage. Could we really afford this wedding? Still, I wasn't ready to concede defeat yet.

"My parents have volunteered to pay for the wedding, and if they don't mind, why should you? Anyway, I'm the last of their daughters to get married, so they'll be home free after this wedding."

I was to learn that if I could be tenacious, my fiancé could be equally so. "Are you really going to ask your parents to pay for an expensive wedding after they just put the five of you through private colleges?"

Okay, now I was feeling a bit on the guilty side, but not so much that I was willing to relinquish my dreams of a wedding altogether. "What about just a small wedding then with only our families and closest friends?" I sensed my advantage as he hesitated. "No wedding, no marriage," I stated firmly, "and that's my final offer."

"Fine," he conceded, "a small wedding it is then." The smile of triumph he tried unsuccessfully to hide convinced me immediately that a small wedding was what he was after the whole time. Now why oh why couldn't he have just said so in the first place?

The ensuing negotiations to hammer out all the details of the wedding felt a bit like bartering for a used car. Our next big decision was who to invite. Every decision it seemed came with its own set of complicating factors. After we settled on the number of wedding guests, it seemed only reasonable that we each be responsible for half the guest list. The problem was that my family far outnumbered his, and what with all my siblings, aunts, uncles and cousins, I would have a difficult time staying within my limit.

"Even though I have to invite them all, most of the East Coast branch of the family won't be able to attend," I quickly assured him, with much less confidence than I was feeling. As I composed my proposed list of invitees, I carefully penciled in next to their names the likelihood that they would actually attend. "There," I crowed triumphantly, when my list was finally compiled, "I predict with an 85% certainty that a maximum of two-thirds of the guests I invited will actually attend."

"And what if you're wrong," he asked suspiciously, "and we end up with double the number we expected?" No doubt he was having some second thoughts about his decision to marry a mathematician.

"Then we hock the family silver, and use the money to elope," I quickly replied. He had the good grace to laugh.

From the guest list, we proceeded to picking the date, no mean feat as all four of my siblings and my mother were tied to academic calendars, either as grad students or professors. Moreover, half were on the quarter system while the other half were on the semester system, so their vacations didn't exactly match up.

"Let's see," I mused, after making a spreadsheet of all possible wedding dates, it being Thanksgiving Day when we announced our engagement. "It looks like we can go with the last weekend in March of next year, or try to work around everyone's summer vacations." March 28th it was to be then, leaving us a mere four months to deal with selecting the facility, the photographer, the band, the flowers, the attire, the meal, the wedding party, and a whole host of other decisions. There was no shortage of details to work out apparently.

"You know," I remarked casually one day, as I was working out a complex calculation of what was the right proportion of marinated mushrooms to bacon-wrapped scallops on the hors d'oeuvres tray, "maybe we should have just eloped and saved all this trouble. Just kidding," I hastily amended, after seeing the expression on the face of my intended.

Well the big day finally arrived, and the details just kind of sorted themselves out. While there were no major crises to deal with, there were plenty of the smaller run-of-the-mill glitches: the head musician fell sick at the last minute, the top layer of cake that we had carefully set aside for our first anniversary landed icing side down on the floor, at least half a dozen guests who hadn't bothered to RSVP showed up anyway, and a family friend accidentally trod on the train of my wedding gown when we were dancing, dislodging all those tiny silk buttons that held it up so nicely. Somehow we managed to deal with those things, and when all was said and done, our wedding went about as smoothly as we could have hoped for.

The sun broke through the clouds just long enough for the photographer to take the formal pictures of the family outdoors, the food and wine were plentiful, and if I never personally got to taste one of the marinated mushroom hors d'oeuvres that were my special favorite, everyone afterwards assured me they were excellent. One of the highlights of the evening was the rousing hora at the end in which everyone partook, from the youngest five-year-old to my octogenarian aunt.

I'm not sure we fully appreciated what we were getting ourselves into that day, as we solemnly uttered our vows. We were both in our twenties, and life's greatest joys and sorrows were still ahead of us. I am firmly convinced however, that the four months of almost constant give and take as we worked through the details of our wedding was the best preparation possible for our ensuing thirty-seven years of married life. Our next major decision was deciding when to start our family, and how many children we would have, he wanting two, and me leaning towards five, but that's a whole other story!

~Cara Holman

婚礼是结合的开始……雨中漫步、沐浴阳光、共享美餐、互相关爱，感受婚姻爱情的开始。

——逸名

　　我和丈夫一起作的最早的决定就是结婚。就在我们真正喜结连理之前，我们一起协商的婚礼细节差一点让婚礼泡汤。

　　首先，我一直梦想有个豪华的大型婚礼，我从头到脚都披着白色蕾丝，挽着让我骄傲的父亲的胳膊，含蓄而庄严地走过通道。无论是谁都不能让我放弃这个遐想，尤其是我未来的丈夫。然而婚姻不是时时都要妥协吗？他和我正好相反，他是个务实的工程师，对这件事有着不同的看法。

　　"你知道就为了这一天的婚礼，我们要砸进去多少钱吗？为什么不拿这些钱去支付房子的首付款呢？这样肯定能更好地利用我们的钱啊！"

　　最让人恼火的是按理来说他是对的。他要还学生贷款，我要还汽车贷款，而且过不了多久，我们就要拿到第一笔抵押贷款了。我们真的有钱办婚礼吗？但是，我还不打算认输。

　　"我的父母主动提出支付婚礼费用，如果他

们没意见，你会有意见吗？不管怎么说，我也是他们最后一个结婚的女儿，婚礼过后，他们就大功告成了。"

我清楚如果我坚持自己的观点，我的未婚夫也会如此："你的父母已经供你们五个孩子在私立大学念完书，你还想让他们支付昂贵的婚礼费用吗？"

嗯，现在我感觉有点内疚了，但是还没有内疚到能够浇灭我对婚礼的梦想。"那我们就办一个小型婚礼，只邀请我们的家人和最好的朋友，怎么样？"他犹豫了，我感觉到自己占了上风，"没有婚礼，就不结婚，"我坚定地说，"这是我的底线。"

"好吧，"他让步了，"那就举行个小型婚礼吧。"他的微笑未能成功地掩饰他的本意，这让我立刻明白了小型婚礼正中他的下怀。那为什么，为什么一开始他不说呢？

接踵而至的敲定各项婚礼事宜的协商，让人感觉有点像在交易一辆二手车。我们要作的下一个重大决定就是邀请谁来参加婚礼。每一个决定似乎都包含着一连串固有的复杂因素。我们商量好婚礼嘉宾的人数后，看起来我们每个人负责邀请一半嘉宾才公道。而问题是我家里的人远远超出了他家里的人，还有我的叔叔阿姨、堂兄弟姐妹和表兄弟姐妹，对我来说，要想把人数控制在范围之内真是太难了。

"即使我都邀请了，住在东海岸的亲戚也来不了。"我很快向他保证，虽然自己也感觉很没底气。写完邀请人员名单后，我仔细在人名旁边写上这些人能来参加婚礼的概率。整理好最终名单后，我带着胜利的喜悦，得意扬扬地说："我有 85% 的把握，预计来的人最多也就三分之二。"

"万一你错了呢？"他狐疑地问我，"万一来的人是我们预期的两倍呢？"毫无疑问，他在考虑要不要娶一个数学家。

"那我们就把家当都典当了，换成钱私奔。"我很快回答他。他儒雅地笑了笑。

根据客人名单，我们开始挑选日子，要让我的母亲和四个兄弟姐妹像研究生或教授一样遵守校历绝非易事。何况一半是按照季度上学，一半是按照学期上学的，所以放假的时间也凑不到一起。

"我们看一看，"我们是在感恩节那天宣布订婚的，在制作了一个所有可能选为结婚日期的电子表格后，我沉思着说，"我们可以选择明年3月份的最后一个周末，或者选择大家都有空的暑假举行婚礼。"这样的话，就是3月28日，我们只有四个月的时间来挑选场地、摄影师、婚戒、鲜花、礼服、婚宴、婚礼和决定其他事宜。显然整个工作不允许遗漏半个细节。

"你要知道，"有一天当我在计算作为开胃菜——腌制蘑菇和裹着培根的扇贝之间的适当比例时，我漫不经心地说，"也许我们应该私奔的，就不会有这麻烦事了。开个玩笑。"看到未婚夫脸上的表情后，我匆匆补充了一句。

重大的日子终于来到了，所有事宜都各就各位了。虽然没有重大危机，但是出现很多常见的小问题：琴师在关键时刻病倒了；为纪念周年结婚日精心准备好的蛋糕顶层的冰块掉在地上了；至少一半的客人为了省事没有回复邀请，却突然出现在婚礼上；跳舞的时候，一个亲戚不小心踩到了我的婚纱，导致婚纱上的丝绸纽扣纷纷掉落。尽管如此，我们都设法应付了，总而言之，我们的婚礼和设想的一样，进展得十分顺利。

等了好久，太阳才穿破云层，摄影师在外面给我们照了全家福，食物和酒水都很充足，虽然我没有亲自品尝我最喜爱的开胃菜之一——腌制蘑菇，但是吃过的人都说做得很好吃。当晚的亮点在于最后令人兴奋的霍拉舞，从最小的只有 5 岁的小孩到我年过八旬的阿姨都跳了起来。

当我们庄严地说出誓词的时候，我不确定我们是否真的感激自己拥有的东西。我们都才二十来岁，未来的生活充满了快乐和悲伤。但是我坚信，在那四个月的时间里我们对婚礼事宜几乎不间断地交流和沟通，可能为我们 37 年之久的婚姻生活作了最充分的准备。我们的下一个重大决定就是什么时候要孩子，要生几个孩子，他想要两个，而我想要五个，这是另一个故事了！

——卡拉·霍尔曼

The Seating Plan
座位表

One hundred people must sit at twelve round tables. I survey the jumbled pile of hand-written response cards in the red shoebox and grin. Soon Steve and I will hold hands as we zoom away from the quaint chapel and glide through the hills in the back seat of our gleaming limousine. Later, we will emerge from the plush interior, flushed with the glow of becoming Mr. and Mrs. I have planned the perfect wedding. Robin Red Breast will alight on the fronds of the lush palm trees standing sentinel before the stately manor's French doors. The sun will beam. My angelic blond niece in her spotless gown will enter first, scattering pink rose petals along the lace-draped entry hall to herald our arrival.

I take a small stack of cards from the shoebox and lay it out before me like a Texas Hold 'em hand. I look up at the calendar, which displays a respectable distance between today and my blessed event. I had suggested a buffet dinner without assigned tables, but our parents prefer that we create a seating plan.

One hundred people divided among twelve round tables shouldn't be so difficult. One hundred guests divided by twelve tables makes eight or nine guests per table. Why buy software for wedding planning? I grab some paper and begin to sketch. I draw twelve globes orbiting an inner blank space that represents the banquet hall's dance floor. I turn the paper clockwise three times to fit them all into my diagram. The sharp pencil makes a satisfying scratching sound.

Names dance through my mind. The Holland cousins and their siblings will all sit together. They all chat amiably. I pencil a letter "H" on the table farthest from the center of the diagram. I select five cards from the hand laid out in front of me, and fish in the shoebox to withdraw two more. I put all the Holland-related cards face down on the floor next to my desk. I exhale.

I grab another stack of cards. My seven Nugent aunts and uncles dance well, I note, and so I write an "N" on a table near the dance floor. Two seats to fill with them. But with whom? My witty cousin Jenny from Boston? Maybe my former boss Kara and her husband Tim Rudy? I vow to show my admiration for my respected, former supervisor by seating her with impressive people. I pick up another card, this one messily scrawled, "M-Flaherty-2." My Flaherty uncles are quiet. Perhaps I will seat Kara with them and talkative people like my cousin and our friend Dr. Carroll for balance. Wait, darn, cousin Jenny likes to drink, so she can't sit near any of my Flaherty uncles; they're all in recovery. Could Kara sit with Aunt Angela? No, Angela likes to sit near the aisle at weddings so she can take a cake-cutting photo. Sighing, I put the card marked "Mr. and Mrs. Rudy" aside on my left.

Then I snatch up a card that reads "Taranto-4 persons". I pause. Are these the Tarantos from New Jersey? No, wait, the Taranto brother is the groom's cousin who crews for NASCAR. Cool. My eyes dart back to my diagram. I look at Kara and Tim's card. I start to move my pencil downward, listing guests in my mind…Danny Taranto. His step-brother Luke Taranto and his wife from San Francisco…Lilly? Lucy! Lucy Taranto who I know from…from that spinning class last year. Small world. Whoa. That means that she's also the Lucy who went out for late night cocktails with her personal trainer. And my swim coach. And that married lawyer. No way! I won't seat her within a mile of sweet, unsuspecting Tim and Kara.

The phone rings, dragging my thoughts and my fingers away from the insistent reply cards.

"Miss Flaherty? I want you to know we have everything in order for your perfect day," purrs my florist. "I must notify you of one slight impediment, though, regarding your lilies."

Alarm bells clang in my cerebral cortex. "Impediment? Did you say impediment?"

"Yes," soothes her honey-soaked voice. "It's nothing really, only the tiniest of delays regarding the centerpieces, Miss-Mrs. Pagan."

"We'll see if it's tiny!" I interject, breathing hard. "What kind of delay are we talking about?"

"Flower crops can be temperature-dependent," she breezes on. "Thus my supplier informs me that the number of lily stems that you requested, may, and I stress may, not be available by the eighteenth of July."

"Let me get this straight. You can't guarantee that we'll get the lilies we want for the tables?" My manicured fingernails drum on the desk. The calendar glares at me. Throbbing pinkish blotches appear on my neck and quickly spread to my cheeks and forehead.

She pauses. "My supplier can't get enough lilies for all twelve tables in time."

"We paaaaiid," I draw the vowel sounds out, "for lily centerpieces for all twelve tables."

"I am very sorry, Mrs. Pagan, and I am aware of our contractual agreement, but I can not control…"

"As you say, we have a contract. We contracted for lilies on all twelve tables at the manor house on July eighteenth." Then I clang down the receiver into the cradle, relishing my rudeness and the dramatic sound of our landline landing hard.

My eyes turn back to the once-promising shoebox of ivory reply cards. Looking in, my eyes catch sight of the card bearing the names of my wacky Uncle John and new, hippie Step-Aunt Star. I gulp. Where the heck do I seat them? Talk about opening a can of worms! Where would they want to sit? Do I care where they want to sit? Who will talk to them? Who knows? I shove the shoebox away.

I awake my hibernating laptop. I image search "July" and "flowers" and "New York". I half-heartedly inspect the search results. I scan pictures of hydrangeas. I steal guilty glances at the shoebox.

Suddenly, I look up. What the heck are we doing? Forget this! I look at my watch, and then back at the accusatory calendar. I fish a calculator out of the top desk drawer. The second hand on my wrist twitches by. I think long and hard about how many miles stand between us and Las Vegas. I wonder if we have enough gas in the Volkswagen to make it all the way to Reno. Blotches fade down my face towards my neck. My fingers dance over the computer keyboard and my grin returns, broad and free. Maybe we should elope.

That night, my future maid of honor stops by to see how our preparations are going. She knocks zealously. No one answers, and friendly concern gets the better of her. She lets herself in with our obviously placed hide-a-key. My future maid of honor frowns at the unnerving silence. There is no bride in the living room consulting magazines. There is no bride in the kitchen tasting cake samples. There is no bride on the phone scolding the florist. There is no bride in the bathroom on the scale. In the office, my future maid of honor finds a trail of ivory cards littering the floor. Her frown deepens into a fretful mask. Tiny shreds of cardstock dot the floor. Her panicked eyes widen as she spies edges of reply cards falling pell-mell from the gaping mouth of a gleaming, silver shredding machine.

***

No, we didn't elope but we came close! Three months later, my new husband and I smile broadly as we peruse the sumptuous buffet line at our lively reception. Savory roast beef and spicy eggplant tempt our senses. The bridesmaids stand behind us in line, cradling the adorable daisy bouquets that they have made for themselves. We have ignored our family and friend's well-meaning advice. We have pleased ourselves. We have the perfect wedding.

~P. A. Flaherty

我等不及成功的来临，所以放弃等待，径直向前。

——乔纳森·温特斯

100 个人必须围着 12 张圆桌入座。我看了看红色鞋盒里堆成一堆的手写的回复卡，咧着嘴笑了起来。一会儿，史蒂夫和我将手牵着手从古色古香的教堂出来，穿过小山，进入闪闪发光的轿车的后排坐椅。然后，我们会从豪华轿车里出

Chapter 5 The Wedding
第五部分　婚礼篇

来，成为光彩熠熠的新郎和新娘。这场完美的婚礼是我策划的。罗宾·瑞德·布里斯特将从车上下来，在森严的庄园的落地玻璃门前，他像哨兵一样站在那片葱郁的棕榈树下。太阳将放出光芒。我那天使般金发碧眼的侄女将穿着一尘不染的长袍走出来，沿着蕾丝装饰的入口大厅撒下粉色玫瑰花瓣，预示我们的到来。

我从鞋盒里拿出一小叠卡片，像玩得州扑克一样摆在我的面前。我看了看日历，今天距离我最重要的日子还很远。我建议吃自助晚餐，这样就不用排座位了，但是双方的父母想让我们画一个座位表。

要把100个人分配到12张圆桌入座应该不难。100个人入座12张桌子，那就是每张桌子安排8个或9个客人。为了这个婚礼，还用买什么软件呢？我拿起几张纸就开始画起来。我画了12个圆，中间是一片空白，表示宴会厅的舞池。我顺时针把这张纸转了3次，让它和我的图对齐。锋利的铅笔发出让人心悦神怡的嚓嚓声。

各种名字在我的脑海中浮现。住在荷兰的堂兄弟姐妹和他们家的兄弟姐妹坐在一起，他们聊得来。我用铅笔在距离图中心最远的地方写了个"荷"字。从手中选出5张卡片放在我面前，然后再从鞋盒里拿出2个。我把所有与荷兰相关的卡片正面朝下放在桌子旁边的地板上。我吐了口气。

我又拿出一叠卡片。我的7个纽金特家的阿姨和叔叔擅长跳舞，我把这点记下了，就在靠近舞池的那张桌子旁边写了个"纽"字。还要再选两个人和他们坐在一起。但是要选谁呢？我那从波士顿来的机智堂妹珍妮？还有我以前的老板卡拉和她的丈夫蒂姆·鲁迪？为了表示我对尊敬的前任上司的钦佩，我发誓要让她和重要人士坐在一起的。我又挑了一张卡片，上面乱七八糟地写着："弗莱厄蒂-2。"弗莱厄蒂叔叔们喜欢安静。也许我应该均衡一下，让卡拉和他们坐在一起，而像我的堂妹这样滔滔不绝的人和我们的朋友卡罗尔博士坐在一起。但是，该死的，堂妹珍妮喜欢喝酒，所以她不能和我的任何一个弗莱厄蒂叔叔坐在一起；他们的身体都在康复中。卡拉和安吉拉阿姨坐在一起怎么样呢？不行，安吉拉想坐在挨着婚礼通道两边，这样她就能在切蛋糕的时候拍照了。我叹了口气，把标有"鲁迪夫妇"的卡片放在我的左边。

然后我抓起一张写着"塔兰托家——4个人"的卡片。我怔住了，他们是住在新泽西的塔兰托家的吗？不是，等等，塔兰托弟弟是新郎的表弟，在全国汽车比赛协会工作。太好了。我的眼睛很快盯住那个表。我看了看卡拉和蒂姆的卡片。把铅笔放下，脑子里不停地想着客人的名字……丹尼·塔兰托。来自旧金山的他的异母兄弟卢克·塔兰托和他的妻子……莉莉？露西！我去年在单车课上认识的露西·塔兰托。这个世界真是小啊！哦，这意味着她就是在大晚上和私人教练一起喝鸡尾酒的露西。还有我的游泳教练，还有那个已婚律师。不行！我不能让她和可爱天真的蒂姆和卡拉坐在一起。

电话铃响了，我将注意力和手指从那烦人的回复卡上收回。

"弗莱厄蒂小姐？我想通知您我们已经为您把那完美的一天安排妥当了。"我高兴得心花怒放，"但是现在我得告诉您百合花出了点小问题。"

我的大脑皮层发出闹铃般的蜂鸣声："问题？你是说有问题吗？"

"是的，"她用如蜂蜜般的声音轻轻说，"不是什么大事，只是装饰品出了一丁点问题，帕根小姐——夫人。"

"到时候就知道是不是小事了！"我打断了她，呼吸变得急促，"我们刚才说什么要推迟了？"

"花卉对温度有依赖性，"她轻声说道，"所以卖花的人告诉我您预订的百合的数量在 7 月 18 日之前可能不够。"

"坦白说吧，就是不能保证每张桌子上都有百合，是吧？"我修剪得整整齐齐的指甲在桌子上敲来敲去。我前面就是刺眼的日历。我的脖子上涨红的印迹不断跳动着，很快就蔓延至我的脸颊和额头。

她停顿了一下："卖花的不能及时为 12 张桌子送够百合花。"

"我们——"我拖着长音说，"已经支付了 12 张桌子百合花的钱。"

"我很抱歉，帕根夫人，我知道我们有合同协议，但是我也没有办法……"

"就像你说的，我们是有合同的。我预订了 7 月 18 日送往庄园的 12 桌的百合花。"然后我把电话听筒挂掉了，为自己的无礼和听筒挂掉的美妙声音沾沾自喜。

我的目光又回到那个曾让我充满希望的鞋盒——那些乳白色的回复卡。看着里面的卡片，我突然看到写着我那古怪的约翰叔叔和嬉皮风格的新阿姨斯达的卡片。我咽了一口唾沫。我要让他们坐在哪里呢？我真是给自己惹出一大堆麻烦。要让他们坐在哪儿呢？他们坐在哪儿有关系吗？谁和他们说话呢？鬼才知道！我把鞋盒扔到一边。

我打开许久未用的笔记本。我搜索着"七月"、"鲜花"和"纽约"，心不在焉地看着搜索结果。看了几张绣球花的图片，充满内疚地瞟了一眼鞋盒。

突然，我明白了。我们到底在做什么？忘了这一切吧！我看了看手表，然后又看了看那个万恶的日历。我从桌子的第一层抽屉里拿出一个计算器。我手腕的秒针不停地抽搐着。我使劲想了很久我们和拉斯维加斯之间有多少公里。我在想如果开大众车到里诺汽油够不够用。我脸上到脖子上的涨红的印迹消失了。我的手指在电脑键盘上飞舞着，又咧着嘴笑了起来，心情开朗，自由自在。也许我们应该私奔。

那天晚上，我的伴娘过来看我们的婚礼准备得怎么样了。她十分热切地敲了敲门，但是没有人回答，最终她对我们的关心占据了上风。她拿着我们藏在隐秘之处的钥匙进来了。令人不安的寂静让我的伴娘紧皱眉头。新娘没有在卧室里翻阅杂志，没有在厨房试吃蛋糕，没有在打电话痛骂花店老板，也没有在浴室里称体重。在办公房间里，我的伴娘看到丢在地板上的一堆乳白色卡片。她的眉头皱得更紧了，仿佛戴着一副令人烦躁的面具。一些卡片的小纸条落在地板上。当她无意中发现从一个闪闪放光的银色粉碎机张开的大"嘴"中，纷纷落下的回复卡时，立刻睁大了她那惊慌失措的眼睛。

……

我们非但没有私奔，反而变得更加亲密了！三个月后，当我和新婚丈夫看着在招待会的自助餐区排起的长长的队伍时，我们都笑逐颜开。萨沃烤牛肉和香辣茄子充满了食欲的诱惑。伴娘们在我们的身后站成一排，手里捧着他们自己动手做的可爱的雏菊花束。我们没有考虑双方的亲人和朋友好心提出的建议。我们完全按照自己的心意来操办。我们的婚礼是最完美的。

——P.A. 弗莱厄蒂

Because of a Fortune Cookie
因为一块幸运饼干

> When you realize you want to spend the rest of your life with somebody, you want the rest of your life to start as soon as possible.
>
> ~Nora Ephron

I ran to the mailbox and opened the lid. There was a letter inside stamped Camp Pendleton, CA and addressed in a familiar scrawling script. I ripped it open and let out a yell.

"Mom, Paul is definitely coming home on leave next week!"

"Well, thank God!" she replied. "You two can work out all the wedding details."

We had been planning a huge wedding through the mail since Paul left for Marine boot camp in January. It was now mid-May and our nuptials were to take place in September. I hadn't seen him since he left; we couldn't talk on the phone, and even writing letters was hard for him. There is a saying in the services, "If the (insert branch of the service) wanted you to have family they would have issued you one." The Marine Corps owned Paul. He confessed that some nights, after writing me a letter by flashlight, he would sneak down the road in his boxers, and deposit it in the base mail slot. We called it "midnight mail". Dangerous at best.

The weekend finally arrived and I was on cloud nine. Paul was taking me to dinner and the theater. I felt like a queen in my new black dress and pearls. He showed up with roses promptly at seven.

"Ready for the time of your life?" he asked after a long kiss hello. I didn't realize how prophetic that phrase was.

"Babe, I've waited for this day forever. Let's go," I replied and with that he whisked me to the car with my parents waving goodbye and smiling at the door.

Paul wouldn't tell me where we were going for dinner but I didn't care; just being with him was enough.

We pulled into the parking lot of General Lee's in Chinatown. Walking up Bamboo Way, I couldn't believe Paul was actually here. As we ate, we kept touching hands across the table reassuring each other that this wasn't a dream.

After the main course the waiter put two fortune cookies down on the table with two orange slices. Paul poured more tea for me while I read my fortune.

"Hmmm...my fortune says 'Don't do anything on the spur of the moment'," I mused. Wonder what that means? "What could we do on the spur of the moment?" I asked.

"We could elope," Paul suggested shyly.

"We can't do that...can we?" My mind raced. "My parents would kill us. My dad has already rented the country club, I have my dress, the bridesmaids have their dresses, the church..."

"You're probably right," Paul interrupted. "Still, it does sound daring."

"Oh, this is crazy," I said. But I knew I loved Paul madly and this was the most thrilling thing I could imagine.

"Where can we elope on a Saturday night?" I asked, still intrigued with this romantic notion of becoming man and wife immediately.

Chapter 5 The Wedding
第五部分　婚礼篇

"Well, I read in the paper that if we go to Yuma, you can get a blood test and then slip back into California to a place called Winterhaven. They marry you right away. But you're right, it's a crazy idea," Paul stated.

"Yeah, crazy," I said, sitting there just staring at Paul.

"Can I get married if I'm only nineteen?" I asked, still intrigued.

"Sure, we'll stop by our houses and pick up our birth certificates on the way." The more we talked the more exciting the idea sounded.

"Well, what are we going to do?" I asked. "Is it the theater or Yuma?"

Paul smiled and whispered, "Yuma".

And with that the idea was set in motion. After paying our tab, we practically ran to Paul's car. We were two love-crazed kids and we were going to be married.

At my house I told my dad I had to have my birth certificate to get into a go-go club and he handed it over, no questions asked. I felt guilty about lying to him, but I was young and in love.

Paul stopped at his apartment and got his certificate, borrowed $50 from his roommate and we hit the road to Yuma. His roommate thought we were doing the most exciting thing in the world and wished us luck.

I was in heaven as we whizzed down the road at speeds approaching eighty. The balmy night air whipped through the open windows as we clung to each other in the front seat. Finally, it dawned on me.

"Paul, I have to let my parents know where I am. When morning comes and I'm not home, they'll be worried sick."

This was before cell phones and e-mail, so we stopped in Indio and sent telegrams to both our parents.

"Have eloped. STOP. Love you both. STOP Sallie and Paul. STOP."

Back on the road, we drove all night except to stop for gas. Paul's Plymouth Fury was guzzling gas like a fiend and our funds were getting low.

We finally pulled into Yuma around six on Sunday morning. We shared a breakfast at a small diner so that we would have enough money left for the blood tests. I was so excited I didn't need much food but my Marine was a hungry guy.

The clinic opened at eight and we were the first in line. We got our results and headed to the Lutes Gretna Wedding Chapel. There before the minister's wife and daughter we said, "I do" with stars in our eyes.

Now I'm not going to lie and say going home to face my parents was easy, but Dad understood, being a romantic at heart himself. He celebrated getting his deposit back from the country club by buying a new Thunderbird. I sold my dress to my best friend, and Paul went back to boot camp a tired, happy, and married Marine. I set up house in a little apartment until we could afford our first home.

It has been forty-five years and guess where we're going to dinner? Here's a clue, it's located on Bamboo Way and serves great fortune cookies.

~Sallie A. Rodman

要是你知道了自己想和谁一起度过余生，你会希望余生开始得越早越好。

——诺拉·伊弗龙

我跑向邮箱，打开盖子。里面有一封信，贴着加利福尼亚彭德尔顿营的邮票，信上是很熟悉的草体字。我撕开信封，大喊一声：

"妈妈，保罗下周要回家休假了！"

"哦，谢天谢地！"她对我说，"你们两个可以在一起商量婚礼事宜了。"

自从保罗一月份去了海军新兵训练营之后，我们就一直通过信件策划一场宏大的婚礼。现在是五月中旬，我们的婚礼在九月份举行。自从他离开后，我就再也没有见过他；我们无法通电话，就是写信对他来说也是件很困难的事。对于服兵役，有一句俗话："如果（兵役分部）想让你有一个家庭，他们会给你分配的。"保罗在海军陆战队。他向我坦白，有时晚上用手电筒给我写完信后，他就穿着短裤偷偷溜到马路上，把信放入邮件投递口。我们称之为"午夜信件"，十分危险。

终于到周末了，我欣喜若狂。保罗要带我去吃晚餐，然后一起看电影。穿上新买的黑色长裙，戴上珍珠项链，我感觉自己像王后一样。他准时在 7 点出现了，拿着几朵玫瑰。

"准备好迎接你生命中的重要时刻了吗？"他深深地吻了我一下，然后问我。我根本不知道这句话预示着什么。

"宝贝，一直在等待这一天的到来。我们走吧。"我回答他说，然后他急忙让我坐进车里，我的父母在车门口微笑着和我们挥手告别。

保罗没有告诉我要去哪里吃晚餐，我也没放在心上，只要能和他在一起我就心满意足了。

我们把车停在唐人街的李将军停车场。沿着竹街走，我简直不敢相信保罗真的就在我身边。吃饭的时候，我们把手放在桌子上，不停地抚摸对方，以此告诉自己这不是梦。

用完主菜后，服务员送上来两块幸运饼干，放在桌子上，还有两瓣橘子。当我估算自己的运气时，保罗给我添了点茶水。

"嗯……我的运气告诉我'做任何事都不要冲动'，"我想了想，想弄清楚这是什么意思，"我们冲动的时候，会做什么呢？"我问道。

"私奔。"保罗腼腆地给我提出一条建议。

"我们不能这样做吧？"我感到不知所措，"我的父母会杀了我们的。

我的爸爸已经租下了乡村俱乐部，我的裙子、伴娘的裙子也都准备好了，还有教堂……"

"也许你是对的，"保罗插了一句，"这个主意听起来确实很大胆。"

"是太疯狂了。"我说道。但是我疯狂地爱着保罗，这是我能想象得到的最让我兴奋的事。

"星期六晚上我们能往哪里私奔呢？"我还是对立刻成为夫妻的浪漫幻想充满好奇，于是问他。

"嗯，我在报纸上看到，如果我们去尤马，可以在那里做一个血液测试，然后回到加利福尼亚一个叫温特黑文的地方，可以马上让我们结婚。但是你说得很对，这个想法太疯狂了。"保罗说。

"是啊，太疯狂了。"我坐下来，盯着保罗说道。

"如果我才 19 岁，能结婚吗？"我还是很好奇，接着问道。

"当然了，我们可以回趟家，然后拿上我们的出生证明。"

我们聊得越多，这个想法就变得越让人兴奋。

"那我们接下来要做什么呢？"我问道，"是去电影院还是尤马？"

保罗笑着小声对我说："尤马。"

我们把心动变成了行动。结账后，我们几乎一路跑向保罗的车。我们像两个被爱情冲昏头脑的孩子要去结婚了。

回到家里，我告诉爸爸我要拿我的出生证明去一个现代酒吧，他什么也没问就把东西给了我。我对他撒了谎，感到很内疚，但是我那时很年轻，而且深陷热恋中。

保罗回公寓拿了他的证明，还跟室友借了 50 美元，然后我们就向尤马启程了。他的室友觉得我们现在所做的是世界上最刺激的事，他祝我们好运。

Chapter 5 The Wedding
第五部分 婚礼篇

我们的车在马路上风驰电掣，速度接近 80 迈，我感觉自己飘到了天上。我们手拉着手坐在前排坐椅上，夜晚宜人的空气透过开着的车窗阵阵袭来。最终，我恍然大悟。

"保罗，我得让父母知道我现在在哪儿。如果天亮了我不在家，他们会因为担心我而生病的。"

那时还没有移动电话和电子邮箱，所以在印第欧停了下来，给我们的父母发了电报。

"我们私奔了。我爱你们。萨莉和保罗。"

我们又上路了，除了加油，我们一路上都没有停。保罗的普利茅斯复仇女神（Plymouth Fury，美国汽车品牌）像魔鬼一样吞噬着汽油，我们的钱越来越少了。

终于，我们在星期日早上 6 点左右抵达尤马。我们在一个小餐馆里一起吃了一份早餐，这样就能剩下足够的钱做血液测试了。我感觉太兴奋了，吃不了太多，但是我的海军饿坏了。

门诊 8 点钟开门，我们排在第一个。拿着结果，我们径直前往卢蒂斯·格雷特纳婚礼教堂。在牧师的妻子和女儿面前我们说道"我愿意"，眼中含着泪水。

我不想撒谎说回家面对父母很容易，但是爸爸也是个内心浪漫的人，所以他很理解我。他拿回在乡村俱乐部的定金，很高兴地买了一辆新雷鸟（Thunderbird，福特汽车）。我把婚纱卖给了我最好的朋友，保罗—— 一个疲惫不堪、满心欢喜、刚刚大婚的海军回到了新兵训练营。我住在一个小公寓的房子里，直到我们有钱买了第一座房子。

45 年过去了，猜猜我们要到哪里去吃晚餐呢？给你个提示，在竹街供应幸运饼干的餐厅。

——萨莉·A. 罗德曼

Ronald

罗纳德

Mirth is God's medicine. Everybody ought to bathe in it.
~Henry Ward Beecher

It was midnight. Richard and I were writing our personal vows for the coming afternoon's wedding ceremony. In addition to the prayers and comments the rabbi would make, my future husband and I wanted to express to one another what we felt and believed about our love and our shared destiny.

June 18th was our wedding day. Richard and I were driven to the synagogue where our ceremony would take place. The setting was breathtaking. The temple was situated on acres of green landscape, and was designed by a Japanese architect. It was starkly elegant and simple, all white inside and outside.

Richard was fifty-one and I was forty-three when we married. It was my first marriage. I chose to walk down the aisle hand in hand with my future husband at my side. That was the way we wanted to start our life together as partners. Literally and symbolically it expressed how we saw ourselves. We were not only lovers but also best friends.

I remember smiling at our guests as we walked toward the rabbi. Everyone there meant so much to us. They smiled back at us, recognizing how special this moment was in our lives. We had waited a long time for this day. It was going to be perfect.

I carried a peach rose, which was the color of the wedding decor and the lettering on our white invitation. Orange had been my favorite color as long as I could remember. The peach roses gave the room a gentle softness that was inviting and delicate. They were breathtaking, their scent exquisite.

Richard allowed me to select our wedding song. I remember the moment I played Barbra Streisand singing "Starting Here, Starting Now" for him. The lyrics expressed what we both were feeling as we were about to begin our life as a married couple. A singer sang that song as we walked down the aisle. In our wedding pictures we were literally glowing.

We had had several discussions with the rabbi about our journey in finding one another. We had likened it to finding a needle in a haystack. The ceremony reflected our appreciation of one another and the future we would now share as husband and wife.

When the ceremony was over, the guests cornered us to extend their congratulations. My sisters somehow broke away from the crowd and walked into the room where tables were set up for our reception.

They gasped at the beauty of more peach-colored roses and the matching tablecloths and napkins. My sister Susan walked over to one of the tables and picked up one of the scripted napkins. She stared at the names and froze.

"Linda, come here," she called out to my sister. "The napkins say Elynne and Ronald."

"Very funny," Linda answered as she walked toward Susan and the napkin. Taking the napkin from Susan's hands, she looked at the names and screamed. "Hurry! Pick up all the napkins on every table!"

While my new husband Richard and I continued greeting our guests in another part of the synagogue, my sisters worked as fast as they could to remove the disaster awaiting us.

They tried their hardest but missed a couple of tables. As fate would have it, this was where Richard's friends sat down to eat. They looked at the napkins in total disbelief. One of his friends told us years later that she thought all the time she had known Richard she must not have known that his real name was Ronald.

Throughout the remainder of our wedding celebration and during our honeymoon I could not resist every now and then calling for Ronald.

~Elynne Chaplik-Aleskow

欢乐是上天所赐的良药，每个人都应该满怀喜悦。

——亨利·沃德·比彻

正值午夜，我和理查德在写第二天下午婚礼上各自的誓词。除了法师的祈祷和评论外，我和未来的丈夫还想表达对彼此的心意，对我们之间的爱和共同的命运坚贞不渝。

6月18日是我们结婚的日子。我和理查德去了犹太教堂，这是我们举办婚礼的地点。婚礼的选景叫人惊叹不已。教堂坐落在一片绿油油的草地上，是由一位日本建筑师设计的。端庄而又

Chapter 5 The Wedding
第五部分　婚礼篇

简洁，教堂里里外外全是白色的。

我们结婚的时候，理查德51岁，而我也43岁了。这是我第一次结婚。我选择与身边未来的丈夫一起牵手走过通道。我们想作为伴侣一同开启我们的生活。无论从表层还是象征意义上，都表示我们对二人关系的理解。我们不仅仅是爱人，还是最好的朋友。

我记得在我们走向法师的时候，我向来宾们微笑。这里的每一个人对我们来说都非常重要。他们也对我们笑了笑，大家都知道在我们的人生中，这是多么特殊的一刻。为了这一天我们等了好久，这一天肯定是最完美的。

我拿着一束桃红色玫瑰，婚礼的装饰和白色邀请卡上的字也是桃红色的。我还记得橙色一直是我最喜欢的颜色。桃红色玫瑰让房间充满了一种诱人的温和气息。这些花香气浓郁，让人心旷神怡。

理查德让我来选择我们婚礼的歌曲。我还记得芭芭拉·史翠珊唱的一句"从这里开始，从现在开始"。歌词流露出我们两个即将作为新婚夫妇开启生活的感情。当我们从通道上走过的时候，有一位歌手唱着这首歌。结婚照片上面的我们璀璨耀眼。

关于寻找对方的旅程，我们和法师商量过好几次。我们把它比作在一堆干草中寻找一根针。婚礼反映出我们对彼此的感激，对今后能够作为丈夫和妻子共同生活的感激。

婚礼结束后，来宾们把我们围起来，表达他们的祝贺。我的姐姐们离开人群，走进已经准备好接待的房间里。

更多的桃红色玫瑰和与之搭配的桌布和餐巾所释放出来的美丽让人赞叹不已。我的姐姐苏珊走到一张桌子前面，拿起一叠餐巾。她凝视着餐巾上的名字，怔住了。

"琳达，过来，"她叫着我的姐姐，"餐巾上写着琳妮和罗纳德。"

"太有意思了。"琳达走向苏珊回答说。

她拿过苏珊手中的餐巾，看着上面的名字，发出一声尖叫："快！把每张桌子上的餐巾都拿走！"

当我和新婚丈夫理查德继续在犹太教堂的另一个地方迎接我们的来宾时，我的姐姐们正尽可能快地消除正在等待我们的灾难。

她们已经尽力了，但还是有几张桌子逃出了她们的法眼。也许是命中注定，理查德的朋友正好坐在这里吃饭。他们看着餐巾，完全不敢相信。很多年之后，他的一个朋友告诉我们，她很早就认识理查德了，但是她居然不知道他的真实名字叫罗纳德。

在我们婚礼的剩余时间里，以及在我们的蜜月中，我总是忍不住时不时叫他罗纳德。

——琳妮·查普里克-阿莱斯科

Chapter 5 The Wedding
第五部分　婚礼篇

Carousels

旋转木马

After all there is something about a wedding-gown prettier than in any other gown in the world.

~Douglas William Jerrold

She seemed to grow taller and more regal as she stood before the three-way mirror.

"That's the one," her twin sister whispered, barely able to breathe.

I nodded as my daughter turned around and slowly smiled. It definitely was THE dress. We found the perfect veil and shoes and left the bridal shop feeling somewhat giddy.

"Okay, what's next?" I asked.

"A dress for you, Mom," was the reply.

We were in the midst of a whirlwind of activity. The bridesmaids' dresses were chosen, so now came decisions about floral bouquets and arrangements, wedding cake, photographer, and music. I hand-addressed the invitations and the reply cards were flooding in.

Then, since I had put it off as long as I could,

I began the search for my dress and managed to find a pale pink one that my daughter approved. Her father purchased a new tuxedo. He joked that he felt like a walking ATM machine, only there to write checks or sign credit slips. It was mayhem, yet we were somehow enjoying that special time.

A few weeks before the May wedding, we rushed in from grocery shopping and the bride's sister greeted us with, "Dad, Mom, can we talk to you?"

I glanced at her holding hands with her boyfriend and suddenly knew what they wanted. A half-gallon of milk slipped from my hand, spilled across the wood floors and spread everywhere, even under the refrigerator.

"Oh, no!" I wailed. "I can't believe this."

"Don't worry, Mom, we'll help you," my daughter said as she rushed to grab the carton to stop the rest of the milk from escaping.

We all grabbed paper towels, crawled on our hands and knees, and spent the next hour together cleaning up the mess. Then we sat, the four of us, staring at one another.

He squirmed and fidgeted and finally sputtered out his love and devotion for our daughter.

"We'd like to get married in December," he said, "with your permission."

"Which December?" I asked in disbelief.

"This one," she finally spoke.

"That's only seven months away," I moaned.

Her father and I stole frantic glances at one another. He then queried and pried as he did a year earlier with her sister and her suitor. Finally he smiled and we gave our blessing. They knew we would.

As I sat there watching them, I felt my life spiraling out of control. Panic spread over me like the milk that had earlier spilled across the kitchen floor. I could do nothing to stop it. Two weddings? The thought of another wedding that year was overwhelming. I felt as if I were on a carousel that would never stop.

"Oh, Mom, this is so exciting!" The girls were thrilled that they would stand together at the altar a second time that year in reverse roles.

I couldn't tell them I was considering a nervous breakdown but didn't have time for one. Meanwhile, their father was wondering about bankruptcy.

Sleep was elusive. My dreams were filled with wedding disasters or mixing up the grooms. I'd wake exhausted only to see a white illusion floating before me. Then I'd realize it was the white satin dress on its padded hanger suspended from a ceiling anchor in the corner of our bedroom. The vision of the long sweep of its pearl-studded, lace-embroidered train evoked all kinds of emotions—joy, happiness, worry, nostalgia, and, at times, sheer panic. Especially as I contemplated a second wedding to come.

The days and weeks flew by in a blur of activity and a long white limousine was in front of our house to whisk the bride and maid of honor off to the church before I could catch my breath.

The wedding was perfect, beautiful and sweet, and everything she had dreamed it would be. The next morning I woke to the vision of yet another dress hanging from the corner. Smooth, creamy, pearl-trimmed silk reminded me that I was still on the wedding carousel.

As I pondered the beauty of the dress and what it represented, I came to realize that we go along the road of life and then, every once in awhile, stop and whirl around in the busyness of the place until it's time to step off and continue on down the road.

We took a double ride that year and found the experiences there tender and sweet, funny and poignant, times that will stay in our memories forever.

Life is change. And filled with carousels. I always try to enjoy the ride.

~Jean H. Stewart

世界上最漂亮的婚纱肯定有一段故事。

——道格拉斯·威廉·杰罗尔德

　　站在三向镜子前，她显得更高挑了，而且更华丽了。

　　"就是它了。"她的双胞胎妹妹小声说道，几乎无法呼吸。

　　我的女儿转过头，轻轻笑了笑，我对她点了点头。肯定就是这件婚纱了。我们都觉得面纱和鞋非常完美，然后离开了婚纱店，感觉有点头晕目眩。

　　"好了，接下来呢？"我问道。

　　我得到的回答是："为你选一套衣服，妈妈。"

　　我们正在准备一场庆祝活动。伴娘的衣服都选好了，现在该商量花束、布置、结婚蛋糕、摄像师和音乐了。邀请卡是我手写的，回复卡如洪水般涌来。

　　因为我已经拖得不能再拖了，就开始找我的衣服，找一件经过女儿同意的浅粉色衣服。她的父亲买了一件新礼服。他开玩笑地说他感觉自己像一个会走路的自动提款机，但是只会写支票或签信用单。虽然有些过分，但是我们在那特殊的时刻都感到很高兴。

五月份的婚礼到来之前的几周，我们从商店购物后急匆匆回到家，新娘的妹妹迎接我们说："爸爸妈妈，我们能谈谈吗？"

我看到她和男朋友手牵着手，突然意识到他们的想法。半加仑牛奶从我手中滑落，洒在木地板上，到处都是，甚至流到了冰箱下面。

"哦，不！"我大叫起来，"我简直不敢相信。"

"不要担心，妈妈，我们来帮你。"我女儿一边说着，一边冲过来拿起纸盒，防止剩下的牛奶也洒出来。

我们都拿着纸巾，双手和膝盖趴在地上，花了一小时清理这个烂摊子。之后，我们四个人坐下来，眼睛盯着对方。

他感到忐忑不安，最终表达了他的爱和对我们女儿的忠贞。

"我们想在十二月结婚，"他说，"如果您允许的话。"

"哪年的十二月？"我感到难以置信，便问他。

"今年。"她最终还是说出来了。

"只剩下七个月的时间了。"我含着抱怨的语气说。

她爸爸和我对视了一眼，然后像一年前对待她的姐姐和求婚的人一样，开始问东问西。最后他笑了笑，我们送上对他们的祝福。他们知道我们会同意的。

当我坐在那看着他们的时候，我感觉自己的生活一发不可收拾。我的内心惊慌失措，就像刚刚洒在厨房地板上的牛奶一样。我无能为力，两个婚礼？我忍不住想到了那年的另一场婚礼。我感觉自己仿佛坐在一个永不停止的旋转木马上。

"哦，妈妈，太让人激动了！"女孩儿们十分兴奋，因为那一年她们可以互换角色，再一次站在圣坛上。

  我没有告诉她们我有点精神衰弱，没有时间操办婚礼。那个时候，她们的父亲也在为破产而担忧。

  睡眠真是让人难以捉摸。我的梦里全是婚礼上出现的灾难或把新郎弄混了。我筋疲力尽地醒来，看到眼前飘浮着白色的幻觉。然后我意识到那是挂在我们卧室一角天花板挂钩上的缎面婚纱。那慢慢挥动着的镶满珍珠、绣着蕾丝花边的裙尾唤起各种情感——快乐，幸福，忧虑，怀旧，还有时不时的惊慌。尤其是我在考虑即将到来的第二场婚礼的时候更是如此。

  随着各种忙碌的准备活动，时间很快过去了，一辆长长的白色轿车停在我们房子的前面，还不等我喘口气，就把新娘和伴娘接到了教堂。

  婚礼温馨完美，一切都和她梦想的一样。第二天早上我醒来，又看到一件婚纱挂在墙角。柔滑的镶满珍珠的米色丝绸让我想起我还坐在婚礼的旋转木马上。

  婚纱的美丽让我深思它象征着什么，我意识到我们经历了一段漫长的人生路，每过一段时间，就要停下来卷入当地的忙碌生活中，然后离开，继续沿着道路前进。

  那一年我们坐了两次旋转木马，旅行的经历既充满柔情蜜意，又滑稽辛酸，那些日子将永远留在我们的回忆里。

  生活瞬息万变，到处都是旋转木马。每一次坐上它，我总是充满喜悦。

——琴·H.斯图尔特

Chapter 5 The Wedding
第五部分 婚礼篇

"一年办两个婚礼？为什么不可以？我已经想不出让我欠债的更好的理由了！"

The Pearl Necklace
珍珠项链

Where there is great love, there are always miracles.

~Willa Cather

It was two days before my wedding. I had promised myself (and my fiancé!) that I wouldn't be one of those brides—the bridezillas who freak out if every detail of the wedding isn't perfect—but I was exhausted from planning, organizing, and coping with too much family and too little sleep.

I decided to try on the pearls my grandmother had given me, but the clasp was stuck. As I tugged, to my horror, the necklace snapped and pearls flew everywhere.

Keeping my cool, I gathered up the errant pearls, consulted a phone book, and began dialing. I received the same reply everywhere: a minimum of two to three weeks to fix. Even when I pleaded that my wedding was in two days, I just received more elaborate excuses: no on-site jeweler, full schedule already, company policy, sorry.

It was the proverbial last straw. I collapsed in tears on the bed, next to my sleeping fiancé. He awoke in confusion, listened to my tale of woe, then suggested, "Borrow my mother's pearls." This set me off into another jag of crying, the only discernible words being, "I want to wear the pearls my grandmother gave me!"

He must have realized I'd passed the threshold of rational thought, so he took charge and did the only thing he could think of under the circumstances: he lied. He phoned a jeweler and told the following story.

"I'm getting married in two days. I was fiddling with my fiancée's grandmother's pearls and broke them. I need them restrung by tomorrow, or else there might not be a wedding."

The necklace was fixed by the next day.

~Sheri Radford

哪里有真爱存在，哪里就有奇迹。

——薇拉·凯瑟

离我们的婚礼就剩两天了。我向自己（当然还有未婚夫）保证过我绝对不会成为像哥拉斯那样的新娘，婚礼有一点不如意就大喊大叫，但是由于忙于婚礼的策划、组织和应对各种家庭问题，睡眠时间又少，我都筋疲力尽了。

我决定戴我祖母给我的珍珠项链，但是项链的扣钩卡住了。我就使劲拽，让我惶恐的是，项链"啪"的一声断了，珍珠散落了一地。

　　我镇定自若，捡起满地的珍珠；查了查电话簿，开始拨号。每个人都是同样的回复：最少需要两到三周才能修好。即使我哀求他们说我的婚礼要在两天之后举行了，但是我得到的只有更加精心编造的借口：缺宝石匠，日程已满，公司政策……抱歉。

　　如谚语所说，这是我的最后一根救命稻草了。我蜷缩在床上痛哭不已，我的未婚夫在旁边睡着。他晕头晕脑地醒来了，听着我悲痛的诉说，然后给我提了一条建议："借我妈妈的珍珠项链吧。"听到之后，我又是一阵痛哭，隐约能听到的话是："我要戴祖母给我的珍珠项链！"

　　他肯定意识到我已经失去理智了，所以他当机立断，做了在这种情况下唯一能想到的事：他撒了谎。他给一个珠宝商打电话，说了下面一个故事。

　　"两天后我就要结婚了。我玩未婚妻祖母的珍珠项链时，不小心把它弄坏了。我想明天之前把它修好，否则婚礼可能就办不成了。"

　　第二天，项链修好了。

——谢莉·雷德福

Dancing in the Kitchen
厨房之舞

To watch us dance is to hear our hearts speak.

~Hopi Indian Saying

I love my husband. I also love dancing. Over the years we learned from experience, however, beginning with our wedding more than forty years ago, that the two were not compatible. We just didn't dance well together. We seemed to have an abundance of left feet.

So when our son announced that he was getting married, I knew something had to be done. I was not about to let us stumble our way through the official parents' dance. I did what I thought was the easiest and fastest way to come up to dancing speed—I signed us up for dancing classes.

My husband grumbled. He complained that it is impossible to count the beats, do the variations, and feel the music at the same time.

"That's multitasking," I told him.

Women are used to it. Folding the laundry and

helping with homework. Cooking dinner and talking on the phone. It comes naturally.

"I'm a focused kind of guy," he said. "I do one thing at a time."

"Good," I said. "Do one thing. Dance."

He was reluctant but, with the wedding approaching in a matter of months, he agreed to go.

Our instructor taught us the basic steps but warned that if we didn't practice, we would forget them by the next class. We knew she was right because by the time we got home that first night we were already struggling to remember everything she showed us.

But where to practice? Our house didn't have an appropriate dance floor. The den was too small, the living room too crowded. We decided to practice in the kitchen. We moved the table and chairs to one side. The room really wasn't big enough for an elegant foxtrot, and it would put a crimp in an enthusiastic swing, but it would do.

It was difficult at first. Our instructor told us that the male and female each have specific parts: he leads, she does the flourishes. Yet between my jittery energy and his resistance, our individual styles, limited as they were, frequently clashed. I would resort to leading when I thought my husband wasn't assertive enough, which irritated us both. With practice, though, we began to sense each other's strengths and respond to each other's timing. Our posture became more confident. We stopped staring at our feet, willing them to go where they were supposed to instead of being surprised by where they ended up.

We noticed that our dancing improved the more we practiced, so we practiced more. We noticed something else, as well. Things seemed to be changing between us—in a good way. We were rediscovering each other. As we accepted our differing approaches to dance, we began to be less critical in other areas. If dinner was a little late, Benny Goodman helped us while away the time. When we held hands as we got ready to dance, the anticipation of our dating days returned. We laughed a lot more when we danced, no longer upset by our mistakes. We started with our instructor's steps and then began making up our own. We were having fun!

We danced at our son's wedding and to our mutual surprise we keep on dancing. Sometimes it is at a party, often just in our kitchen. I can tell when my husband wants to take a swing around the kitchen floor. His eyes light up. I love the grin on his face when we finish a pattern and come out on the right step. I am even more delighted at our laughter when we don't.

Dancing has drawn us closer, renewed our intimacy. There is a lot more hugging, more innuendo, more delight. Maybe it's just our endorphins running wild. Dancing is, after all, an aerobic exercise that releases those wonderful chemicals of euphoria.

The wedding was the excuse to dance but the result was more than a physical exercise. It helped us remember the excitement of who we are together. And as we continue dancing in the kitchen, wrapped in each other's arms and looking into our happy faces, we rekindle our love.

~Ferida Wolff

看我们跳舞吧，这就等于在聆听我们的心声。

——霍皮印第安人的俗语

我爱我的丈夫。我也爱跳舞。但是，自从 40 年前的婚礼开始，多年的经验告诉我们这两种爱不能兼容。我们就是不能好好地一起跳舞，总是感觉好像多了一只左脚。

所以当我们的儿子宣布他要结婚的时候，我知道我得做点什么了。我不会让我们俩在正式跳双亲之舞的时候出丑的。我找到一个能够让我们跟上节拍的最简单快捷的方法——给我们两个人报了舞蹈课。

我的丈夫为此一直抱怨。他说要数着节拍，做着各种造型，还要听着音乐，根本不可能做到。

"这是个多重任务。"我告诉他。

女人已经习惯了一边叠洗过的衣服，一边给孩子辅导功课；一边做饭，一边打电话。都是顺其自然的事。

"我是个专注的人，"他说，"一次只能做一件事。"

"好啊，"我说，"那就只做一件事：跳舞。"

他很不情愿，但是因为再过几个月就要举行婚礼了，他还是同意去了。

我们的教练教会我们一些基本舞步，同时警告我们如果我们不练的话，下节课就会忘的。我们都知道她说的是对的，因为第一天晚上我们刚回到家，就开始绞尽脑汁地回想她教给我们的动作。

但是在哪儿练习呢？我们的房子里没有跳舞专用的地板。储藏室太小，卧室太挤了。于是我们决定在厨房里练习。我们把桌子和椅子都移到一边。房间太小了，很难跳一个优雅的狐步舞，而且在我们热情地舞动的同时，还要缩着身子才行，但还能凑合。

一开始很难。我们的教练告诉我们男士和女士都有自己特定的角色：他起引导作用，我来配合舞动。我一推他一闪，我们的动作都受到限制，所以不停地产生冲撞。我觉得我的丈夫缺乏自信，就毛遂自荐来引导他，两个人都很生气。但是通过练习，我们开始感觉到对方的优势，互相配合。我们的姿势变得更加自信了。我们也不再一直盯着脚看了，不再为放错位置而一惊一乍，而是随着感觉让双脚自由移动。

我们注意到，练习得越多，跳得就越好，所以我们就更加努力地练习。我们也注意到我们之间的关系发生了一点变化——是朝好的方向转变。我们开始重新审视彼此。因为我们已经接受了在跳舞方式上的差异，所以在其他方面也不再那么吹毛求疵。如果晚饭做得晚了，班尼·古德曼就陪着我们一起打发时间。当我们手牵着手准备跳舞的时候，对约会的那份期盼又重现了。我们跳舞的时候，欢笑更多，不再为犯的错误恼火。我们先从教练教我们的舞步开始跳，然后开始形成我们自己的风格。我们感觉很开心！

我们一起在儿子的婚礼上跳舞，而且让我们双方都惊讶的是，我们就这样一直跳了下去。有时候是在晚会上，但大多数时候都是在我们的厨房里。如果他想在厨房的地板上跳上一段，我能看得出来，他的眼睛突然一亮。我很喜欢看到我们成功跳完一支舞后他脸上露出的笑容。如果我们没跳好，我甚至笑得更高兴。

跳舞让我们越来越近，恢复了我们之间的亲密关系。彼此间的拥抱更多了，打趣更多了，欢乐也更多了。也许是我们体内的内啡肽在猖狂作乱。但是跳舞是一种能够释放兴奋化学物质的有氧运动。

婚礼是我们跳舞的一个借口，可是结果却远不止是身体锻炼。它让我们记住了我们在一起的激动时光。我们继续在厨房跳舞，抱住彼此的手臂，凝望着幸福的脸颊，重新点燃了爱情火花。

——法丽达·沃尔夫

Meet Our Authors
见见我们的作者

Jack Canfield is the co-creator of the *Chicken Soup for the Soul* series, which Time magazine has called "the publishing phenomenon of the decade." Jack is also the co-author of many other bestselling books.

Jack is the CEO of the Canfield Training Group in Santa Barbara, California, and founder of the Foundation for Self-Esteem in Culver City, California. He has conducted intensive personal and professional development seminars on the principles of success for more than a million people in twenty-three countries, has spoken to hundreds of thousands of people at more than 1,000 corporations, universities, professional conferences and conventions, and has been seen by millions more on national television shows.

Jack has received many awards and honors, including three honorary doctorates and a Guinness World Records Certificate for having seven books from the *Chicken Soup for the Soul* series appearing on the New York Times bestseller list on May 24, 1998.

You can reach Jack at www.jackcanfield.com.

杰克·坎菲尔德是《心灵鸡汤》丛书的创作者之一,《时代》杂志把《心灵鸡汤》系列称为"近十年来出版界的神话"，杰克也是许多其他畅销书的合著者。

　　杰克是加利福尼亚州桑塔芭芭拉市坎菲尔德培训集团的首席执行官，也是加利福尼亚州卡尔弗市自尊心基金会的创立人。他在二十三个国家为超过一百万人举行了成功原理的个人专业发展讲座，在一千多家公司、大学、专业会议和国际大会上的成千上万的人面前发表过演讲，还上过无数的电视节目。

　　杰克获得过很多奖项和荣誉，包括三项荣誉博士称号以及一份吉尼斯世界纪录证书，以表彰他编辑的七本《心灵鸡汤》系列丛书于 1998 年 5 月 24 日登上《纽约时报》的畅销书榜单。

　　你可以登录 www.jackcanfield.com 与他取得联系。

Mark Victor Hansen is the co-founder of *Chicken Soup for the Soul*, along with Jack Canfield. He is a sought-after keynote speaker, bestselling author, and marketing maven. Mark's powerful messages of possibility, opportunity, and action have created powerful change in thousands of organizations and millions of individuals worldwide.

Mark is a prolific writer with many bestselling books in addition to the *Chicken Soup for the Soul* series. Mark has had a profound influence in the field of human potential through his library of audios, videos, and articles in the areas of big thinking, sales achievement, wealth building, publishing success, and personal and professional development. He is also the founder of the MEGA Seminar Series.

Mark has received numerous awards that honor his entrepreneurial spirit, philanthropic heart, and business acumen. He is a lifetime member of the Horatio Alger Association of Distinguished Americans.

You can reach Mark at www.markvictorhansen.com.

　　马克·维克多·汉森和杰克·坎菲尔德一起创办了《心灵鸡汤》。马克是一名受欢迎的主题发言人、畅销书作家、市场专家，他的有关可能性、机遇和行动方面的强有力的信息已经使得全球成千上万的组织和个人产生了强有力的变化。

马克是一个多产的作家，除了《心灵鸡汤》，他还有很多畅销书。通过自己收藏的音频、视频资料和有关大胆思考、销售业绩、财富累积、成功出版、个人职业发展方面的文章，马克已经对人类潜能领域产生深刻的影响。他还是米加讲座系列的创始人。

马克曾被授予无数的奖项，以表彰他的创业精神、博爱的心和敏锐的商业眼光，他是霍雷肖杰出美国人协会的终身会员。

你可以登录 www. markvictorhansen.com 与他取得联系。

Amy Newmark is the publisher and editor-in-chief of *Chicken Soup for the Soul*, after a thirty-year career as a writer, speaker, financial analyst, and business executive in the worlds of finance and telecommunications. Amy is a magna Cum laude graduate of Harvard College, where she majored in Portuguese, minored in French, and traveled extensively. She and her husband have four grown children.

After a long career writing books on telecommunications, voluminous financial reports, business plans, and corporate press releases, *Chicken Soup for the Soul* is a breath of fresh air for Amy. She has fallen in love with *Chicken Soup for the Soul* and its life-changing books, and really enjoys putting these books together for Chicken Soup's inspiring readers. She has co-authored more than two dozen *Chicken Soup for the Soul* books and has edited another two dozen.

You can reach Amy through the webmaster@chickensoupforthesoul.com.

艾米·纽马克是《心灵鸡汤》的出版人兼主编，她在财务和电信领域工作了三十年，身兼数职，如作家、发言人、财务分析和商业主管。艾米以优异的成绩毕业于哈佛大学，她主修葡萄牙语，副修法语。她喜欢到处旅游。她和丈夫有四个孩子。

长期撰写有关电信的书籍、长篇财务报告、商业企划和公司新闻发布稿，

Meet Our Authors
见见我们的作者

《心灵鸡汤》令艾米耳目一新。她爱上了《心灵鸡汤》和改变人生的书籍，很喜欢为受到《心灵鸡汤》启发的读者们编写这些书籍。她已经与人合著了超过十二本的《心灵鸡汤》，还编辑了其他十二本。

你可以通过 webmaster@chickensoupforthesoul.com 联络艾米。

Thank You
感谢词

We owe huge thanks to all of our contributors. We know that you pour your hearts and souls into the thousands of stories and poems that you share with us, and ultimately with each other. We appreciate your willingness to open up your lives to other *Chicken Soup for the Soul* readers.

We can only publish a small percentage of the stories that are submitted, but we read every single one and even the ones that do not appear in the book have an influence on us and on the final manuscript.

We want to thank *Chicken Soup for the Soul* Assistant Publisher D'ette Corona for reading the thousands of stories and poems that were submitted for this book. She shaped the initial manuscript and this book is as much hers as it is ours. We also want to thank our editor and webmaster Barbara LoMonaco and editor Kristiana Glavin for their expert editorial and proofreading assistance.

We owe a very special thanks to our creative director and book producer, Brian Taylor at Pneuma Books, for his brilliant vision for our covers and interiors. Finally, none of this would be possible without the business and creative leadership of our CEO, Bill Rouhana, and our president, Bob Jacobs.

Thank You
感谢词

　　我们向所有的投稿者致以最真诚的感谢。我们知道，你们把最真实的情感投入到了数以千计的故事和诗歌中去，你们与我们分享，最终会与大家一起分享。我们感谢您愿意把您的生活展示给所有《心灵鸡汤》的读者。

　　我们只能在收到的故事中择取一小部分发表于书中，但是我们阅读了每一个故事，包括那些没有出现在书里的故事。它们也深深地影响了我们，也影响了最终的书稿。

　　我们想要感谢《心灵鸡汤》发行社副社长狄爱特·科罗拉，她阅读了向本书投稿的数以千计的故事和诗歌。她完成了最初的书稿，与其说这本书是我们的，不如说是她的。我们也要感谢我们的编辑和网站管理员芭芭拉·洛摩纳哥，以及编辑克里斯蒂安娜·格拉文，他们为本书提供了专业的编辑和校对。

　　我们要特别感谢我们的创意总监和书的生产监督，精神书屋的布莱恩·泰勒，他对书籍的封面和内里都具有杰出的眼光。最后，如果没有商业和创意领导人、我们的首席执行官比尔·鲁哈纳和我们的主席鲍勃·乔布斯，就没有《心灵鸡汤》系列。

Chicken Soup for the Soul
Improving Your Life Every Day

Real people sharing real stories—for fifteen years. Now, Chicken Soup for the Soul has gone beyond the bookstore to become a world leader in life improvement. Through books, movies, DVDs, online resources and other partnerships, we bring hope, courage, inspiration and love to hundreds of millions of people around the world. Chicken Soup for the Soul's writers and readers belong to a one-of-a-kind global community, sharing advice, support, guidance, comfort, and knowledge.

Chicken Soup for the Soul stories have been translated into more than forty languages and can be found in more than one hundred countries. Every day, millions of people experience a Chicken Soup for the Soul story in a book, magazine, newspaper or online. As we share our life experiences through these stories, we offer hope, comfort and inspiration to one another. The stories travel from person to person, and from country to country, helping to improve lives everywhere.

心灵鸡汤
每天改善你的生活

这十五年来，真实的人们分享他们真实的故

Improving Your Life Every Day
每天改善你的生活

事。现在,《心灵鸡汤》已经超越其书本的本身价值,成为改善生活的世界领导者。通过书本、电影、DVD、在线资源以及其他合作关系,我们将希望、勇气、灵感和爱心带给全世界千千万万的人们。《心灵鸡汤》的作者和读者都是全球独一无二的社区中的一员,他们分享建议、相互扶持、接受引导、安慰彼此、共享知识。

《心灵鸡汤》里的故事已被翻译成四十几种语言,在一百多个国家出版发行。每天都有成千上万的人通过书本、杂志、报纸或是网络阅读《心灵鸡汤》的故事。我们通过这些故事来分享自己的人生经历,给予人们希望、安慰和灵感。这些故事口口相传,不分国界,它们在世界的每一个角落帮助人们改善生活。

Share with Us

We all have had *Chicken Soup for the Soul* moments in our lives. If you would like to share your story or poem with millions of people around the world, go to chickensoup.com and click on "Submit Your Story." You may be able to help another reader, and become a published author at the same time. Some of our past contributors have launched writing and speaking careers from the publication of their stories in our books!

Our submission volume has been increasing steadily—the quality and quantity of your submissions has been fabulous. We only accept story submissions via our website. They are no longer accepted via mail or fax.

To contact us regarding other matters, please send us an e-mail through webmaster@chickensoupforthesoul.com, or fax or write us at:

Chicken Soup for the Soul
P.O. Box 700
Cos Cob, CT 06807-0700
Fax: 203-861-7194

One more note from your friends at *Chicken Soup for the Soul*: Occasionally, we receive an unsolicited book manuscript from one of our readers, and we would like to respectfully inform you that we do not accept unsolicited manuscripts and we must discard the ones that appear.

与我们一同分享

我们的人生中都经历过"心灵鸡汤"一刻，如果你愿意和世界各地的人们分享你的故事或是诗歌，请登录 chickensoup.com，点击"提交你的故事"。或许你在帮助另一名读者的同时，自己也能成为一名作者。我们过去的一些撰稿人在我们的书中发表了自己的作品后，开始了写作和演讲的职业生涯。

稿件递交量在稳步上升，你们提交的稿件的质量和数量都令人难以置信。我们只接受网络作品递交，邮件或是传真方式恕不接纳。

有关其他事项，请发邮件至 webmaster@chickensoupforthesoul.com，或传真或给我们写信，联系方式如下：

心灵鸡汤

P.O. Box 700

Cos Cob, CT 06807-0700

传真号码：203-861-7194

你的"心灵鸡汤"朋友的另一个特别提醒：偶尔我们会收到读者主动提供的书稿，我们在此郑重地提醒您，这些书稿是不被接受的，一旦收到，我们只能弃置不用。

Share with Us
与我们一同分享